The Cooking of Japan

TIME LIFE BOOKS ®

THE ART OF SEWING
THE OLD WEST
THE EMERGENCE OF MAN
THE AMERICAN WILDERNESS
THE TIME-LIFE ENCYCLOPEDIA OF GARDENING
LIFE LIBRARY OF PHOTOGRAPHY
THIS FABULOUS CENTURY
FOODS OF THE WORLD
TIME-LIFE LIBRARY OF AMERICA
TIME-LIFE LIBRARY OF ART
GREAT AGES OF MAN
LIFE SCIENCE LIBRARY
THE LIFE HISTORY OF THE UNITED STATES
TIME READING PROGRAM
LIFE NATURE LIBRARY
LIFE WORLD LIBRARY
FAMILY LIBRARY:
THE TIME-LIFE BOOK OF THE FAMILY CAR
THE TIME-LIFE FAMILY LEGAL GUIDE
THE TIME-LIFE BOOK OF FAMILY FINANCE

Foods of the World

The Cooking of Japan

by

Rafael Steinberg

and the Editors of

TIME-LIFE BOOKS

photographed by Eliot Elisofon

TIME-LIFE BOOKS, NEW YORK

TIME-LIFE BOOKS

FOUNDER: Henry R. Luce 1898-1967

Editor-in-Chief: Hedley Donovan
Chairman of the Board: Andrew Heiskell
President: James R. Shepley

Vice Chairman: Roy E Larsen

MANAGING EDITOR: Jerry Korn
Assistant Managing Editors: Ezra Bowen, David Maness, Martin Mann, A. B. C. Whipple
Planning Director: Oliver E. Allen
Art Director: Sheldon Cotler
Chief of Research: Beatrice T. Dobie
Director of Photography: Melvin L. Scott
Senior Text Editor: Diana Hirsh
Assistant Art Director: Arnold C. Holeywell

PUBLISHER: Joan D. Manley
General Manager: John D. McSweeney
Business Manager: John Steven Maxwell
Sales Director: Carl G. Jaeger
Promotion Director: Paul R. Stewart
Public Relations Director: Nicholas Benton

FOODS OF THE WORLD

EDITORIAL STAFF FOR THE COOKING OF JAPAN:
EDITOR: Richard L. Williams
Picture Editor: Kaye Neil
Designer: Albert Sherman
Assistant to Designer: Elise Hilpert
Staff Writers: Peter M. Chaitin, James A. Maxwell, Geraldine Schremp, Ethel Strainchamps, Carolyn Tasker, L. Robert Tschirky
***Chief Researchers:* Sarah B. Brash, Helen Fennell**
Researchers: Malabar Brodeur, Marjorie Chester, Doris Coffin, Helen Isaacs, Barbara Leach, Myra Mangan, Monica Suder
Art Assistant: Gloria duBouchet
Test Kitchen Chef: John W. Clancy
Test Kitchen Staff: Fifi Bergman, Sally Darr, Leola Spencer

EDITORIAL PRODUCTION
Production Editor: Douglas B. Graham
Assistant Production Editor: Gennaro C. Esposito
Quality Director: Robert L. Young
Assistant Quality Director: James J. Cox
Copy Staff: Rosalind Stubenberg (chief), Eleanore W. Karsten, Florence Keith
Picture Department: Dolores A. Littles, Joan Lynch

The text for this book was written by Rafael Steinberg and the editors; recipe instructions by Helen Isaacs, directed by Michael Field; picture essays and appendix material by members of the staff. Valuable assistance was provided by the following individuals and departments of Time Inc.: Editorial Production, Norman Airey; Library, Benjamin Lightman; Picture Collection, Doris O'Neil; Photographic Laboratory, George Karas; TIME-LIFE News Service, Murray J. Gart; Correspondents Jerrold L. Schecter, Frank Iwama, Erik Amfitheatrof, S. Chang, Shoichi Imai and Yasuo Kitaoka (Tokyo).

THE AUTHOR: Rafael Steinberg *(above, left),* who joined with the Editors of TIME-LIFE BOOKS in producing the text, first went to the Orient as a correspondent in the Korean War, shortly after graduating from Harvard. Later he was a TIME correspondent in Tokyo and London, and he spent several years as *Newsweek*'s Tokyo bureau chief. He is the author of *Postscript from Hiroshima,* a book about survivors of the nuclear bombing.

THE PHOTOGRAPHER: The late Eliot Elisofon *(above, right)* first went to Japan in 1955 as a lecturer on photography. He returned five times, twice to take pictures for major stories for LIFE. A painter as well as a photographer, Elisofon was in Tokyo for an exhibit of his watercolors while completing work for this book.

THE CONSULTING EDITOR: The late Michael Field *(above, left)* supervised the adapting and writing of recipes for this book. One of America's foremost food experts and culinary teachers, he wrote many articles for leading magazines. His books include *Michael Field's Cooking School* and *All Manner of Food.*

THE CHEF: Toshio Morimoto *(above, right)* started as an apprentice in Osaka's famous Kitcho Restaurant when he was 15 and was an experienced chef when he left for the United States 12 years later. In 1964 he opened his own restaurant in New York, naming it, by special permission, after its Japanese prototype.

THE CONSULTANTS: Fumie Adachi, director of exhibits programming for the Japan Society in New York City, reviewed the text for accuracy. Rand Castile, educational director of the Japan Society, studied the tea ceremony in Kyoto under Sochitsu Sen and served as the expert on the subject. Fumi Inokuma, wife of a distinguished Japanese painter, helped plan the still-life food photography. Eiko Yuasa, head of the International Conference Hall in Kyoto, assisted in Japan.

THE COVER: *Togan-to ebi,* soup with shrimp, winter melon and lime *(Recipe Index).*

Sixth printing.
Published simultaneously in Canada.
Library of Congress catalogue card number 75-84632.

Contents

	Introduction	6
I	The Heritage of a Remarkable Past	8
II	Foods to Suit the Seasons	24
III	The Logic of Japanese Cookery	40
IV	The World's Greatest Seafood	74
V	Simple, Satisfying Foods of Home	106
VI	A Ceremony That Sired a Cuisine	136
VII	Eating Out as a Way of Life	150
VIII	Magnificent Meals in Elegant Settings	182
Appendix	*How to Use Japanese Recipes*	198
	A Guide to Ingredients in Japanese Cooking	199
	Recipe Index: English	200
	Recipe Index: Japanese	201
	General Index	202
	Mail-Order Sources	207
	Credits and Acknowledgments	208

The Recipe Booklet that accompanies this volume has been designed for use in the kitchen. It contains all the 84 recipes printed here plus 31 more. It also has a wipe-clean cover and a spiral binding so that it can either stand up or lie flat when open.

Solving the Mysteries of Japan's Marvelous Cuisine

As a boy in landlocked, then lakeless Oklahoma, I had dreamed of the islands of Japan, but both Lafcadio Hearn and Giacomo Puccini were curiously reticent about Japanese *food.* Rumors of "raw fish" fought their way through dust storms and tornados, but that whole, salty, underwater world of "sea-food" was for the most part a trickle of misinformation. Squid and octopus. (Any difference? Don't they both squirt black ink and who counts tentacles anyway?) Sea urchins and anemones. (What the devil are they? Kids? Flowers?) Secrets of the sea eluded canning processes, frozen foods hadn't come along yet, and refrigerator cars were fairly unknown. (Or did they simply stop at Kansas City and refuse to go on?)

The time finally came for me to visit my dream of Japan, and as soon as I set foot on the good ship *Hikawa-maru* in Seattle—oh yes, airplanes were invented but they weren't flying the Pacific—I was confronted with what the passengers called "The Choice." You could either have a full Western meal or a full Japanese one. I asked for Japanese food, got it three times a day and stuck to it for all 21 days of the voyage to Yokohama. My motives were mostly brummagem, but partly too, I like to imagine, good sense. I was determined to learn Japanese for, as I now tell the story, I knew war was coming. I have never believed that "you are what you eat" (in Japan they drink snake's blood for longevity); however, I am convinced that you can't learn a language without enjoying the food of the nation. Just think of the loss of idiom an English-speaking Japanese might feel if he didn't understand things like a lover being "cream in my coffee," or someone or something else being "as American as apple pie."

Now, in retrospect, I must admit I explored Japan's gustatory and culinary arts the hard way. I tortured myself with *umeboshi,* ultrasour plums, on deck while watching the sun rise. I snacked on odorous, fermented soy beans *(natto)* at night before retiring. I even tried again and again those little cakes printed in the shape of flat flowers, which taste dry as chalk and crumble into sandy powder with every bite. But along the way I encountered myriads of delights and miracles of surprise pleasures. *Sukiyaki* and *tempura,* it goes without saying, and noodles too, and *tonkatsu,* which loses totally in translation if you say "pork cutlet." The warmth of bean soup, the dewlike freshness of thin soup, the brilliant clarity of good, first-quality soy sauce, and the thousands of other sauces, each bound, like a marriage, to its own particular mate. Where else in the cooking world can you have so light, so greaseless, so sparkling a set of flavors and textures that turn into aromas or almost melt as soon as they reach your mouth?

The day soon came when raw fish was on the ship's table d'hôte, and I discovered that it didn't taste raw, or even like fish. And with this conclusion I joined the ranks of astonished foreigners whose numbers increase, like school children and textbooks, year by year. By now the last threshold was crossed, and I was enslaved to Japanese cooking.

My life in Japan proper during those prewar years was one long restaurant tour. After all, I persuaded myself, I was learning Japanese and it was important to say *kaki* (which means both "oyster" and "persimmon") and wait to see whether the waitress asked, "Raw or fried?" or, "Fresh or sugar-dried?" I shared afternoon teas of *mitsumame* with pretty young girls lapping up rainbow cubes of transparent gelatins swimming in fragrant, sugary water dotted for artistic emphasis with a brown bean or two. Evenings, I learned to mix *sake* with beer (never touching, of course, the *sake* cup with my left hand—*hidarikiki*—that's the sign of a drunkard so eager to get at the booze he forgets formality and uses either hand in careless haste), drinking and eating with the best of the men until the liquor was gone and the concluding rice and soup came on. Back in the homeland here, when Japan had turned from a dream into a memory, I found myself missing the very foods that I had not particularly liked but not exactly hated. *Mitsumame,* for example.

Several years later I returned to Japan. I was a soldier and, as it happened, was living at the American Embassy where I had a large apartment, a small kitchen, and two cooks—one for Western food and one for Japanese. This wasn't entirely my own idea, because it was General MacArthur's policy to rehire all the old, prewar Embassy staff (one of whom had cooked Western style); but it suited my plans very well. I did a lot of entertaining and invariably offered guests "The Choice." One evening George Sansom, dean of Japanophiles and great scholar, came to dinner. I had known how good Japanese food was, but I hadn't before then known that it was good *for* you, too. Sir George had just arrived after a long absence and hadn't climatically adjusted yet. Still he insisted on coming, provided I could give him raw fish. "Whenever I have a tummy upset," he explained, "I eat nothing but raw fish for a day and then I'm fine." And so he was.

Today I often find myself "hungry" for Japan, and once it got so bad I cooked up an excuse for a quick trip back just because I was hungry. So, there are dangers in becoming habituated to this great cuisine. However, a book such as this one at last makes possible the impossible: You can now do it yourself in your own home. Here, too, be careful. My own son said to me recently, "Please, Dad. Not *tofu* again!" But just wait until he grows up.

—Faubion Bowers, author, world traveler and aide-de-camp to General Douglas MacArthur during the early years of the postwar occupation of Japan.

I

The Heritage of a Remarkable Past

During all the years I lived in Japan, my delight in the foods of that fascinating land grew more intense at every change of season and almost at every meal. This may sound strange to those other Westerners who still labor under long-standing misconceptions that make this distinguished cooking seem utterly and impossibly alien. Before I encountered it and later, through my Japanese wife, became a member of the family, I too shared the misimpression that Japanese cooking is simply many little dishes with an overdose of fish—that it is mainly an esthetic production in which palatability is sacrificed in favor of beautiful effects and finicky etiquette.

Japanese food is indeed served in small, meticulously prepared portions —but if the portions served at any one meal are less than most Westerners are accustomed to, there are enough of them to approach an average Western meal in total volume. I also grant that fish plays a featured role in Japanese cooking. But while fish, shellfish and seaweed appear frequently on the menu, they never become monotonous because the Japanese have devised an astonishing number of mouth-watering ways of preparing them.

As for the emphasis on appearance, it is certainly true that the Japanese are adept at imparting additional excitement to food through the use of exquisite dishes and bowls selected for their harmony with particular foods. This dedication to visual appeal actually enhances a meal. For, as your palate is captivated by tastes calculated to set off each other, your eye is intrigued by contrasts of color, shapes and texture.

As a journalist, I have friends in the profession whose work has taken them to other countries famous for fine cuisine. When at last they sampled Japanese

A young mother picnics with her hungry baby in a Kyoto setting that combines two familiar symbols of Japan. Behind her is a cherry tree in blossom; at left is a box of *sushi*. Sometimes called the sandwich of Japan, *sushi* consists of rice delicately flavored with sweet rice vinegar, then shaped and wrapped in fish or nutritious seaweed.

cooking and compared it with the food they had enjoyed elsewhere, these world travelers invariably characterized Japanese cuisine as uniquely refined, fastidious and subtle; the Japanese themselves refer to it as *sappari*—clean, neat, light, sparkling with honesty. Gourmets have ranked the cooking of Japan with that of France and China as one of the world's truly great cuisines. In Japan *grande cuisine* is every bit as *grande* as it is in France; and if Japanese cooking has a relatively limited range of foodstuffs to work with, it compensates for this lack through great versatility in methods.

A reflection of Japanese sensitivity toward food is the great attention paid to each material being processed—even more consideration than is shown by the French, which is very much indeed. Whereas the French and the Chinese tend to meld together many ingredients in one dish, the Japanese generally strive to preserve the intrinsic properties of each so that all may have about equal importance in taste as well as in appearance. In clear Japanese soup, for example, that bit of carrot used as garnish is quite distinct in taste, color and shape from the pale-gold sliver of pungent lemon that flows up against your lips as you drink the soup. Each ingredient in the soup is to be relished separately, for its own special character. Moreover, if a dish calls for a strong-tasting garnish such as chopped scallions or grated ginger, this is added only at the last moment—usually by the diner himself—so that its taste will not permeate the other ingredients.

Equally important in Japanese opinion as cooking method and artful presentation is the message or mood that certain foods are intended to convey. One example is a dish, made for the spring fish festival, whose many ingredients include finely textured slices and cubes of raw tuna and sea bream, crisp cucumber strips and shredded radish, sections of boiled lotus root, a spray of cherry blossoms and a willow twig—all arranged to suggest the trees, mountains, rivers and flowers of Japan in springtime. The decoration of the room in which food is served is regularly changed to suggest a mood or to remind a diner of the rhythm of the seasons. In the coldest days of January, for instance, a painting of plum blossoms may be hung in the *tokonoma*—the alcove found in virtually every principal Japanese room—to remind you that the first flowering tree will be in bloom next month.

Often a Japanese chef will go still further to make his dishes visually ap-

A Note about This "Different" Volume

In reading and using this book you will find certain differences between it and other FOODS OF THE WORLD *volumes. For one thing there is a preponderance of seafood in the Japanese repertoire, and the recipes and illustrations reflect this. For another, the recipes are organized into four major sections (see pages 54, 90, 122 and 168) instead of appearing as appendages to text chapters. These recipe sections contain explanatory notes at the beginning of each category of dishes. By reading these and the discussion of menu planning on page 198 in the Appendix—as well as the author's enlightening text—you will find that many aspects of Japanese cuisine that may have seemed mysterious become perfectly clear.*

There is a culinary glossary in the Appendix, but for your convenience, near the beginning of text chapters there are also brief glossaries that translate Japanese terms not fully defined in the text. There is no chapter glossary with this opening chapter because Japanese terms are defined in it when first used.

—The Editors

A Land in a Few Brushstrokes

This stylized map, done in brush-and-ink calligraphic style, suggests the general shape and comparative size of the four islands that make up the major part of Japan. The island chain, about 1,000 miles long, lies in the same latitudes as the North American coast from Georgia to Nova Scotia and has a similar variation in climate. The waters that surround Japan are among the world's richest fishing grounds. Honshu is the most temperate and has the largest proportion of arable land; it grows three quarters of Japan's rice and has three quarters of the population. Hokkaido, comparatively cold and thinly populated, is important for dairy products. The islands of Shikoku and Kyushu are subtropical, producing mandarin oranges and other citrus fruits.

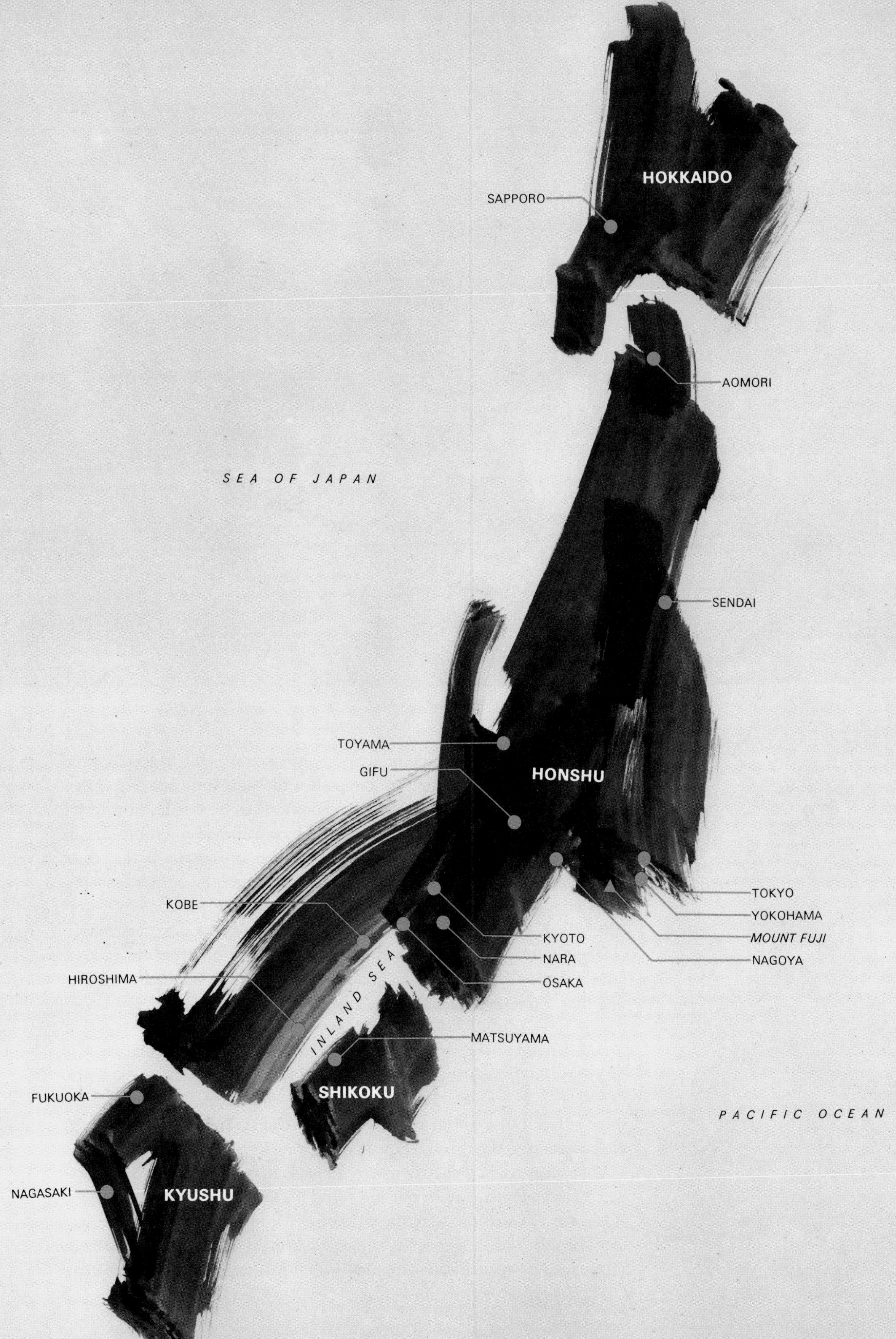
HOKKAIDO
SAPPORO
AOMORI
SEA OF JAPAN
SENDAI
TOYAMA
GIFU
HONSHU
TOKYO
YOKOHAMA
MOUNT FUJI
NAGOYA
KOBE
KYOTO
NARA
OSAKA
HIROSHIMA
INLAND SEA
MATSUYAMA
SHIKOKU
FUKUOKA
PACIFIC OCEAN
NAGASAKI
KYUSHU

petizing, perhaps by cushioning a plate with several freshly washed maple or chrysanthemum leaves or by adorning it with a pine sprig or a crisp green leaf scissored into a series of arrowlike points. Then he decides how to set the food within the pattern of the plate and its ornamentation, sometimes at an angle to lead the eye to an accompanying dish, or squarely in the center to emphasize the food's self-containment. Moreover, he aims at making every arrangement unique, and in this way keeps himself constantly creative. As Kaichi Tsuji, chef and owner of one of Tokyo's outstanding Japanese restaurants and the author of many books on Japanese cuisine, once declared: "A great presentation is fine the first time, but less so the second time. To repeat a third time . . . that's kindergarten."

To understand how this unique approach to eating developed and reached its present high sophistication, we must know something about the forces that shaped its growth. For like the culinary habits of all other nations, those of Japan are a reflection of the country's climate and geography, its ethnic inheritances, the ebb and flow of its history, its religious beliefs.

While their origin is uncertain, it seems likely that most of Japan's early settlers were immigrants from the arid, wind-blown steppes of northern Asia. When they crossed the water from Siberia or from Korea, they found verdant islands with a generally temperate climate and abundant rainfall, surrounded by coastal waters teeming with fish. The gratitude that the early

On a sunny day in May, women workers harvest the first (and best) crop of green tea leaves on a plantation in the Ujidawara district, near Kyoto. The shears they are using, with a bag attached to the right-hand blade to catch the snipped leaves, are an innovation in tea harvesting. They are used mainly to cut the outer leaves; the rest are still gathered by hand. A second crop will be picked in July and a third one in September. The women's identical costumes are similar to those worn by rural women throughout Japan.

Overleaf: Reflected in the shallow water that covers paddies of newly transplanted rice shoots, a farmer *(foreground)* carries a pail of insecticide to scatter over his rice paddies. He and his neighbors cooperated in creating the irrigation system, but the paddies are individually owned. Thatched roofs like those in the background are still found in parts of rural Japan.

settlers must have felt for the beneficence of their new land probably helped create a desire to live in harmony with nature; these feelings became a fixed characteristic of the emerging Japanese people, a trait that has left an indelible imprint on every aspect of Japanese culture.

In time, this simple reverence for nature developed into a cult dedicated to the worship of a pantheon of natural spirits. Wherever there was a tree or rock with an unusual shape or a stream murmuring over stones, there a divine presence was said to dwell and a primitive temple was erected; there the people made offerings of rice—Japan's staple crop in antiquity as it is today—and *sake,* a beverage made by fermenting rice and then distilling it.

The nature worship of the archaic Japanese—which eventually evolved into the Shinto religion still widely practiced in Japan—was essentially a hymn to the god-given fertility of the land. At spring and autumn festivals, prayers asking for good planting weather and bountiful harvests were directed to the appropriate deities. One of the most important of these deities was the food goddess, Ukemochi-no-kami. Also held in high esteem was Inari, the rice god. Even today hundreds of thousands of miniature shrines dedicated to him can be seen throughout rural Japan.

The food goddess yielded first rank to the goddess of the sun, legendary grandmother of Jimmu, the first Emperor of Japan and founder of the dynasty that has reigned for more than 2,600 years. Nonetheless the food goddess remained an important figure of worship, a symbol of the respect with

Continued on page 16

which a hard-working, frugal people regarded their most vital resource. For the ancient Japanese, like their descendants today, could not afford to be casual about food. Japan has never produced crop surpluses, for only about 16 per cent of this mountainous land is suitable for cultivation. Consequently the earliest Japanese diet was sparse and simple, consisting mainly of rice, fish, vegetables, seaweed, salt and fruit, augmented occasionally by venison or wild boar or game birds.

Even in modern Japan the ancient respect for the sacredness of food still prevails. The poetic Shinto Prayer for Harvest is regularly recited, beseeching the gods for "crops in ears long and in ears abundant, things growing in the great moor-plain, sweet herbs and bitter herbs, things that dwell in the blue sea-plain, the broad of fin and the narrow of fin, seaweed from the offing, seaweed from the shore. . . ." Every year the Emperor and Empress of Japan observe the chief national festivals, celebrations centuries old that give thanks for plentiful crops. These are called *Niiname Sai,* or "The Tasting of the First Fruits", and *Kanname Sai,* or "The Divine Tasting." In modern industrialized Japan with its ability to import needed food from all over the world, the Emperor and Empress observe the festivals largely as a matter of form because it gives a sense of continuity to their line. But in the past, royal participation was a much more serious matter, for a poor rice crop could mean severe hardship to millions of Japanese.

Other nations with natural resources as limited as Japan's have compensated by importing the things they lacked. But the Japanese, an insular people whose sea-bordered archipelago lies three times farther from the Asian continent than the British Isles lie from the continent of Europe, pursued a policy of either enthusiastically accepting ideas from the outside world, or shutting the world out entirely for centuries at a time.

This oddly vacillating policy profoundly affected not only Japanese eating habits but Japanese life in general. During those periods when the country's doors stood open, the free flow of ideas, products and techniques from abroad enabled the Japanese to be selective, sifting out and retaining only those features of other cultures that they found especially attractive or useful. And in their centuries of withdrawal, they concentrated on reshaping what they had borrowed, blending it with the best of their own native civilization to create an exquisitely refined Japanese way of life that was manifest in its art and literature, architecture and gardening, and the preparation and serving of food.

Japan's first and most significant period of contact with the outer world began around the Sixth Century when Japan, still semibarbaric despite centuries of sporadic contacts with China, suddenly awoke to the merits of its neighbor's highly sophisticated civilization. In the Seventh and Eighth Centuries, when T'ang Dynasty China was becoming the world's most advanced nation, Chinese cultural influence on Japan—especially with regard to the beliefs and practices of Chinese Buddhism—reached astounding proportions. The impact of China is still evident in Japanese art and architecture, ideographic written language, literature, techniques of government, taxation and city planning, and—not least—cuisine.

Perhaps the most important food innovation contributed by China was the soybean, which in various guises is still the foundation stone of Japanese cooking. Another acquisition from China was tea, which became Japan's national beverage. Tea reached Japan around the year 800 and was first used there in powdered form as a medicine or as a drink reserved for aristocrats and priests. Tea was to have an important impact on Japanese cooking, but this would not be felt until the 15th Century.

This flow of influences from China came to a near-total end toward the middle of the Ninth Century, when the T'ang Dynasty approached collapse. But as the Japanese moved into a long era of insular seclusion they began to refine their borrowings and turn them into an elegant Japanese civilization.

The focus of that civilization was the imperial court at Japan's ancient capital of Heian-kyo (later known as Kyoto), and the 400 years following the city's founding in 794 are known as the golden age of Japanese culture. The Heian age was a time of aristocratic ideals, and never perhaps in the history of any people have the poetic and the practical been so intimately married. Many of the interests that preoccupy Japan to this day took shape during that era, among them poetry, subtle color combinations, graceful manners, beautiful ceramics. The Heian nobles wrote and exchanged poems on paper whose shade was chosen to convey their moods, practiced scent-blending as a fine art, held banquets in lovely gardens beside flowing streams and often followed them with excursions to admire wildflowers, to view the moon or to listen to the almost imperceptible sounds of falling snow. Every aspect of their lives, from their amorous affairs to their dining habits, was governed by an almost incredibly elaborate code of etiquette.

But while the Heian age was ultrarefined, it was not gastronomically opulent. The diet of its aristocrats and common people alike was mostly the rice, fish, fruit and vegetables eaten by their ancestors. To make this simple fare as poetic as possible, the Heian nobles added romantic ingredients such as fern-frond tips and devised various ways of presenting food that were calculated to enhance its visual appeal, thus infusing Japanese cuisine with one of the qualities that forever after would mark it as unique.

After Japan's golden age came centuries of violent civil strife that saw the rise to power of a class very different from the poetry-oriented Heian courtiers —the warriors called samurai. Although these fighting men were realistic and hard-bitten in the field, they were not averse to adopting the imperial court's elegant table etiquette and artful presentation of foods during their leisure time. Since their ranks included men of lesser birth as well as nobles, refined practices began to reach lower levels of Japanese society, a process that was speeded during the 15th Century with the perfection by the Japanese imperial court of a Buddhist-inspired ritual known as the tea ceremony. In the tea ceremony, a small gathering of friends enjoy tea and food served in a mannered, graceful fashion by their host amid simple but beautiful objects and in a tranquil atmosphere. Over the centuries this ceremony not only became the basis of a whole branch of cooking called *kaiseki ryori* (tea-ceremony cooking), the *grande cuisine* of Japan *(Chapter 6),* but also influenced Japan's architecture, decorative style and much of its dining etiquette.

The standards of dining were also refined in that they reflected the tastefully frugal quality of Japanese life. Even noblemen were expected to leave their bowls and plates absolutely clean, to the extent of tucking fruit pits and fish bones into the sleeves of their kimono. The Japanese still consider a

dish with unfinished food unsightly, although inedible remains are no longer hidden in one's sleeve but are replaced in the dish as tidily as possible.

Toward the mid-16th Century, Japan was brought face to face with a totally new influence—this time from the Western world. The first Westerners known to have reached Japan were three Portuguese traveling in a Chinese junk that was blown ashore by a typhoon in the early 1540s. The Japanese received the Europeans cordially, and their warlords quickly duplicated Portuguese firearms, thus adding a new element to samurai warfare. After the castaways returned home with news of their welcome by an agreeable, highly cultivated people, other Portuguese soon were sailing to Japan to begin a lucrative trade between Chinese and Japanese ports.

While the early Portuguese traders were enchanted by the Japanese and their civilized ways, the Japanese saw the newcomers as little better than barbarians. They invited the Europeans to their homes but were appalled by the manners of these pale, long-nosed, meat-gobbling foreigners. A provincial lord, writing his impression of the Portuguese traders, described them as understanding "to a certain degree the distinction between Superior and Inferior, but I do not know whether they have a proper system of ceremonial etiquette. They eat with their fingers instead of with chopsticks such as we use. They show their feelings without any self-control. . . . They are people who spend their lives roving hither and yon. They have no fixed abode and barter things which they have for those they do not, but withal they are a harmless sort of people."

This condescending view of Europeans changed for the better after 1549 when well-educated Jesuit missionaries, backed by the Portuguese Crown and determined to convert the Japanese to Christianity, began to arrive in Japan. The Jesuits noted that the Japanese, following Buddhist beliefs, still ate practically no meat but a good deal of fish, and that they cultivated a variety of grains—notably rice—and many kinds of vegetables. They also noted that the Japanese made plentiful use of herbs and fruit, including dried fruit, in their meals. What the Japanese ate was obviously good for them, for a leading Jesuit reported: "These people live wonderfully healthy lives and there are many aged."

But the European missionaries and traders unfortunately made the error of meddling in Japanese politics. This threat to the feudal system, plus Japanese fears of an invasion by Spaniards based in the Philippines resulted in the expulsion in 1638 of all Westerners except a few Dutch traders, who were permitted to remain but were kept under close watch. An occasional Dutch merchant ship was allowed to land its cargo, but all other foreigners were forbidden to enter Japan, and no Japanese could leave on pain of death. The islands' doors were now locked more securely than ever against the rest of the world, and they remained so until Commodore Perry's arrival more than two centuries later.

Although the Portuguese were gone, they left behind their recipes for deep-fat-fried foods that came to be known as *tempura*. The word *tempura* itself provides a clue to its origin. In his book *Talking Your Way around the World*, the eminent philologist Mario Pei says: "The Portuguese, as good Catholics, rejected meat on Ember Days, which they called by the Latin name of Quattuor Tempora, the 'four times' of the year. They asked instead for sea food,

Shintoism, the ancient religion of a nature- and ancestor-worshiping people, is still closely identified with the bounties of land and sea in Japan. On the opposite page, Shinto priests stand before bottles and casks of *sake* that they have blessed. This rite takes place annually in April at Kyoto's Matsunoh Shrine.

Overleaf:
A newly built oyster boat has been purified in a Shinto ceremony that includes placing a lacy bamboo stalk trimmed with straw and paper in the stern. Presumably, the boat will now be protected as it lowers the racks of scallop shells in which oysters are cultivated in Hiroshima Bay.

Continued on page 22

usually shrimp. Eventually the name *tempura* became attached to the fried shrimp the Portuguese favored on these days. Thus did the ancient Latin word for 'times' turn into the Japanese word for shrimp fried in batter."

In characteristic fashion, the Japanese refined the Portuguese method, using a lighter batter and lighter oil and also enlarging the scope of foods prepared in this fashion. Today Japanese deep-fried foods have a delicacy unmatched anywhere in the world.

After the 1850s, when Japan ended an almost unbroken millennium as a tightly sealed nation, the Japanese found much to admire in the dynamic civilization of the West. They rushed headlong into learning all they could about the ways of Westerners, especially their advanced science and technology, and by the early 20th Century Japan was well on its way to becoming the industrial giant it now is.

Along with Western technology and science, the eclectic Japanese also borrowed Western food styles, including the eating of meat. As new dietary ideas took hold and most of the people gradually abandoned Buddhist regulations forbidding meat consumption, chicken and pork and beef appeared more and more frequently on the Japanese menu. Before very long the Japanese were raising some of the world's finest beef cattle, and beefsteak and chicken had become principal ingredients in the most internationally famous dish of Japanese cuisine—*sukiyaki (Recipe Index).* In Japan's principal cities restaurants serving dishes patterned on those of the West are now enormously prosperous, and the chefs of some of the better ones learned the art of Western cooking in France. By the early 1960s Tokyo alone had more than 2,000 restaurants that served Western-style foods exclusively. And the fact that such restaurants are rivaled in popularity by those specializing in a Japanese version of Chinese cooking reflects a growing cosmopolitanism of Japanese tastes in food.

Since their wide exposure to American eating habits during the United States occupation of Japan following World War II, the Japanese have been particularly enthusiastic about American-type foods. A United States food fair held recently in Tokyo drew half a million people, and today you can have *aisukurimu*—Japanese for ice cream—or ham and cheese sandwiches almost anywhere in Japan. Bread, toast and fried eggs, similarly, have made inroads on the traditional diet. But these changes in food preferences have had at least one serious side effect: an increasing number of Japanese are fat; until a few years ago it was unusual to see an overweight person in Japan. The notable exception were the *sumo,* Japan's professional wrestlers, who deliberately attain their enormous girth through a special diet.

While Japanese appetites have become cosmopolitan, the traditional fine cooking of Japan is still widely practiced by present-day Japanese, who treasure it as an integral part of their national character. A Japanese separated from his national diet for any length of time feels lost, listless and uprooted. Only with his traditional dishes featuring freshly caught fish and nutritious seaweeds, steamed rice, succulent mushrooms gathered in the uplands and the shimmering white curd made from soybeans can a Japanese feel the verities of his homeland's sea, mountain and plain.

It seems surprising, in this rapidly shrinking world of the 20th Century, that only recently have Westerners—and Americans more than others—reversed the usual order and begun to borrow gastronomically from the Japanese. Japan's manufactured products have been known nearly everywhere for years. Movies, television and the ease of travel by plane have familiarized millions of foreigners with many aspects of Japanese culture. But it was not until relatively recently that Japanese cooking began to be widely appreciated abroad for what it really is—a unique and highly refined art to be relished by both palate and eye. There were only one or two Japanese restaurants in New York City until the Korean War, when thousands of American troops discovered and admired Japanese dishes on their native ground. As a result of exposure to Japanese food during the 1950s, the number of Japanese restaurants in New York multiplied dramatically. And there has been a similar increase in Japanese restaurants in other large American cities.

There are various reasons for this belated appreciation. One of them is that Americans for a long time confused Japanese with Chinese food, which has been known in America ever since the laborers from southern China helped build the transcontinental railways during the latter part of the 19th Century. Japanese immigration, on the other hand, was slight until 1900, and so Japanese cooking had little opportunity to reveal its distinctiveness. Another factor has been the long-standing devotion of most Americans to their own way of cooking or to those of such well-known countries as France, Germany and Italy. Until World War II forced Americans into large-scale contact with Japan and other very different cultures and infused them with a new, adventurous spirit in eating, they were generally not eager to test the unfamiliar.

Probably the most significant reason for our tardy recognition of Japanese cooking, however, has been the Japanese themselves. While they eagerly assimilated Western technology, in matters pertaining to their traditional culture they tended to regard "things Japanese" and "things foreign" as lovers without a common language. This attitude still prevails, often keeping the casual tourist from discovering the finest in Japanese cuisine.

The emphasis on subtlety of taste, esthetic appearance and traditional ways of serving may make Japanese cuisine seem too formidable to be attempted at home. The surprising truth is that it should be every housewife's delight, for most of its dishes, far from being difficult, actually allow great freedom and rich opportunities for creativity in cooking.

All cookbooks devoted to Japanese cooking stress this freedom. The recipe for a specific dish will give methods and seasonings and then add "this method can be used on shrimp, crab, lobster, any white fish, etc."—often listing as many as eight or 10 possible foodstuffs for which the method might be applicable. Where different foodstuffs require a slight variation in method, this is also noted and may consist of signals telling you to "cook only until it changes color" or "cook until transparent white but not opaque white." It is such telling signals that will enable you to recognize those crucial small differences that add up to perfection.

An old Japanese saying holds that if you have the pleasant experience of eating something that you have not tasted before, your life will be lengthened by 75 days. I like to believe that there is truth in this, and that the pleasures of discovering the cooking of Japan will prolong by many years the lives of those who explore its many byways.

II

Foods to Suit the Seasons

Young maple leaves and a red felt picnic cloth provide a springtime setting for this 300-year-old *bento* box and its nested contents. The food has been meticulously prepared for a festive picnic by a professional chef. It includes chestnuts, duck, fish cakes, shrimp balls, kelp and such seasonal favorites as clams *(at left of the main box)* and quail eggs *(in the tray, center front).*

Suddenly, on a raw day in early February, the strawberries arrive in a torrent. Fruit vendors all over Japan shove other products into a corner and cover their shelves with a rich, red carpet—boxes and boxes of the biggest, juiciest, sweetest strawberries in the world—while editorial writers and television commentators remind readers and listeners of the seasonal thing to do. For a few weeks it seems as if no other fruit exists in Japan.

In elegant restaurants, when most of the dishes have been cleared away and the geisha are tuning up their samisen, the sated diners are revived by the sight of five or six huge, glistening strawberries, set before them on a black or dark-green dish. (If the occasion is informal enough and sufficient *sake* has been consumed, the attending geisha and the waitresses will obligingly spear the strawberries with toothpicks and pop them seductively into the mouths of the weary customers.) In tiny noodle shops, in *fugu* restaurants, which generally limit their menus to varied preparations of the globefish called *fugu*, even in the *sushi* snack shops, which normally serve no dessert at all, strawberries are presented at the end of the meal as a matter of course. No housewife in Japan would feel that she was doing right by her family unless she offered strawberries as often as she could afford them.

Almost as abruptly as they come, the strawberries disappear, not to be seen again until a little later in the year. The Japanese do not often preserve them or make jam out of them, and only recently have frozen strawberries reached a few luxury shops. Strawberries are eaten fresh or not at all; to the Japanese they are as much a part of the late winter season as pumpkins are to Halloween in the United States. The Japanese would be as startled to be

Japanese-English Glossary

DAIKON: *giant radish*
MOCHI: *rice cake*
OBI: *broad sash worn with kimono*
SASHIMI: *slices of raw fish*
SHOYU: *soy sauce*
SUSHI: *vinegared rice topped with raw fish or wrapped in laver*
SUKIYAKI: *simmered beef dish*
TOKONOMA: *alcove with decorative items*
YUZU: *citrus fruit similar to lime*

served strawberries in late summer as we would be to find eggnog at a Fourth of July picnic.

It's not just because strawberries are at their best in February that the Japanese go on a strawberry binge every year; hothouse cultivation could make the berries available for most of the year with little sacrifice of taste. To the Japanese, in their unending quest for harmony with nature, a food simply cannot be separated from its season: to do so would risk throwing the universe ever so slightly out of its foreordained rhythm. There are scores of Japanese foods—fruit, fish, vegetables, even sweets—that belong unalterably to certain seasons, and whose enjoyment, at the right time, the Japanese approach with almost reverent fervor. In Japan every season has its food and, to some extent, every food has its season. Some years ago a Japanese friend of mine was dumfounded when I happened to mention the variety of frozen foods available in American supermarkets. "But is it safe to eat foods out of season?" she asked.

We of the West go to such lengths to defeat and "tame" nature that it is hard for us to appreciate a culture and a cuisine that still swing with the elements. The Japanese ride the seasons instead of battling them. To a Westerner shivering in an unheated Japanese house in the wintertime this "oneness with nature" may seem absurd, but if he can survive until dinnertime, a hot bowl of soup with *tamago dofu* (seasoned egg custard) and a few cups of hot *sake* may give him a different perspective.

Eating egg soup and eating strawberries in season may not be a mystical experience for us, but by responding to the rhythm of the seasons the Japanese unite themselves with the divine forces of the universe. Even nonreligious Japanese feel the need for this. Nowadays, many Japanese have abandoned such traditional seasonal pastimes as moon viewing, firefly catching, and listening for the pop of the first lotus blossoming: there's just too much noise and smog and concrete in the way. Cut off from nature's manifestations by central heating, air conditioning and urban sprawl, urban Japanese have come to rely even more heavily on their seasonal foods to keep the channels open to the cosmos. And as might be expected, their emphasis on foods in season produces some gastronomic miracles.

But merely serving foods at certain times of year is not enough. To squeeze every possible drop of seasonal mood and meaning out of a meal, the best Japanese restaurants maintain separate sets of dishes and serving utensils for each season. They insist that the patterns of their waitresses' kimono and *obi* always reflect the season—red leaves in autumn, for example, and blossoms in the spring—and they carefully change the flower arrangement and the hanging scroll in the *tokonoma* of each guest room every few days (or more often), not only to harmonize with the food to be served and to suit the particular guest but to match the season outside.

Many Japanese dishes, moreover, are prepared and arranged to look like some seasonal symbol. It is in tea-ceremony food *(Chapter 6)* that this combination of taste, ingredients and appearance reaches its artistic peak, but the idea shapes and colors a wide range of ordinary Japanese foods, adding another esthetic dimension to the Japanese enjoyment of the seasonal parade.

One of the first signs of spring, for instance, is the *uguisu mochi,* or nightingale cake. You see it (usually clutched in the fist of a small, happy child) only when the nightingale breaks his winter silence. Like other sweet rice cakes this soft and chewy confection is made of pounded rice meal and sugar and is filled with sweetened bean paste. This one, however, is cut roughly in the shape of the bird and lightly dusted with green bean powder.

A few weeks later, when the cherry trees are about to blossom, a sweet *mochi* wrapped in cherry leaves appears. The leaves are removed before eating, but their delicate fragrance permeates the cake and lingers on the tongue.

By cherry-blossom time the season is well under way and the Japanese have already eaten many spring foods. Bamboo shoots, for instance. Although these crisp, refreshing slivers of young bamboo are now available canned all year round, the fresh ones are at their tenderest in the spring, and their appearance in *sukiyaki,* in one of the compartments of the *bento* picnic boxes, and in various kinds of rice dishes always signifies this season.

Early in the spring some elegant restaurants take a trout called *kawamasu,* which happens to be at its best when the plum trees are in bloom, and doubly commemorate that brief moment of the year by producing a dish in which chunks of the salt-broiled trout *(Recipe Index),* garnished with seasonal leaves, are arranged on a blossom-shaped plate so that they look like part of the plum blossom itself.

To Toyama Bay, on the coast of the Japan Sea, April brings the tender "firefly squid," a tiny phosphorescent creature that appears nowhere else in Japan. Every evening for three or four weeks the bay sparkles with millions of the squid coming in to shallow water to spawn. Toyama residents and sightseers from the cities swarm out in boats to marvel at the display and watch the fishermen pull in their full, glittering nets, which look like huge clusters of diamonds. Most of these squid are consumed raw, as *sashimi,* right at Toyama, since they cannot be kept fresh long enough for shipment.

In May the Japanese gourmet turns his attention to tea, for it is then that the *shincha,* the highly prized first new leaves of the tea bush, are plucked and sent to market. This is not the leaf for the tea ceremony (which is taken from special ancient plants), but the everyday green tea that the Japanese drink morning, noon and night, at home and at work, before meals, with meals and after meals—and when offered to a visitor, must be sipped before any business can be done. Green tea (Japan tea, or *Nihon-cha,* as the Japanese themselves call it to distinguish it from *kocha,* or black tea, that most of the rest of the world consumes) is considered so essential a beginning that most Tokyo coffee shops will serve you, unasked, a free cup of tea before they bring your coffee, even if you have ordered nothing else.

Shincha, new tea, makes a brighter-colored brew than tea picked later in the year, and the Japanese claim that it has a mellower flavor. If the new leaves lie around too long, they lose their unique freshness, so *shincha* can be enjoyed only in May. During the season, tea lovers from all over Japan descend on the tea plantations in Shizuoka, about 110 miles southwest of Tokyo, to taste *shincha* brewed fresh from the plucking. Tens of thousands of tea connoisseurs who can't make the trip order growers to ship them, every year, a choice selection of new leaves as soon as they are picked.

The Japanese can be just as fussy about their tea as the crustiest English lord. *Shincha,* they say, must be brewed for one to two minutes in water between 140° and 160° F., and the cups must be warmed to the same temperature

Onlookers, including a local policeman, watch Japanese school children salvage frostbitten persimmons for their owner after an early snowstorm in October. This particular species of persimmon—a small, astringent type—is usually picked in the fall, peeled and dried, but these were allowed to ripen on the tree and fell victim to the cold.

beforehand. Ordinary tea requires about 180°, and only the cheapest grades, *bancha,* are exposed to water near the boiling point. If, when the tea is poured, the leaves and stems float on the surface, then the tea has not steeped enough; if they sink and lie flat on the bottom, it has been steeped too long. Ideally, the particles should remain suspended near the bottom of the cup—preferably, say the purists, in a vertical position!

From the tea sipping at Shizuoka, the traveling epicures might journey on to Gifu, between Nagoya and Kyoto, to be on hand for the first taste of the finest seasonal food on the Japanese calendar: *ayu.* The *ayu* is a small fresh-water sweetfish that looks like nothing but a brook trout and tastes like nothing but a fish for the gods. From mid-May, when the *ayu* season opens, until the season peters out in various parts of the country at different times in the fall, the *ayu* and its praises are literally on everyone's lips. It has such a distinct, sweetish, satisfying taste that the first time I had it I found it hard to believe that I was not eating some carefully concocted culinary masterpiece; it didn't seem possible that the unprepossessing little fish lying before me with skin and bones intact had produced all that flavor by itself. But the only thing the chef had done (after gutting the fish) was *shioyaki (Recipe Index),* salt-broiling the fish, the simple Japanese cooking method *(Chapter 3)* that brings out the best in any fish; it was merely my untrained palate that had looked for artifice where nature had already achieved perfection.

The *ayu* is an egalitarian fish. In the cities the greatest restaurants serve it proudly on proper dishes, surrounded by just the right seasonal herbs and grasses. But it tastes just as good in the dozens of flimsy, temporary stalls that pop up every summer along the banks of Japan's rivers to serve fresh-caught *ayu* to the common folk—and to unlucky fishermen.

It is not the *ayu* alone that attracts visitors to Gifu in the *ayu* season (for the fish is found almost everywhere in the country), but the remarkable technique of catching *ayu* with trained cormorants, large, long-billed aquatic birds remarkably skilled at catching fish under water. The technique has survived at Gifu centuries after falling into oblivion in other parts of the world.

Cormorants work on moonless nights, tethered to their handlers by long strings. Rings around their necks prevent them from swallowing any but the smallest fish they catch. In the eerie light from torches on the handlers' boats, the obedient birds swoop low over the river, diving in a twinkling to snatch fish from the water, darting back and forth in apparent confusion. A handler may run as many as 12 cormorants at once, somehow managing to prevent his birds from snarling each other's lines or the lines from other boats. One at a time he pulls them back to disgorge their gulletfuls of *ayu*—which are transferred immediately to accompanying restaurant boats and served afloat, salt-broiled or raw, to foreign tourists who have come to look and marvel and to Japanese tourists who have come to eat and look.

Connoisseurs believe that the *ayu* is at its best in late August and early September, when cooling weather puts a layer of fat on the fish. But the Japanese are so eager to get at the *ayu* early in the season and they consume so many of the fish before midsummer, that by August they are slightly fed up with it —although they will never admit to being tired of *ayu.*

Before that happens, the Japanese have briefly abandoned *ayu* for a midsummer fling with eels. Unlike ordinary fish, eels don't lose their fat in the summer, and since fatty fish is considered superior, eels are preferred over other leaner seafoods during the hot weather. What is more, they are fantastically rich in vitamin A. Split, boned, skewered on bamboo and broiled over charcoal in a special sweetened soy sauce *(tare),* the eels become a toasty-brown dish called *kabayaki,* which in any season, with or without rice, is pungent, heady fare. It is easy to understand why it is so popular.

What is harder to understand, however, is why so many modern Japanese slavishly obey an old superstition that orders them to eat eels on a particular day of the year. On the Chinese lunar calendar, eel day is *Ushinohi,* the Day of the Ox in the *Doyo* season (the dog days), and it falls in late July or early August. For reasons lost in antiquity, the Japanese believe that eels eaten on *Ushinohi* cure illnesses and enable one to survive the heat of summer. Some authorities suggest that the custom derived from the idea that eels would drive out evil spirits on a day that is astrologically propitious. A more likely explanation is that the whole thing was dreamed up a couple of centuries ago

Overleaf: The patchwork quilt of land on Innoshima Island in the Inland Sea shows the manner in which Japanese farmers rotate their crops to best advantage. The white sections are fields of chrysanthemums, which are processed into an agricultural insecticide that is sold throughout Japan. These plants do not thrive if they are planted in the same soil year after year. Therefore next season's chrysanthemums will be planted where the brownish-yellow wheat and green leafy vegetables now grow.

by an eel-shop proprietor in Edo (old Tokyo). If the latter story is true, it was the most successful promotion scheme in Japanese history.

On *Ushinohi* eel restaurants are jammed from morning to midnight, and some customers have to eat standing up. Politicians and other celebrities get themselves photographed smiling over skewered *kabayaki,* and television comedians work eels into their routines. "Have you had your eels yet?" is the standard greeting when meeting friends on *Ushinohi.* Office workers, having eaten eels at lunch, stop off at eel restaurants again on the way home to pick up a package of precooked *kabayaki* for the wife and kids, for eels are too slippery and difficult for the ordinary housewife to handle.

Oddly, eel eating on *Ushinohi* is one old custom that flourishes more strongly in the sophisticated cities than in rural districts. Country folk don't seem to need a special day to remind them of the seasons. But the vast majority of Japanese in the cities really seem to believe that they must eat a portion of eels on the appointed day or else risk illness, and so they happily devour about 865 tons of eels in a 24-hour period every year. And lo, most of the eel eaters do indeed survive the summer heat.

While eels are keeping the Japanese healthy, a variety of other summer dishes are keeping them cool. *Tofu* (soybean curd), cooked with other foods during most of the year, finally becomes a dish in its own right in the hot weather. Served on ice, and flavored with soy sauce and flakes of *katsuobushi* (dried bonito), chopped scallions and ginger, the cold, custardlike *tofu* makes an excellent—and nonfattening—light summer lunch. Another favorite food for fighting the heat is *zarusoba,* iced buckwheat noodles. The slithery greenish-brown noodles are piled on a little bamboo tray, dipped before eating into a sauce made of soy sauce and *dashi* (all-purpose Japanese soup stock, *Recipe Index)* and garnished with chopped scallions and bits of seaweed.

The Japanese have too high a regard for their green tea ever to imbibe it cold. Instead, on hot summer days, they drink a kind of cold "tea" made by brewing roasted barley grains in a teapot. Just what makes their *mugicha* so refreshing I cannot say, but it does have a tonic aftereffect. Nowadays, carbonated beverages and ice cream are as popular in Japan as anywhere else, but a plate of *zarusoba* and a cup of *mugicha* still win my vote as the best aids to comfort on one of those awful, sultry Tokyo August afternoons.

Autumn arrives suddenly, in early September, and not even in the concrete jungle of Tokyo do you need a menu to tell you that the season has changed. The summer vanishes overnight and you wake up to what most Japanese consider the finest season of the year—cool, dry air, the sky scrubbed blue, and a hint of changing colors on the trees, on the kimono of the women, and on the cup that holds your morning tea.

The first—and perhaps the most important—gastronomic event of autumn is the September appearance of *matsutake,* which may very well be the world's most delicious mushroom. Certainly no other mushroom I have eaten ever tasted like steak. A smaller product called *shiitake* (available dried in the United States) is by far the most common mushroom in Japanese cookery, but to the Japanese the huge *matsutake* (often eight inches across) is the mushroom king, and they properly make as much fuss over it as they do about strawberries in the spring and *ayu* and eels in the summer.

Matsutake grows in red pine forests. In districts thus favored, such as the

Continued on page 36

This "frost spotted" model house suggests winter, the season when abalone strips are broiled at table on a hot stone.

The Right Food Honored at the Right Season in the Right Setting

The Japanese reverence for nature, which manifests itself at every turn, is perhaps most frequently perceived in the serving of food. For to the Japanese food is the most essential product of nature and therefore an especially favored object of respect. Kaichi Tsuji, a noted chef and master teacher of Japanese *grande cuisine,* puts it this way: "Food should be prepared to do honor to the essence of the materials chosen." By this he means that food is appropriately honored when it is served in season and when its full flavor is brought out without the addition of anything alien to its inherent taste. Great chefs like Kaichi Tsuji further enhance the delights of fine food by devising exquisite presentations that please the eye as well as the palate; seen above is one example of their skill in this regard and others are pictured overleaf. While certain Western dishes depend on seasonal foods for their excellence, seasonal Japanese dishes go a step further by creating a subtle interplay of substance and symbolism. To be sure, the season dictates the food to be used, but it is the chefs who invent compatible settings that make the finished dishes charming salutes to a particular time of the year.

MAY: FESTIVAL FOOD

In Japan the fifth day of May is Children's Day. But the day was formerly dedicated to boys, and some of the festive food still reflects this emphasis. Special stress is laid on manliness and courage. The serving pictured—an artistic still life complete with a teak frame—consists of prawns shaped like a samurai warrior's helmet *(center, top)* and accompanying green circlets made of cucumber slices cut to simulate an ancient coat of arms suitable for an adventurer. Other foods are rice and sea bream wrapped in bamboo leaves and seaweed, and crisp ginger spears *(left)*; roast duck, mushrooms and green soybeans *(right)*. The box above the plate holds a special candy.

AUGUST: HORS D'OEUVRE

To combat the debilitating effect of summer on the appetite, this meal uses psychological as well as culinary weapons. The cool appearance of the glass plate sets the mood for this light hot-weather meal. Green maple leaves placed beneath a transparent tray are a summery base for *(counterclockwise from top edge)* smoked salmon, sea urchin and white meat of sea bream, bean curd, green soybeans and fried chicken. Next to this array is a pitcher of *sake*. The lacelike crystal plate offers visual refreshment with its green *nori* seaweed, cucumber stuffed with plum paste, and raw prawns. At right on the yellow dish are salted, dried bonito. On the long green leaf are cucumber and river trout.

SEPTEMBER: MOON FOOD

The autumnal colors of this traditional meal, together with warm *sake,* bring joy to Japanese viewing the moon during the semi-annual Tsukimi Festival. The red lacquer bowl contains *akadashi* soup, whose base of *dashi* and red soybean paste is the starting point for many variations. Above it are steamed abalone and cucumber with a special soy sauce. In the quartered tray, the red dish holds broiled rock trout. The chicken made of rice has an eye made of a green pea. In the blue-rimmed dish are fern fronds, boiled bamboo shoots and two bean-curd balls. At upper right are shrimp, eel-and-burdock cylinders and half an egg that represents the moon surrounded by clouds.

DECEMBER: EXOTIC CASSEROLE

Winter brings a solid dinner whose somber colors befit the season. In the pot on the upper tray are thick slices of white *daikon* radish, reddish octopus and *konnyaku,* a jellylike food made from devil's tongue. The fluted bowl contains a hot prepared mustard —stinging by Japanese standards; numbing to unwary Westerners —with which morsels are gingerly anointed. The uncovered bowl holds *akadashi* soup, also encountered above, here varied by addition of bits of mushroom and *daikon.* In the covered bowl is rice. The oblong plate offers raw sea bream surrounded by three different garnishes. Diners dip the raw fish into the grated *daikon* in the tiny bowl to add a tangy flavor.

area around Osaka and Kyoto, *matsutake* gathering is one of the happiest festivals of the year. Thousands of local people, their ranks swelled by many salivating Tokyoites who zip down on the new superexpress, swarm through specially reserved forest areas carrying *sake,* rice and cooking pots. There are family groups, factory and office excursions paid for by the boss, and clusters of businessmen, accompanied by geisha or bar hostesses hired for the day (on the expense account) to provide even more zest to the outing. They pick their *matsutake,* preferably those with the crown only half opened, cook them on the spot and savor the taste, with *sake* and laughter, under the trees. It's a delightful and often ribald way to harmonize with nature.

Most Japanese, who can't afford the time and money to go to the *matsutake,* need only wait and the *matsutake* will come to them. At the peak of the season the *matsutake* turns up everywhere. Even restaurants that never serve another mushroom all year offer *matsutake* to keep their regular customers from straying. Housewives cook it at home, *sukiyaki* houses add it to their ingredients, restaurants offering a Japanese version of Western cookery serve it like a meat dish, on a platter with vegetables, while chefs at the great restaurants spin webs of subtle taste adventure to complement the hearty flavor of the mushroom. Often *matsutake* will be cooked only with *tofu,* which is bland, so that no extraneous taste will mar the mushroom's purity. To many Japanese, however, *matsutake* marinated in soy sauce and sweet *sake,* and then grilled, is a filling, satisfying meal in itself. Others prefer it in *dobin mushi,* steamed with chicken, fish and ginkgo nuts in small earthenware pots, one for each person. *Matsutake meshi,* rice cooked with the mushroom, is the simple dish of the pine-forest picnics and is popular wherever rice is served.

In Japan as elsewhere, autumn is also the season for fruits and nuts. In modern times, Western fruits such as apples, pears, grapes and (for late-summer eating) peaches have been introduced to the country, and Japanese orchards produce fabulously delicious crops. But for the tradition-minded Japanese, the fruit that truly says autumn is the bright orange *kaki,* or persimmon, ripening in farmyards and on hillsides all over Japan.

Fresh, the *kaki* is segmented and served as dessert all autumn long; its taste lies somewhere between apple and apricot. Dried, the *kaki* becomes a winter staple, excellent for between-meal nibbling, and an indispensable part of the New Year holiday. *Kaki* is rich in vitamin C, and since ancient times the Japanese have recognized its medicinal properties as well as its seasonal beauty and taste. Persimmons are said to be an effective, quick antidote for overindulgence in *sake.* Oldtimers in some parts of the country still prescribe *kaki* leaves for coughs, high blood pressure and various digestive upsets.

October brings chestnuts and the ginkgo nut, the latter peculiar to the Orient. In the Kansai (the Osaka-Kyoto area), chestnuts go into an autumn dish called *fukiyose,* a colorful melange of nuts, shrimp, *matsutake* and vegetables, arranged to suggest a pile of autumn leaves. Some rural areas celebrate a chestnut festival, cooking the nuts in rice and making a special sweet rice cake flavored with chestnuts. In some poorer mountain districts of Japan, boiled and mashed chestnuts are made into dumplings and eaten as a staple food.

The little ginkgo nut is used in soups and cooked dishes all year round, but the Japanese eat it for its own flavor in the fall. Before they can get to the meat of the nut they must wash off a soft, outer covering. Then a hard white shell is cracked. Finally, after roasting, a filmy inner skin comes off, revealing the green gem within. Traditionally a family gathers around the hibachi on autumn evenings to roast ginkgo nuts over charcoal and eat them hot. Nowadays the nuts are also used to bring a whiff of autumn and a mood of nostalgia to some of Tokyo's sleek, Western-style bars.

For those Japanese who care deeply about every aspect of their food, November is the memorable moment when rice *(gohan* in Japanese), fresh from harvest, tastes best. Country people who have moved to the city send home in November for a sack of the early rice of their district, and even housewives who have lived all their lives in town know that the moist new rice (distinguished by a special name, *shinmai*) requires less water for cooking than last year's dried-out grains.

Rice is something more than a staple food for the Japanese. For centuries it was their standard of wealth; feudal fiefs were ranked according to their rice yield and samurai were paid in rice. Even today shrines to Inari, the rice god, are the most ubiquitous in Japan and an integral part of the folk culture. The very word for "meal" in Japan is *gohan*—rice—and a Japanese doesn't feel he has eaten until he's had his bowl of rice, regardless of how many other good foods may have led up to it.

Sometimes, for variety, the Japanese will pour different sauces over their rice or cook it with other ingredients. But the freshly harvested *shinmai* is al-

Imposing a decorative design, the crisscrossed bamboo strips form the protective wrapping of carefully boxed fresh *shiitake* mushrooms. Harvested both in the spring and fall, *shiitake* are much in demand, fresh or dried, for their subtle flavoring and visual interest.

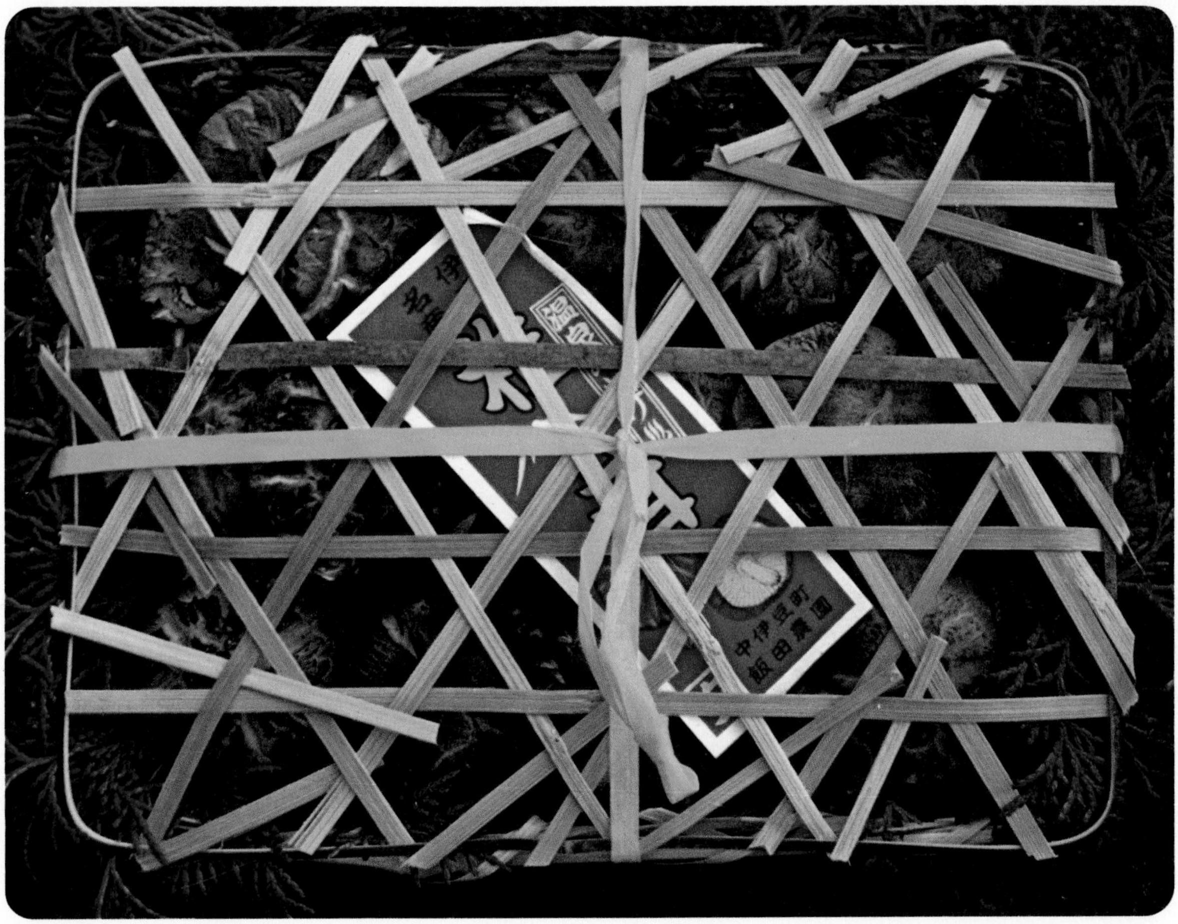

most never "spoiled" this way, for the Japanese insist that they find in it a taste and goodness that speak of the season, the land and their heritage in pure and elemental voice.

All through the autumn, as the ocean waters cool and spawning ends, fattened fish check in on schedule and take their places on the Japanese menu. One of the first to arrive is the *kamasu,* a species of barracuda, followed quickly by *samma,* a mackerel-pike. By December, most of the scores of varieties of sea creatures that nourish Japan are plentiful *(Chapter 4).*

Winter is the time for white-meat fishes, raw, broiled and deep-fried *(tempura).* It is the season for warming fish stews, like the *sampei jiru* of far-northern Honshu and Hokkaido: a thick salmon soup with vegetables. In winter, *fugu,* the dangerous globefish *(Chapter 4),* is at its best and hot *sake* at its most effective. And it is on winter evenings that you are most likely to hear the plaintive, reedy wail of the noodle vendor's horn; for although the Japanese eat noodles—both buckwheat *soba* and the heavier wheat variety called *udon*—all year round, hot noodles, served in dozens of combinations of fish, meat and vegetables, are particularly appropriate to cold weather.

Foods cooked at the table, like *sukiyaki* and *mizutaki (Recipe Index),* flourish in the winter months. *Mizutaki* is made with chicken; a similar dish, made with beef, is called *shabu shabu (Recipe Index),* because that is the sound the sliver of raw meat makes as you hold it in your chopsticks and swish it around in a pot of boiling chicken stock and *dashi.* When the meat is lightly cooked you remove it, dip it into a special sauce of *shoyu,* grated *daikon,* ground sesame seeds, *yuzu* juice and other ingredients, and enjoy it. Then the winter vegetable *hakusai* (which we call Chinese cabbage) and *tofu* are boiled in the same liquid and, after they are consumed, *udon* noodles are sometimes added to the rich broth remaining and eaten as a final course. The secret of *mizutaki* lies in the dipping sauce, and many restaurants specializing in the item guard their formulas jealously.

The seasonal star of the winter scene is something much more simple: the tangerine, or mandarin orange, called *mikan* in Japanese. The *mikan* is one of several citrus fruits grown in Japan, but except for expensive imported delicacies it is just about the only fresh fruit of any kind available through the winter—until that magic moment when the strawberries arrive. Legend has it that there were tangerines in Japan 2,000 years ago; history records the presence of the fruit for at least 600 years, and centuries before science discovered vitamin C the Japanese were using *mikan* juice as a tonic for colds.

From late December until early spring, tangerines are on every table, on sale in little net bags at subway newsstands, and often served with the cup of tea that precedes all business discourse. On New Year's they join rice cakes on the Shinto god shelves as standard holiday offerings—and if the deities are at all like their descendants, the offerings are hugely appreciated, for the Japanese devour the fruit in tremendous quantities. (I have seen a family group of about 10 children and adults, gathered on the New Year, casually polish off an entire crate of *mikan* in one happy, chatty, informal—and eminently healthy—afternoon.) In a way, the Japanese regard the *mikan* through the winter as a flame-colored symbol for the rising sun that will come back again in springtime to warm the earth and its people, and signal the ever-recurring miracle of the rhythm of the seasons.

Opposite:
The best, biggest and most expensive strawberries of the season reach the markets in February and signal winter's waning. These berries grow on steep terraces in the mild Pacific climate of Shizuoka Prefecture on the main island of Honshu. The box containing the 11 giant specimens in the foreground sells for about $2.50. The 20 smaller berries in the other box bring considerably less.

福羽

III

The Logic of Japanese Cookery

A variety of cutting and cooking techniques produced the displays in this delightful autumn *bento* box. The foods range from the simple *kimeyaki (top left)* and *temarizushi (top right)* to the elaborate *igaguri (below left)*. The carrot "maple leaf," the lime "flower" cradling red caviar, and the ginkgo-nut leaf made of *fu* all serve to carry out the autumn theme.

After thinking about the reluctance of some of my friends to venture into Japanese cooking, I have decided that their hesitancy is largely a matter of nomenclature. I have complete sympathy with them, for the unfamiliar language can create difficulties with the names both of the ingredients and of the techniques. It takes effort of will to keep in mind that—despite the similarity in sound—*shioyaki* means food sprinkled with salt prior to broiling, while *sukiyaki* is a dish prepared by simmering, and has nothing to do with broiling. In time the pieces do fall into place as it becomes clear that there is a logic to the organization of Japanese cooking, and to its language.

The most important lesson to be learned deals with the ubiquitous role of the soybean. Generally considered by Westerners to be the most humble of vegetables, the soybean is in fact the king of the Japanese kitchen. One might almost say that Japanese cuisine is built upon a tripod of soybean products: *miso,* a fermented soybean paste; *tofu,* a custardlike soybean cake; and soy sauce, used both to season foods as they are being cooked and to make dipping mixtures that enhance the flavors of foods as they are being eaten.

Miso has a distinctive taste that sets its mark on other ingredients. And it forms a vital part of hundreds of Japanese dishes. *Miso* appears in many guises on Japanese menus starting with a favorite breakfast dish, *misoshiru,* the rich soup for which *miso* is essential. *Miso* may be an ingredient in a marinade for vegetables and fish and is also used in some recipes as part of a dressing in which foods are broiled. Because every maker of *miso* varies the proportions of the ingredients according to his taste, because *miso* improves with age (it can be kept in wooden vats for as long as a decade without spoiling) and also because it varies in strength, no two *miso* will taste exactly alike to a sensitive palate.

The second great soybean product in Japanese cooking is *tofu,* which looks like and has the consistency of firm but fragile cakes of whitish custard. To Westerners, *tofu* comes close to being tasteless; the Japanese consider it a blotter for other flavors as well as a separate taste. It is sautéed, boiled, broiled; used to garnish soups; rolled in cornstarch and deep-fried; scrambled with eggs; mixed with sesame seed. So versatile is it as an accompaniment to almost the entire range of Japanese foods that some restaurants take great pride in preparing only dishes that make use of *tofu.*

Until recently the American wishing to cook with *tofu* had to find an Oriental food store whose owner gets his own supply. For *tofu,* even when refrigerated, spoils after three or four days. Happily, the Japanese have learned how to make instant, powdered *tofu,* which is reconstituted by mixing with boiling water and a coagulating agent included in the package. The powder can be stored, without refrigeration, almost indefinitely, and reconstituted *tofu* will stay fresh in the refrigerator for as long as 10 days. The flavor of reconstituted *tofu* is at least as satisfactory as the fresh variety. *Tofu* is also now available in cans, and although slightly less flavorsome than the instant product, its texture makes it desirable for certain dishes.

The third member of the soybean triumvirate is *shoyu,* or soy sauce, whose ingredients include not only soybeans but also wheat or barley, salt, water and malt. Its preparation is rather complicated and hardly worth the effort, for it can be bought at almost any supermarket. The Japanese, like the Chinese who invented it, use soy sauce as a dip, as a seasoning for cooking liquids, and as an ingredient in marinades. But for the Japanese, soy sauce is their all-purpose seasoning, as important to their country's cuisine as salt is to Western foods. One word of caution: Insist on soy sauce imported from Japan; neither the artificially flavored domestic nor the heavier Chinese versions are at all satisfactory in Japanese cooking.

The soybean's only important rival is rice. In Japan, rice occupies an even more important place than wheat and wheat products do today in the West. In fact, a repast without rice in some form would be just about unthinkable; it is hardly surprising, therefore, that a great deal of space is devoted to rice recipes in Japanese cookbooks. But since rice is so intimately connected with family eating, we will discuss its preparation in Chapter 5.

Other ingredients frequently used in the preparation of vegetables, seafood, meat and fowl include: mild rice vinegar; sesame oil; the sweet rice wine called *mirin;* the stronger rice wine called *sake;* a green horseradish powder called *wasabi; daikon,* the giant white radish that resembles the white turnip in taste; the strips of dried gourd called *kanpyo; gobo,* or burdock root; and *shirataki,* a preparation made from a yamlike tuber.

Japanese cooks also use such familiar seasonings as salt, pepper, mustard, sugar, chives, scallions, onions and other foods found in most American kitchens. But there was a time, not so very long ago, when an American interested in preparing Japanese meals had to write to importers in order to obtain the unfamiliar ingredients. Today, however, the situation has markedly improved. While fresh ginger root and *shiitake* (dried Japanese mushrooms) are hardly staple items in every supermarket, an amazing variety of Japanese ingredients is now readily available in the Oriental and gourmet food stores found in almost every major American city.

Once the Westerner who has decided to explore Japanese cooking has been introduced to the ingredients that are unique to this cuisine, the time has arrived to learn the methods by which the people of Japan prepare their meals. As they usually cook meat and vegetables in small pieces, the Japanese have never developed the arts of baking and roasting; they do, however, broil, boil, steam, fry and grill, using techniques quite similar to Western ones but with just enough variation to produce their own distinctive cuisine.

Take broiled fish, for example. In most of the world, it is usual to baste fish with butter while it is broiling to assure its moistness. This is never the case in Japan. There, fish is often salt-broiled by the method called *shioyaki,* and I have never eaten elsewhere a moister or more flavorful broiled fish. Like so many Japanese cooking methods, this is very simple. The fish is salted and then set aside for 20 to 30 minutes before cooking. Then it is placed in the broiler, skin side up, where it remains until the skin becomes golden brown. The fish is then turned over so that its flesh is exposed to the flame. The dish is ready to eat when there is a flow of milky-white juices from between the flakes of the flesh. At precisely this point, the fish must be removed from the broiler; another minute or two of the heat will dry it out.

This method of broiling works with just about any kind of fish one can name. The only requirement is that there be some skin on the fish, for under the skin lies a thin layer of fat that is worked on by the salt. The fat melts and protects the flesh from the heat and moistens and flavors the fish. From their experience with the *shioyaki* method, Japanese cooks have learned to avoid fish that has been skinned and boned. A great deal of flavor lies in the bones and under the skin, flavor that is imparted to the flesh during broiling. The Japanese know this and therefore do very little filleting. But the Japanese do cut away the skin and bones when a fish is to be deep-fried for *tempura,* or on most occasions when it is served raw as *sashimi,* or in some dishes that require boiling with strong soy sauce.

Shioyaki broiling is not limited to fish. A number of other foods, particularly chicken, are enhanced by this quick and simple method. But there are other types of broiling done in Japan. One sure-fire method, relatively well known in the United States, is *teriyaki,* which translates as "shining broil." This is almost as simple as salt broiling, but it does require a marinade made up of soy sauce and *mirin,* usually in equal proportions, although proportions and ingredients may vary and sometimes chicken broth is added for delicacy and to prevent scorching. With some *teriyaki* dishes the marinade does triple or even quadruple duty, serving as a flavoring agent before cooking, a basting sauce during cooking, a glaze to complete the dish, and sometimes as a dipping sauce after cooking. The final results of *teriyaki* broiling *(Recipe Index)* are dishes with a mild, delicate and sweet flavor.

As in all Japanese cookery, timing is of the utmost importance in *teriyaki* broiling. It matters not whether foods are broiled, boiled, steamed or fried, the relationship between the thing being cooked and the degree of heat it is receiving remains uppermost in the minds of Japanese cooks. A good example of this principle is the care with which some Japanese prepare so simple a dish as eggs fried sunny side up. First they brush the pan with sesame oil and heat it until it is sizzling. This done, they break the egg into the pan

Basic Japanese Ingredients

The Japanese ingredients listed below and illustrated overleaf are described further on page 199. Nearly all are available in the U.S.

1 *Kome* (Japanese rice)
2 *Sake* (rice wine)
3 *Su* (rice vinegar)
4 *Mirin* (sweet *sake)*
5 Canned vegetables: *top left, konnyaku; center, shirataki* (both made from the same plant root); *right, takenoko* (bamboo shoot); *bottom,* sliced *renkon* (lotus root)
6 *Junsai* (slippery vegetables)
7 *Gobo* (burdock)
8 *Azuki* (red) and *kuromame* (black) beans
9 *From left: Goma* (black and white sesame seeds), *ginnan* (ginkgo nuts)
10 *Goma-abura* (sesame oil)
11 *Tsukemono* (pickles): *clockwise from top left,* large pickled plums, pickled yellow radish, red pickled ginger, small pickled plums
12 Mushrooms: *from left, nameko, matsutake,* dried *shiitake*
13 *Fu* (wheat gluten croutons)
14 *Udon* (thick wheat noodles)
15 *Hiyamugi* (thin noodles served cold)
16 *Somen* (thin wheat noodles)
17 *Harusame* (cellophane or transparent noodles)
18 *Daikon* (white radish)
19 *Uni* (pickled sea urchin)
20 *Aonoriko* (powdered green seaweed)
21 *Shoga* (ginger root)
22 *Kona sansho* (Japanese pepper)
23 *Hichimi togarashi* (seven-pepper spice)
24 *Clockwise from top right: sansho* (Japanese pepper leaf), Aji-no-moto (MSG), *takano tjume* (small whole red peppers), *karashi* (mustard)
25 *Shoyu* (Japanese all-purpose soy sauce)
26 *From top: aka miso* (red soybean paste), *shiro miso* (white soybean paste), *tofu* (soybean curd)
27 *Kombu* (dried kelp)
28 Preflaked *katsuobushi* (dried bonito)
29 *Katsuobushi* (dried bonito)
30 *Nori* (dried laver)
31 *Wakame* (dried seaweed)

SAKIGAKE OZEKI
MITSUKAN
RICE VINEGAR
MITSUKAN BRAND
ミツカン酢
IMPORTED BY
IMPORTED BRANDS INC.
NEW YORK, N.Y.
SESAME OIL
1
2
3
4
5
6
7
8
9
10
11
12
14

31
29
30
18
17
28
27
19
15
20
26
21
13
16
ALL-PURPOSE
Kikkoman
SOY SAUCE
24
25
22
23

and move the pan around so that the heat is evenly distributed. When the egg white is solid, the Japanese pour one teaspoon of cold water around the egg. The reason for this is simple: the egg whites, being thinner than the yolk, cook much faster. The cold water retards the cooking of the whites, preventing them from getting too hard while the thick yolk slowly heats through. Thus the entire egg cooks at a single speed.

Until comparatively recently, eggs as they are eaten in the West played a rather small part in Japanese cuisine. But the popularity of egg dishes has been growing. In fact, a wide variety of egg dishes is now available in the better restaurants and in sophisticated households. One of my favorites is the Japanese version of the omelet. Called *tamago dashimaki (Recipe Index),* the dish consists of layer upon paper-thin layer of egg, each layer cooked in an oblong pan for a few seconds and then rolled around the previous layer. Although it requires painstaking attention to cooking time and a dexterity that comes only with practice, the result is worth the effort. Served either hot or at room temperature and garnished with grated *daikon,* it makes a perfect brunch or lunch dish, light, delicate and delicious.

Beef, like eggs, is not an important element in the diet of most Japanese because it is just too expensive—good cuts are about $1.50 a pound, while the best cost as much as $10 a pound—but there is no better or more tender beef in the world. The best cuts are cooked very plainly. One way is to fry the steaks in an iron skillet or on a griddle and then serve them with a dipping sauce called *ponzu,* which is half soy sauce and half lemon or lime juice. Another popular method is to broil the steaks on a wire net over charcoal, the meat having been dipped in a sauce made of equal parts of thickened soy sauce and *mirin.* Whether fried or broiled, the steaks themselves are always cut thin, no more than a quarter inch thick. Any thicker and the outside would get done before the inside—a desecration to the Japanese palate.

It is ironic that beef *sukiyaki (Recipe Index),* the most widely known Japanese dish, should come from a cuisine that makes relatively little use of meat. The word *sukiyaki* (pronounced *skee-yah-kee*) means "broiled on the blade of a plow." This name reveals the origins of the dish, for in ancient days farmers in the field, or hunters in the wild, often killed animals and cooked their meat over an open fire on whatever utensils were available, such as a plow blade. However, modern *sukiyaki* is misnamed, for *yaki* refers to broiled foods and today's dish is not broiled. In fact it straddles two categories of Japanese cooking: *nabemono,* which applies to dishes cooked at the dining table, and *nimono,* which means boiling in seasoned liquids. *Sukiyaki* is both cooked at the table and simmered in seasoned liquids.

As an element of *nabemono* cooking, *sukiyaki* is a rather important dish; within the gargantuan *nimono* category it is merely one of hundreds. There are at least 15 major subdivisions of this boiling method—each characterized by a different kind of seasoned liquid, and each embracing a host of dishes. One familiar *nimono* technique is merely to cook meat or vegetables in lightly salted water. However *nimono* liquids run the gamut from stocks strongly flavored with seasonings that include ginger, sugar and *sake* to broths so mild that only the barest hint of their taste is present in the cooked food.

Nimono methods can be used with nearly every kind of foodstuff. One of the simplest, yet most flavorful, *nimono* dishes is called *kimini (Recipe Index).*

In this dish, shrimp are quickly blanched and then rapidly cooked in a boiling liquid containing *niban dashi* (an all-purpose stock), *sake,* sugar and salt. After the few moments it takes for the shrimp to become pinkish white, indicating that they are firm and almost done, beaten egg yolks are poured over them, the pot is covered, and the shrimp steamed for two minutes. In that short time the egg yolks form a rich glaze that both beautifies the shrimp and adds savor.

One *nimono* subdivision combines two categories of the art: *umani,* which means boiling in a liquid that is quite sweet, and "interrupted cooking," in which one of several means is used to halt the cooking process, permitting the food to cool before cooking is completed. To make one of my favorite *umani* dishes *(Recipe Index),* vegetables such as carrots, bamboo shoots, *shiitake* and green peas are combined with strips of boned chicken breast and all are lightly sautéed together in oil. Then the ingredients are taken off the heat and boiled in a mixture of *dashi,* sugar and soy sauce until the liquid has evaporated and the vegetables and fowl are coated with, and penetrated by, the cooking liquid. This dish is great for picnics, for it can be made in advance, eaten at room temperature and requires no dipping sauces.

Interrupted cooking—which may seem unnecessarily complicated—has two purposes: to cook out the bitterness of some foods in one liquid and then to complete the preparation in a second; and to maintain an exact control over the preparation process so that the ingredients cook evenly on the outside and within. This awareness that the inside and outside of foods cannot cook at the same speed explains why the Japanese and other Oriental peoples avoid working with large pieces of meat and vegetables.

Another cooking technique that is very popular in Japan is steaming. This method is simple and the foods prepared in this manner are both flavorful and nutritious. Properly steamed vegetables are crisp and their natural flavors and nutrients virtually intact. For the Japanese, steaming takes the place of American casserole cooking when all the ingredients are to be prepared together. But instead of the American casserole's blending of tastes, each element in the steamed Japanese "casserole" retains its own unique flavor though it may be subtly modified by the other ingredients.

There are two basic methods of steaming Japanese style. The first, called *mushi,* involves food suspended on a plate over boiling water. In many *mushi* dishes, the ingredients are simply seasoned with salt before being steamed, and the end product is a dish that is rather mild in taste. However, the Japanese dip each morsel into one of several sauces before eating it. The dipping sauce imparts a distinct flavor while the steamed ingredient provides texture and body, together with just enough taste of its own; each *mushi* food is clearly different from all others, even when the same dipping sauce is used in every case. Most *mushi* dipping sauces are easy and quick to prepare; if you make several for a *mushi* meal, your guests can experience a wide variety of flavor-and-texture combinations. (See Recipe Index for *mushi* recipes.)

Mushi foods acquire slightly more taste during steaming when they rest in a bath of *sake.* As the food steams so does the wine, and the vapors of the *sake* permeate the meat, vegetables or fish, imparting to them a flavor so subtle that the dipping sauce remains an essential element of the final product.

A second kind of steamed foods, *chawan mushi,* or foods steamed in egg custard *(Recipe Index),* requires no dipping sauces. Since the ingredients to

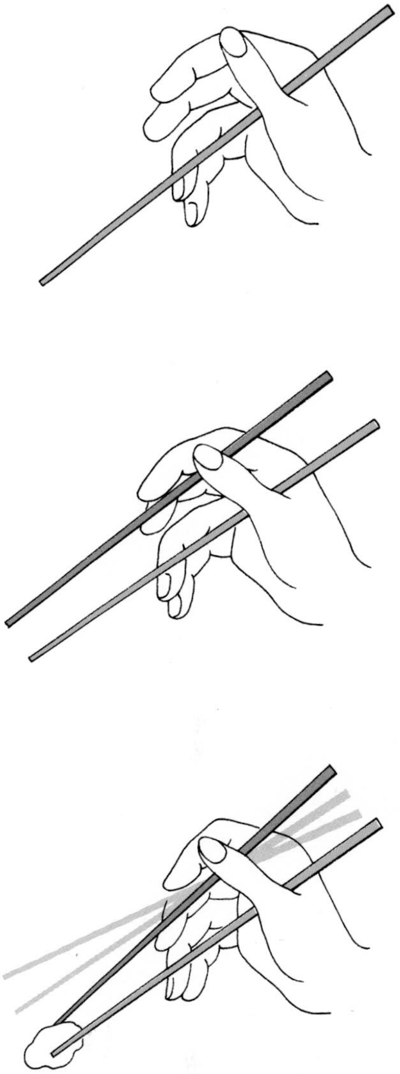

AT EASE WITH CHOPSTICKS

As the top drawing shows, place a chopstick in the crook of the thumb, about one third of the way down from the thicker end of the stick. It should rest on the inside tip of the ring finger. Then *(center),* place the second chopstick so that it lies between the index and middle fingers like a pencil; press it against these fingers with the cushion of the thumb. Keep the point of the top stick extended a little past the point of the lower stick. Keeping the lower stick motionless, move the upper stick down to meet the lower, and grasp the food by bending the index and middle fingers as in the bottom drawing. (This is but one of several workable ways to use chopsticks.)

MSG and the Oriental Food Syndrome

In many of the recipes throughout this book, MSG—a crystalline powder—is called for in the ingredient list as a flavor enhancer. You may have read of the "Chinese restaurant syndrome," in which MSG, monosodium glutamate, was identified as the culprit. After eating in Chinese restaurants—which use MSG more extensively than do Japanese—some diners have on occasion complained of burning sensations, a feeling of pressure in the chest, and facial tightness or numbness. Usually these symptoms occur after eating soup or another first course on an empty stomach. They rarely last more than an hour. The cause appears to be the use of 1/4 teaspoon or more of MSG per serving, a greater amount of the substance than is ordinarily specified for portions in this book.

be bathed in custard are properly seasoned before cooking, dipping sauces are unnecessary, for they would interfere with flavor rather than enhance it.

Whichever method of steaming is used, the key to success is to prevent the steam that condenses on the lid from falling on the ingredients, for this would dilute the delicate flavors. The Japanese employ several specially designed kinds of steaming pots to forestall this dire possibility, but an ordinary lidded pot is a satisfactory substitute; merely place a folded dish towel over the pot before covering it, and the towel will catch the condensate as it falls from the lid. As the towel becomes saturated, it should be replaced. For *chawan mushi* dishes, the Japanese use a special lidded ceramic cup; coffee or custard cups, tightly covered with aluminum foil, do just as well.

One Japanese cooking technique that is rarely attempted by foreigners (yet is simple enough) is called *mushiyaki.* As the name implies, this is a hybrid form, combining elements of steaming and broiling. Unlike other steaming techniques *mushiyaki* uses no water; instead the steam is supplied by the food's own moisture. I particularly enjoy one form of this category called *horakuyaki.* In Japan this is made in a *horoku,* a thick, unglazed pottery bowl hardly ever found in America; a conventional unglazed casserole with a tight-fitting lid makes a perfectly adequate alternative.

In *horoku* cooking a layer of salt is spread across the bottom of the pot, which is then heated to a high temperature. Bits of beef, fish, shellfish or vegetables are placed on the salt, and the pot is covered and returned to the heat. The hot salt causes the moisture inside the food to turn to steam, and this steam, in turn, cooks the ingredients. *Horakuyaki* dishes *(Recipe Index)* are both colorful and flavorful, affording a double pleasure.

When the Japanese serve the steamed or broiled or fried dishes that we might consider main courses, they usually accompany them with a kind of salad. Of salads there are two basic types: *aemono* (mixed things) and *sunomono* (vinegared things). In *aemono* dishes, several raw or cooked ingredients are tossed together with one of many dressings or sauces that are sticky and thick, much like mayonnaise in texture, though not in ingredients. These dressings generally use *tofu* or *miso* or ground sesame seeds as their major ingredient. A very simple but tasty *aemono* dish is spinach dressed with toasted sesame seeds and *miso.*

Although some *aemono* recipes do contain vinegar, it is in the *sunomono* category that vinegar shines. Most *sunomono* dishes have as their main ingredients raw, crisp vegetables—such as sliced cucumber or grated white radish—and a cold cooked fish or shellfish. *Sunomono* dishes take a thin dressing made of rice vinegar, plus *dashi,* sugar and soy sauce.

I have left for last a discussion of *agemono,* or fried things, according to many the pride and glory of Japanese cuisine. The Japanese deep-fry in batter, they deep-fry without batter and they pan-fry in oil. While these methods are familiar to us, there is little similarity between the results achieved by Japanese and Western cooks. American fried foods tend to be heavy and greasy. Japanese fried foods, on the other hand, are as light as air and as delicate as a soft spring breeze. The difference lies in the centuries-old techniques that bring out the most subtle of flavors inherent in each food.

Take *tempura* for example. This Japanese dish is known throughout the world, though mostly in the form of deep-fried batter-coated shrimp. In fact, almost any food can be used to make *tempura*—chicken, fish and all vegetables save for those that are particularly watery, such as white radish, cabbage and cucumbers. *Tempura (Recipe Index)* is almost the perfect dish to explore, for its preparation combines many of the principles of Japanese frying and its taste puts it at the very apex of Japanese cuisine. For the Japanese the preparation of oil for frying is almost an art in itself; they blend various kinds of oils with all the painstaking care that a perfume manufacturer takes in blending scents in order to impart to the ingredients the exact taste favored by the chef. Every *tempura* cook has his own favorite blend of oils. One blend I know of is a mixture of 85 per cent cottonseed oil, 10 per cent olive oil and 5 per cent sesame-seed oil. Another combines peanut oil with sesame-seed oil and olive oil in proportions of 75 per cent, 20 per cent and 5 per cent respectively. My own favorite blend is simple indeed: 70 per cent peanut oil to 30 per cent sesame oil.

While the oil is heating up, the Japanese cook coats the *tempura* ingredients with batter, which may contain a variety of ingredients but almost always includes egg, ice-cold water and flour. The trick here is to get the batter as cold as possible; generally the batter is placed in a glass bowl surrounded by ice. Each morsel of food is lightly coated with this thin batter—so thin that the colors of the food show through, thus adding a visual element to the gastronomical delight—and the morsels are quickly popped into the hot oil, which should be 375° F. As it hits the hot oil, the icy batter literally explodes, puffing up and swelling so that the food inside is partly cooked in its own self-generated steam and partly cooked by the oil.

Tempura is one of the very few Japanese dishes that should always be served right out of the pan. Anyone preparing it should cut the ingredients beforehand, divide them into individual portions, and cook one portion at a time. The deep-frying process is so rapid that the first guest to be served will hardly have gotten well under way before the last guest has received his plate. After each portion has been prepared, do as the Japanese do and skim off whatever residue of batter and food may remain in the oil. In this way the oil is kept fresh for longer use, there is no malodorous smoke from leftover bits of batter and food, and most important, there is no possibility of including bits of overdone residues in successive servings.

One other point must be taken into consideration. Never attempt to cook too much food at one time; the *tempura* ingredients should never cover more than half the pan, for overloading will lower the oil temperature and thus slow the cooking with the sad end product of soggy morsels.

If the rules are followed, *tempura* is indeed easy to prepare. So easy, in fact, that there is no need to shy away from making a true *tempura* feast. Pork and chicken, eel and red snapper, shrimp, scallops and mussels, snow peas, green pepper, okra and mushroom, eggplant and sweet potatoes—all these and more can be included. An authentic *tempura* meal comprises at least six ingredients and can have as many as 14, picked not only for their variety of tastes but also for their varieties of color, shape and texture. All are eaten with dipping sauces (see the Recipe Index for *tempura* dips).

Despite the ease and speed with which *tempura* can be made, it ranks among the great dishes of the world. If Japanese cookery had produced nothing of note other than *tempura*, this alone would be sufficient to secure Japan a place of honor in the gourmet's affections.

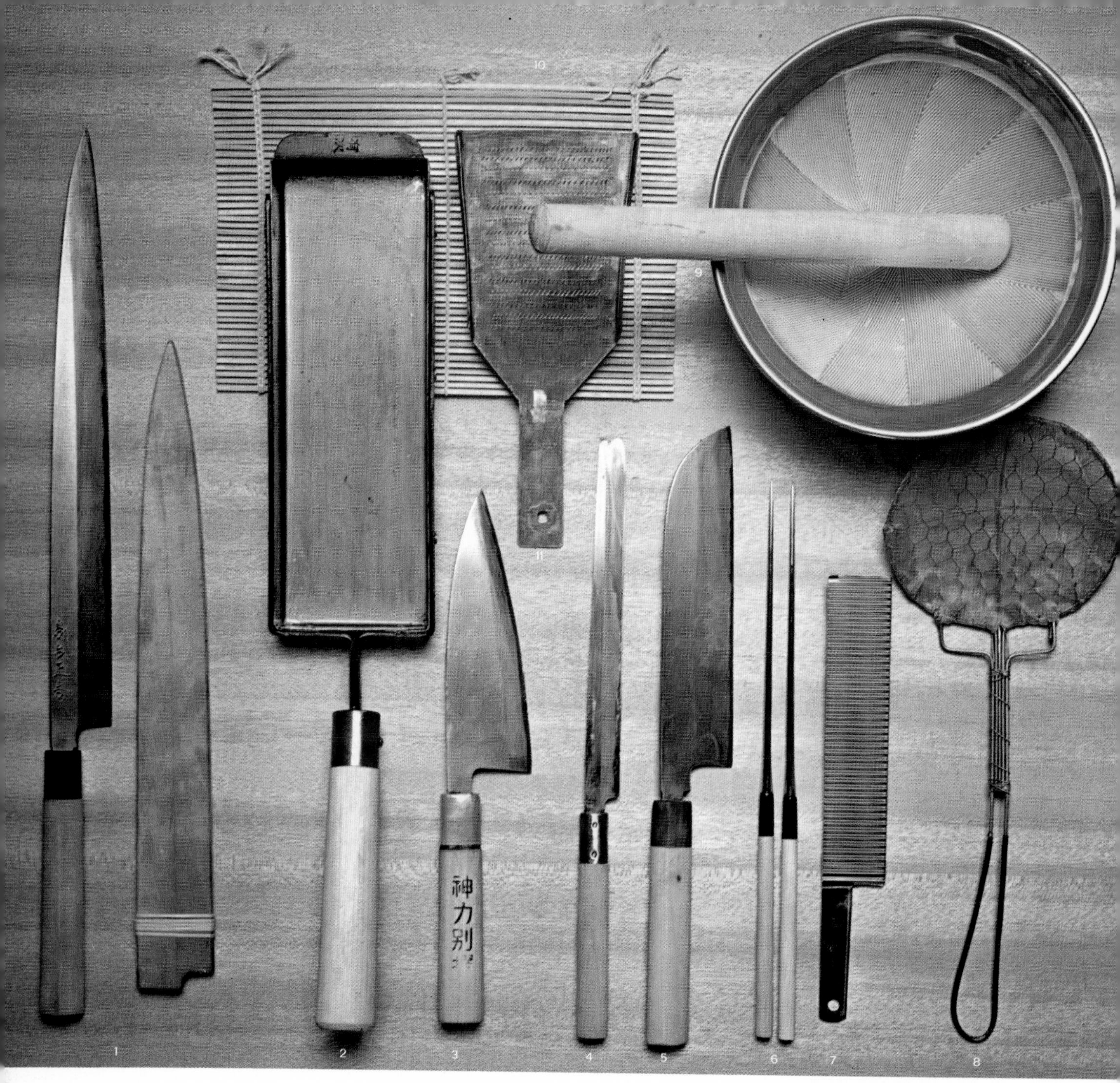

Shown above is an array of some of the specialized knives and cooking utensils used by Japanese cooks.

1 Sashimi knife and scabbard
2 Rectangular omelet pan
3 Boning knife for fish
4 Slicing knife for fish
5 Cutting knife for vegetables
6 Cooking chopsticks
7 *Tofu*-slicing knife
8 Skimmer
9 *Suribachi* (serrated mixing bowl) and wooden pestle
10 *Sodare* (bamboo) mat
11 Grater

Basic Japanese Kitchen Tools

The Japanese treat their tools used for cooking with the same respect they pay to the ingredients themselves. There are special knives for raw fish, for boning fish, for slicing vegetables and for slicing *tofu*. Although many of the kitchen tools shown here are available in the United States, Western knives, mixing bowls, graters and skimmers make perfectly acceptable substitutes. At right, chef Toshio Morimoto, consultant for *The Cooking of Japan*, uses the cutting knife for vegetables as he demonstrates how to peel a *daikon* in a single thin, continuous sheet; the end result, illustrated by the rolled-up carrot, is then finely shredded.

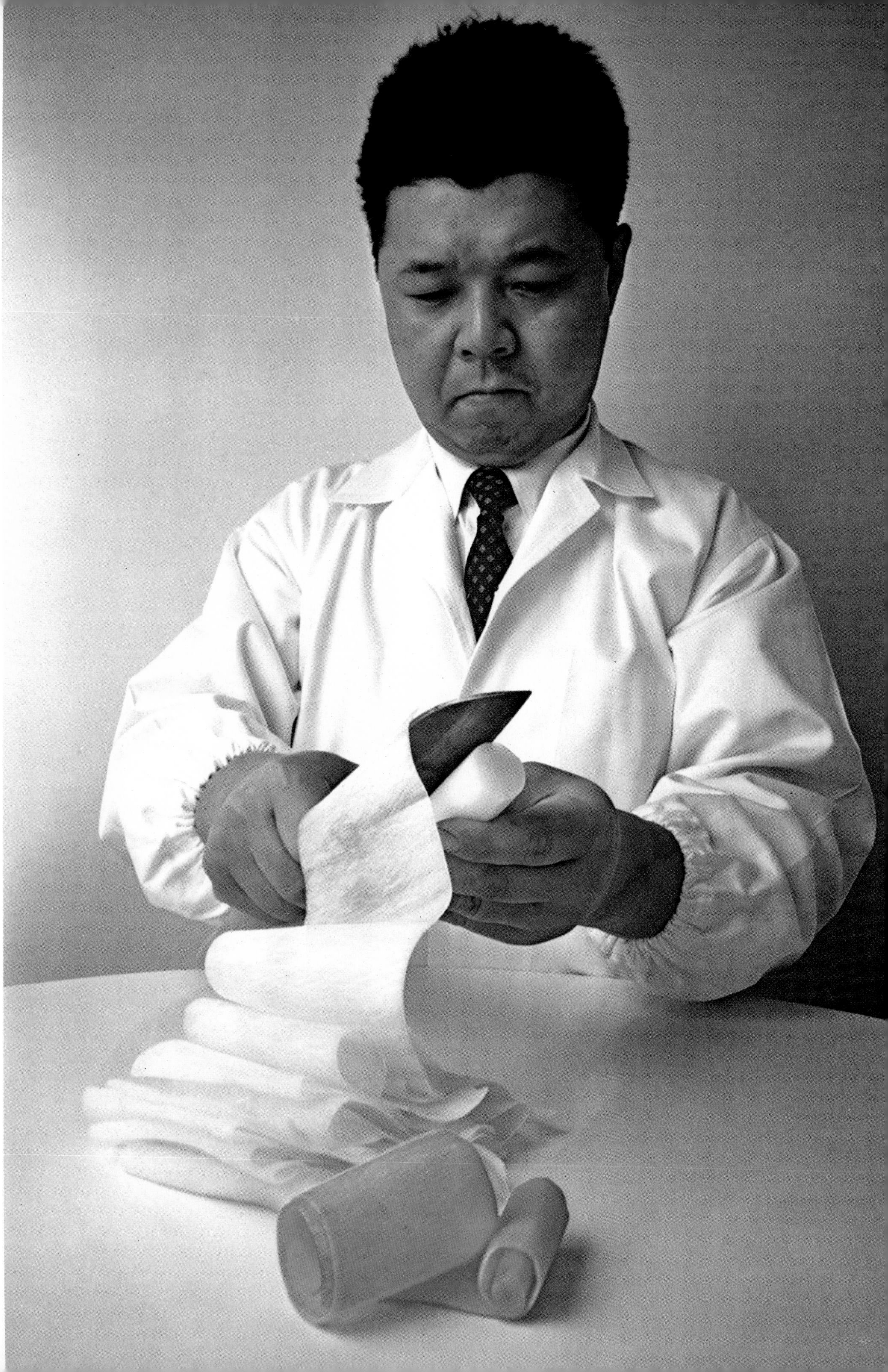

The Fine Art of Cutting and Slicing

Three of the vegetables in the vertical rows at right and opposite should be instantly recognizable to the Western cook, even if some of the end products of their cutting are not. Others are unashamedly exotic—in appearance as well as flavor—but all are basic to Japanese cooking.

1 In the first row is a *daikon,* the workhorse of Japanese vegetables. A small section of this giant white radish is shown on top; just below it is a round slice. This can then be halved, quartered, trimmed and shaped into a square or into dice. Or it can be held in the hand and cut into one thin continuous sheet *(page 51),* which is then finely shredded *(bottom pictures).*

2 The carrot in the second row also can be cut in many ways, the simplest being thin rounds. To cut obliquely, as in the bottom half of the long carrot, make a diagonal slice straight down, roll the carrot a quarter turn, and slice again. Besides being decorative, the oblique cut also provides a greater surface area for seasonings to permeate. The sheet of carrot has been cut as on page 51; this can then be shredded or cut into various-sized strips.

3 The first step in preparing cucumber is almost always to cut it in half lengthwise and to scoop out the seeds and pulp. The smaller section has been partially peeled, leaving strips of green skin that will add color to a dish. Cucumber most frequently appears in thin slices.

4 A canned bamboo shoot appears at the top of the fourth row, the second picture from the top showing a whole bamboo shoot cut obliquely. More frequently, however, the base of the bamboo shoot is cut off and the tapering top cut in half lengthwise. The base of the bamboo shoot then can be halved or quartered.

5 In row five is a lotus root—at top, a fresh root, and below it a slice, available canned. This can be trimmed or cut in any of the ways shown.

6 The last rows show the long, tapering *gobo* root, of which the economical Japanese use even the parings, shown at the tip. To the right of the whole root are *gobo* sections and various ways of slicing them.

7 The bottom picture in each of the three last rows is of an ordinary turnip—cut in an extraordinary way. The whole turnip is peeled and placed between two chopsticks. It is sliced thin to within ⅛ inch of the other side—the chopsticks help to prevent cutting through—and then turned a half turn and cut similarly. Then it is quartered.

3
4
5
6
7

Dashi and Owanrui: STOCKS AND SOUPS

Aemono and Sunomono: MIXED FOODS AND VINEGARED SALADS

Bento and Zensai: PICNIC FOOD AND HORS D'OEUVRE

DASHI AND OWANRUI: There are three basic types of soup in the Japanese cuisine: the clear soup usually served at the beginning of a meal; the slightly thicker and sweeter "miso" soups, flavored with red or white soybean paste, often served toward the end of a Japanese meal; and the more elaborate soups—almost ragoûts—which are substantial main courses at lunch or dinner.

Ichiban Dashi 一番出汁

BASIC SOUP STOCK

"Ichiban dashi" is a cornerstone of Japanese cooking—the Japanese equivalent of our chicken and beef stocks. Like them, it is used as the cooking stock for many meat, poultry and fish dishes and becomes a soup in itself with the addition of various garnishes. "Ichiban dashi" is made easily and quickly from packaged, easy-to-store items.

To make 2½ quarts

- 2½ quarts cold water
- A 3-inch square *kombu* (dried kelp), cut with a heavy knife from a sheet of packaged *kombu* and washed under cold running water
- 1 cup preflaked *katsuobushi* (dried bonito)

Pour 2½ quarts of cold water into a 4- to 6-quart pan and, over high heat, bring it to the boil. Drop in the *kombu,* let the water come just to the boil again, then immediately remove the *kombu* from the pan with tongs or a slotted spoon and set it aside. Stir the *katsuobushi* into the boiling water and turn off the heat. Let the stock rest undisturbed for about 2 minutes, or until the *katsuobushi* sinks to the bottom of the pan, then skim any surface scum with a large spoon. Place a double thickness of cheesecloth or a clean cloth napkin in a sieve set over a large bowl, pour in the stock and let it drain through undisturbed. Remove the *katsuobushi* and set it aside.

The stock may now be used as the base for a soup or stew, or as a cooking base. Although best if freshly prepared for each occasion, *ichiban dashi* can remain at room temperature up to 8 hours without appreciable loss of flavor. Or it can be cooled to room temperature, covered with plastic wrap and refrigerated for as long as 2 days.

NOTE: The cooked *kombu* and *katsuobushi* may be discarded, or they can be used in the preparation of *niban dashi (below).*

Niban Dashi 二番出汁

COOKING STOCK FOR VEGETABLES

"Niban dashi" is an economical way to use the leftover ingredients of "ichiban dashi" for an equally good but weaker stock. "Niban dashi" is used in place of water to cook vegetables.

To make 5 cups

- A 3-inch square cooked *kombu* (from *ichiban dashi, above)*
- 1 cup cooked *katsuobushi* (from *ichiban dashi, above)*
- 5 cups cold water
- ¼ cup preflaked *katsuobushi* (dried bonito)

Combine the cooked *kombu* and *katsuobushi* with 5 cups of cold water in a 2- to 3-quart saucepan, and bring almost to a boil over high heat. Add the additional 1/4 cup of uncooked *katsuobushi,* reduce the heat to its lowest point and simmer uncovered for about 5 minutes. Place a double thickness of cheesecloth or a clean cloth napkin in a sieve set over a large bowl, pour in the entire contents of the pan and let the stock drain through undisturbed. Discard the *kombu* and *katsuobushi.*

Although *niban dashi* can be used at once as a cooking stock for vegetables, it can also be kept for 8 hours at room temperature. Or it can be cooled to room temperature, covered with plastic wrap and refrigerated for as long as 2 days. Because *ichiban* and *niban dashi* look nearly the same, it is best to label their containers if they are not to be used at once.

Sumashi Wan すまし椀

CLEAR SOUP WITH TOFU AND SHRIMP

To serve 6

A 6-ounce cake fresh, canned or instant *tofu* (soybean curd), cut into 6 equal parts
A 2-inch square *kombu* (dried kelp), cut with a heavy knife from a sheet of packaged *kombu* and washed under cold running water
Salt
MSG
6 spinach leaves
6 medium-sized shrimp (16 to 20 per pound), shelled and deveined *(see page 168)*
1/4 cup cornstarch
6 cups *sumashi (page 58)*
A 2-inch piece lemon peel, cut into long, very narrow strips

ALTERNATE GARNISH

1/2 pound ground white meat of chicken
1 tablespoon Japanese all-purpose soy sauce
1/2 teaspoon sugar
A dash of *kona sansho* (Japanese pepper), or substitute freshly ground black pepper
1 egg yolk
1 tablespoon *sake* (rice wine)
A 2-inch square *kombu* (dried kelp), cut with a heavy knife from a sheet of packaged *kombu* and washed under cold running water

PREPARE AHEAD: 1. In a small saucepan, bring 2 cups of water to a simmer over high heat. Add the cubes of *tofu* and the square of *kombu* and let the water return to a simmer. Then immediately remove the pan from the heat and set it aside until ready to serve.

2. In another saucepan, bring 2 cups of lightly salted water to a boil. Drop in the spinach, sprinkle lightly with MSG, and let the water return to a boil. Then remove the spinach with a slotted spoon and run cold water over it. Squeeze the spinach to remove its excess water and dry on paper towels. Reserve the pan of cooking water.

3. To butterfly the shrimp, first cut them three quarters of the way through along the length of their inside curves. Then spread them out and gently flatten them with the side of a cleaver or the flat of a large, heavy knife. Dip the shrimp one at a time into the cornstarch to coat them lightly and evenly, then shake off any excess.

Bring the reserved pan of spinach water to a boil over high heat. Add the shrimp and boil them briskly for about 30 seconds. Drain them through a sieve and set them aside.

TO COOK AND SERVE: In a 2-quart saucepan, bring the *sumashi* to a boil. Add the shrimp, return to the boil, boil about 15 seconds, and drain.

Arrange 1 shrimp, a spinach leaf, a cube of *tofu* and a thin strip of lemon peel in the bottom of each soup bowl. Fill each bowl three-quarters full with the hot soup, pouring it carefully down the side of the bowl to avoid disturbing the decorative arrangement.

THE ALTERNATE GARNISH for the *sumashi wan* is a chicken ball instead of the butterflied shrimp. Prepare the chicken balls as follows:

Combine the 1/2 pound of ground chicken, 2 teaspoons of the soy sauce, 1/2 teaspoon sugar, a dash of *kona sansho* (or finely ground black pepper) and 1 egg yolk in a *suribachi* (mixing bowl) or mortar and mix vigorously with a pestle until the mixture is smooth. With lightly moistened hands, roll the mixture into 6 small balls.

In a 1-quart pan, combine 1 cup of cold water, 1 tablespoon *sake,* 1 teaspoon soy sauce and a 2-inch square of *kombu,* and bring to a simmer over moderate heat. Drop in the ground chicken balls, lower the heat, and poach gently for about 6 or 7 minutes, or until firm. Place 1 chicken ball in each soup bowl in place of the shrimp, add the spinach and lemon, and fill the bowls as described above.

A Selection of Soups–from Morn to Night

The red and white *miso* soups shown directly below—clear soups flavored with soybean paste—are favorite breakfast foods for the Japanese, although they may also play a savory role at lunch or at dinner. Opposite are examples of more formal clear soups, elaborately garnished with seafood, eggs and vegetables. The garnishes in the *miso* soups below are only suggestions—other possibilities, together with the recipes for the soups and garnishes, are found on page 59.

AKADASHI
Red *miso*-flavored soup, garnished here with thinly sliced white *daikon* radish and tiny rings of scallion.

SHIRO DASHI
White *miso*-flavored soup, with a neat tie of *kanpyo* —gourd shavings—topped by a dab of hot mustard.

HAMAGURI USHIOJITATE
Clear clam soup *(page 58)* accompanied by a garnish of a tiny mushroom and a paper-thin round of lime.

UMEWAN
Clear soup *(page 60)* with a slice of rolled egg, porgy, shrimp, mushroom, carrot and aromatic *sansho* leaf.

Hamaguri Ushiojitate 蛤うしを仕立

CLEAR CLAM SOUP WITH MUSHROOMS

To serve 6

1 teaspoon salt
12 sprigs fresh watercress or young spinach leaves stripped from their stems
A 3-inch square *kombu,* cut with a heavy knife from a sheet of packaged *kombu* and washed under cold running water
12 small fresh cherrystone clams, scrubbed under cold running water
6 small white mushrooms
1 tablespoon Japanese all-purpose soy sauce
MSG
6 very thin slices lime or lemon

PREPARE AHEAD: In a small saucepan, combine 1 cup of cold water, ½ teaspoon of salt and the watercress or spinach leaves. Bring to a boil over high heat and boil 1 minute. Drain through a sieve and set the leaves aside.

TO COOK: In a 2-quart saucepan, combine the 6 cups of cold water, the *kombu* and the clams. Bring to a boil over high heat, then remove the *kombu* with a slotted spoon or tongs, and discard it. Let the soup boil for about 2 minutes, or until the clams open, meanwhile skimming off any scum that rises to the surface. Stir in the mushrooms, soy sauce, ½ teaspoon salt and a few sprinkles of MSG. Boil for 30 seconds, then remove from the heat.

TO SERVE: In each of 6 soup bowls place 2 clams in their shells. Garnish with 2 sprigs of the watercress or spinach, a mushroom and a slice of lemon or lime. Fill each bowl with the hot broth, pouring it down the side of the bowl to avoid disturbing the decorative arrangement. Serve at once.

Togan-to Ebi 冬瓜と海老

CLEAR SOUP WITH WINTER MELON AND SHRIMP

To serve 6

SUMASHI (clear soup)
6 cups *ichiban dashi (page 54)*
1½ teaspoons salt
½ teaspoon Japanese all-purpose soy sauce
1 teaspoon *sake* (rice wine)
MSG

GARNISH
A 1¾-pound winter melon or honeydew melon
6 medium-sized raw shrimp (16 to 20 per pound), peeled and deveined *(see page 168)*
1 teaspoon salt
A 2-inch piece lime rind, cut into 6 very thin strips

PREPARE AHEAD: 1. Cut the rind off the melon. Score the peeled side of the melon with cuts ⅛ inch deep lengthwise and then crosswise at ⅛-inch intervals. Then cut the melon into six 1½-inch squares.

2. Drop the shrimp into 1½ cups of boiling water, add 1 teaspoon of salt, and boil uncovered for 5 minutes, or until they are pink and firm. Drain and plunge the shrimp into cold running water to cool them quickly. Drain again and set the shrimp aside.

TO COOK THE SUMASHI: In a 2-quart saucepan, bring 6 cups of *ichiban dashi* just to a simmer over moderate heat. Immediately reduce the heat to low, stir in the salt, soy sauce, *sake,* and sprinkle with MSG.

TO ASSEMBLE AND SERVE: Drop in the melon squares, and simmer them uncovered for 15 minutes, or until they are tender and show no resistance when pierced with the tip of a small, sharp knife.

Place a square of melon in each of 6 soup bowls and top with a shrimp and strip of lime rind. Fill each bowl with soup, pouring it down the side of the bowl to avoid disturbing the decorative arrangement.

Botan Wan 牡丹椀

CLEAR SOUP WITH SEA BASS

To serve 4

A 2-pound sea bass, filleted but with the skin left on
½ teaspoon salt
2 tablespoons cornstarch
1 tablespoon *sake* (rice wine)
A 7-ounce bottle *junsai* (wild vegetables)
1 quart *sumashi (above)*
4 very thin slices lime

PREPARE AHEAD: 1. Cut the fillets in half crosswise and place them skin side down on a cutting board. With a sharp, heavy knife, cut them crosswise at ⅛-inch intervals almost down to the skin, but do not cut through it. The sliced fish will open up when poached and resemble a peony, or *botan* in Japanese.

2. Sprinkle the fish lightly with ½ teaspoon of salt; then, through a sieve or sifter, sift 2 tablespoons of cornstarch evenly over it.

TO COOK: In a 1-quart saucepan, bring 2 cups of water to a boil. Poach the fish, one piece at a time, by placing it on a wide spatula, lowering the spatula into the boiling water for 15 seconds, then sliding the fish onto a heatproof platter. When all the fish has been poached and arranged side by side, sprinkle the pieces evenly with 1 tablespoon of *sake*. Now steam the fish for

5 minutes, either in an Oriental steamer or in the improvised steamer on page 180.

Meanwhile, bring 2 cups of water to a boil in a small saucepan. Add the *junsai* and return to a boil. Strain at once and discard the water.

TO SERVE: Cook the *sumashi* over moderate heat until it reaches a simmer. Divide the *junsai* evenly among 4 soup bowls, add a piece of the steamed fish to each and garnish with a thin slice of lime. Fill each bowl with the hot soup, pouring it down the side of the bowl to avoid disturbing the decorative arrangement. Serve at once.

Misoshiru 味噌汁

CLEAR SOUP WITH SOYBEAN PASTE

"Miso" soups—clear soups flavored with white and/or red soybean paste—are sweeter than other Japanese soups and usually are served toward the end of a formal Japanese meal. All are made in precisely the same way, and may be garnished with a selection of appropriate garnishes listed below.

To make 6 cups of each type

AKA MISO (summer *miso* soup)
6 cups *ichiban dashi (page 54)*
½ cup *aka miso* (red soybean paste)
MSG

SHIRO MISO (winter *miso* soup)
6 cups *ichiban dashi (page 54)*
1 cup *shiro miso* (white soybean paste)
MSG

AWASE MISO (combination *miso* soup)
6 cups *ichiban dashi (page 54)*
½ cup *shiro miso* (white soybean paste)
½ cup *aka miso* (red soybean paste)
MSG

PREPARE AHEAD: Place the 6 cups of *dashi* in a 2-quart saucepan and set a sieve over the pan. With the back of a large spoon, rub the *miso (aka, shiro* or a combination of the two) through the sieve, moistening it from time to time with some of the *dashi* to help force it through more easily.

TO COOK AND SERVE: Bring the soup to a simmer over moderate heat. Then remove from the heat and stir in a small pinch of MSG.

Pour the soup into bowls, add the garnish of your choice *(below)* and serve at once. If the soup seems to be separating, stir to recombine it.

Misoshiru No-mi 味噌汁の実

MISO SOUP GARNISHES

To serve 6

WAKAME AND SCALLIONS
½ ounce *wakame* (dried seaweed)
1 scallion, including the green stem, sliced into very thin rounds

TOFU AND SCALLIONS
A 6-ounce cake of fresh, canned or instant *tofu* (soybean curd), cut into ¼-inch dice
1 scallion, including the green stem, sliced into very thin rounds

DAIKON AND SCALLIONS
A 1-inch piece of *daikon* (Japanese white radish), peeled, or substitute 1 large icicle radish or white turnip, peeled
1 scallion, including the green stem, sliced into very thin rounds

FU AND MUSTARD
18 *kohana-fu* or *yachiyo-fu* (pressed wheat-cake croutons)
1 teaspoon powdered mustard, mixed with just enough hot water to make a thick paste and set aside to rest for 15 minutes

Prepare the garnishes for *miso* soups before the soup is heated.

WAKAME AND SCALLIONS: Soak the firm *wakame* in a bowl of warm water for 15 minutes. When soft, strip the leaves from the tough center vein and discard the vein. Chop the leaves coarsely and set them aside. Bring the *miso* soup to a simmer, drop in the *wakame,* simmer for 1 minute, then pour into individual soup bowls. Garnish with the sliced scallions and serve.

TOFU AND SCALLIONS: When the soup simmers, drop in the *tofu* and simmer 1 minute. Pour into soup bowls, garnish with scallions, and serve.

DAIKON AND SCALLIONS: Cut the 1-inch piece of *daikon* (or the icicle radish or turnip) into strips ⅛ inch wide by about 2 inches long. Cover the strips with cold water in a 1-quart pan and bring to a boil over high heat. Reduce the heat to low and simmer for about 5 minutes, or until the vegetables are tender but still slightly firm. When the *miso* soup begins to simmer, drain the *daikon* and add it to the soup. Pour into individual soup bowls, and garnish with the scallions.

FU AND MUSTARD: Soak the dried croutons in cold water for about 10 minutes, or until they are soft. Squeeze them gently to rid them of their moisture. Bring the *miso* soup to simmer, drop in the croutons and simmer for 1 minute. Pour the soup into individual soup bowls, add a drop of the mustard paste to each bowl, and serve at once.

Umewan 梅椀

CLEAR SOUP WITH ROLLED EGG, VEGETABLES AND FISH

"Umewan," known as a "large 'sumashi,'" is a delicate but satisfying full-meal soup. Although there are many steps involved in its preparation, many of them may be done in advance.

To serve 6

4 eggs, well beaten
Salt
MSG
1 tablespoon vegetable oil
3 large *shiitake* (dried Japanese mushrooms)
½ teaspoon sugar
1 tablespoon Japanese all-purpose soy sauce
1 small carrot, scraped and shredded
¾ cup *niban dashi* *(page 54)*
6 medium-sized raw shrimp (16 to 20 per pound), in their shells
¼ pound fillet of porgy, with skin left on
2 tablespoons cornstarch
6 cups *sumashi* *(page 58)*
12 young spinach leaves or 6 sprigs watercress
A 2- to 3-inch strip of lemon rind, cut into 6 small circles

PREPARE AHEAD: 1. In a mixing bowl, beat 4 eggs with ⅛ teaspoon of salt and a sprinkle of MSG until they are well combined. With a pastry brush or paper towel, lightly coat the bottom and sides of a heavy 10- to 12-inch skillet with 1 tablespoon of oil. Heat over moderate heat until a drop of water flicked onto the surface evaporates instantly.

Pour about ¼ cup of the eggs into the pan, and tip it back and forth gently for a few seconds until the bottom is evenly covered and the eggs have coagulated into a thin film. Tilt the pan up over the heat, and with chopsticks or the side of a table fork, roll the omelet into a tight, thin cylinder. Then slide it on a paper towel to drain and make similar rolled omelets with the remaining eggs.

One at a time, place the omelets on the edge of a bamboo mat or heavy cloth napkin and roll the omelet in the mat 2 or 3 turns. Squeeze the mat tightly around the omelet roll to firm it, then remove the mat and set the omelet roll aside to cool.

2. In a 2-quart saucepan soak the *shiitake* in 4 cups of water for at least 1 hour. Then bring to a boil over moderate heat. Add ½ teaspoon of sugar and 1 tablespoon of soy sauce, and boil 20 minutes uncovered, or until the liquid is a deep brown and has reduced to about ⅓ cup. Cool to room temperature.

3. Drop the carrot shreds into 1 cup of boiling water and boil 2 to 3 minutes. Pour off the liquid and replace it with ¼ cup of the *niban dashi.* Add a pinch of salt and a sprinkle of MSG and cook another 2 to 3 minutes, stirring from time to time. Set aside.

4. Drop the 6 shrimp into 1½ cups of boiling water, add 1 teaspoon of salt, and boil uncovered for 5 minutes. Drain and plunge into a bowl of cold water to cool them quickly.

Shell the shrimp and, with a small, sharp knife, devein them by makng a shallow incision down their backs and lifting out the black or white intestinal vein. Set the shrimp aside.

5. Sprinkle the fleshy side of the fillets with ½ teaspoon of salt and dip them into the cornstarch to coat them lightly and evenly. Shake them to remove the excess cornstarch, then drop them into 2 cups of boiling water. Boil 1 minute, then add ½ cup of *niban dashi* and ⅛ teaspoon of salt. Cook another 3 to 4 minutes, remove the fish from the water with a slotted spoon, and set aside on a plate.

TO SERVE: Slice the rolled egg cylinders crosswise into rounds 2 inches long and place 3 pieces in the bottom of each soup bowl. Add 1 shrimp per bowl, 1 sliver of fish, 2 sprigs of spinach or watercress, ½ *shiitake* and a few strips of the carrot.

Heat the 6 cups of *sumashi* to the simmering point. Fill each bowl three quarters full with the hot soup, pouring it carefully down the side of each bowl to avoid disturbing the decorative arrangement; garnish with a circle of lemon rind and serve at once.

Satsuma Jiru 薩摩汁

MISO-FLAVORED PORK-AND-VEGETABLE STEW

To serve 6

1/2 pound boned loin of pork, cut into 1/4-inch dice
1 pound pork neck bones
1 section canned *konnyaku* (gelatinous vegetable root), cut into strips 1/4 inch wide and 2 inches long
2 *shiitake* (dried Japanese mushrooms)
1 *gobo* (burdock), washed (optional)
1 medium-sized carrot, scraped and cut into strips 2 inches long and 1/4 inch wide
A 1-inch piece *daikon* (Japanese white radish), scraped and cut into strips 1/4 inch wide and 1 inch long, or substitute 1 large icicle radish or white turnip, peeled and cut into 1/4-inch-wide strips
1/4 pound sweet potato, peeled and cut into 1/2-inch dice
1/2 cup *aka miso* (red soybean paste)
MSG
1 scallion, including its green stem, sliced into thin rounds (about 1/4 cup)
Hichimi togarashi (seven-pepper spice)

NAGASAKI JIRU (alternate seasoning)
6 tablespoons Japanese all-purpose soy sauce
MSG
2 tablespoons *sake* (rice wine)
Ground white pepper

PREPARE AHEAD: 1. In a small pan, bring 1 cup of water to a boil and drop in the pork dice. Cook uncovered 10 seconds, then drain and set aside.

2. In a heavy 4-quart pot cover the pork bones with 6 1/2 cups of cold water. Bring to a boil uncovered, then reduce the heat to its lowest point and simmer for 30 minutes, skimming off the foam as it rises to the surface. Strain the broth through a sieve lined with a double thickness of cheesecloth or a clean cloth napkin. Return the broth to its pot and set aside.

3. In a 1-quart saucepan, bring 1 cup of water to a boil and drop in the *konnyaku*. Return to the boil, then drain immediately and set aside.

4. Steam the mushrooms for 4 minutes in an Oriental steamer or in the steamer substitute described on page 180. While the mushrooms are still hot, cut away and discard the stems and slice the caps into the thinnest possible strips. Cool to room temperature.

5. If you are using the *gobo*, peel it with a rotary vegetable peeler to make 1/4 cup of peel. Discard the root.

TO COOK: Drop the *konnyaku* into the reserved pot of pork broth and over moderate heat bring to a slow boil. Add the carrot and *daikon* strips and raise the heat. Bring to a full boil, and add the diced sweet potato and mushroom strips. Skim off the foam with a large spoon and add the pork. Cook 5 minutes, then reduce the heat to moderate and, with the back of a spoon, rub the *miso* through a sieve directly into the soup. Stir in a few sprinkles of MSG. Stir in the optional *gobo* peelings just before serving.

TO SERVE: Transfer the soup to a large serving bowl, sprinkle scallions over the top and add a few sprinkles of seven-pepper spice.

TO MAKE NAGASAKI JIRU: Omit the *miso* flavoring. In its place, stir in 6 tablespoons of soy sauce. Lower the heat and add a sprinkle of MSG. Stir in the *sake*, and the optional *gobo* peelings. Serve as above, substituting a few sprinkles of white pepper for the seven-pepper spice.

Ushio Jiru うしを汁

CLEAR SOUP WITH PORGY

"Ushio jiru" is an unusual soup, deriving its delicate flavor from the fish head, which Westerners usually discard. The body of the porgy may, of course, be used for another purpose (see "umewan," opposite).

To serve 4

A porgy head (from a 2-pound porgy), split open and cut in half
Salt
3 cups boiling water
A 2-inch square of *kombu* (dried kelp), cut with a heavy knife from a sheet of packaged *kombu* and washed under cold running water
MSG
A 5-inch piece of celery stalk without leaves, cut lengthwise into the thinnest possible strips and chilled in a bowl of iced water
4 very thin slices lime

PREPARE AHEAD: Discard the bony jowl part of the porgy head and cut the rest of the head into 2-inch chunks. Sprinkle lightly with salt, drop into the boiling water, and let it cook for 10 seconds. Drain and rinse the fish thoroughly under cold running water.

TO COOK: In a 1 1/2- to- 2-quart saucepan, combine 4 cups of cold water, the fish chunks and the *kombu*. When the water comes to the boil, remove and discard the *kombu*. Regulate the heat so that the stock barely simmers, and skim the scum from the surface with a slotted spoon. Simmer about 3 minutes, then stir in 1 1/2 teaspoons of salt and the MSG.

TO SERVE: Place a few pieces of fish in each bowl and garnish with a slice of lime and a few slivers of celery. Fill each bowl with the hot soup, pouring it down the side so as not to disturb the decorative arrangement.

AEMONO AND SUNOMONO: "Aemono" means mixed things: fresh or lightly cooked vegetables, fish or poultry mixed and tossed with dressings and sauces. "Sunomono" means vinegared things: vegetables alone or with fish in vinegared dressings. The categories overlap somewhat, but both encompass small dishes meant to accompany main dishes and to complement them in taste, texture and color. Westerners might experiment with them as first courses or salad courses.

Kani Sunomono 蟹酢の物

CRAB MEAT IN VINEGARED DRESSING

To serve 6

1 large cucumber
1 teaspoon salt
12 ounces fresh or canned crab meat or abalone
3 tablespoons coarsely grated fresh ginger root

DIPPING SAUCE
½ cup *sambai-zu (page 64)*

PREPARE AHEAD: 1. Peel the cucumber partially, leaving occasional ¼-inch strips of green peel to add color to the finished dish. Cut the cucumber in half lengthwise, scoop out the seeds with a small spoon, and slice the halves crosswise into paper-thin slices.

Combine ½ cup of cold water and 1 teaspoon of salt in a small bowl, and add the cucumber slices. Let them soak for at least 30 minutes at room temperature. Then drain the cucumbers and, with your hands, gently squeeze them to rid them of any excess moisture.

2. If you are using crab meat, pick over it and discard any cartilage and bits of bone. With a large, sharp knife, shred it fine. If you are using abalone, slice it very thin.

TO ASSEMBLE AND SERVE: Divide the cucumber and crab meat or abalone into small individual bowls. Wrap the grated ginger in a piece of cheesecloth and squeeze the ginger juice over each bowl. Serve with the *sambai-zu* dipping sauce, as a first course or as part of a Japanese meal.

Goma Joyu-ae 胡麻醤油和え

SOY-AND-SESAME-SEED DRESSING WITH STRING BEANS

To serve 6

1 pound string beans, or 1 pound fresh or defrosted frozen snow peas
Salt
1 cup *niban dashi (page 54)*
1 tablespoon sugar
MSG
2 teaspoons *sake* (rice wine)
¼ teaspoon Japanese all-purpose soy sauce

DRESSING
½ cup white sesame seeds, toasted and ground into a paste *(see shir-ae, step 5, opposite)*
3 tablespoons *sake* (rice wine)
2 teaspoons sugar
2 tablespoons Japanese all-purpose soy sauce

PREPARE AHEAD: 1. Snip off and discard the ends of the green beans (or snow peas) and cut them into ½-inch lengths. Drop the beans into 2 cups of lightly salted boiling water, reduce the heat to moderate and cook briskly, uncovered, for 8 to 10 minutes, or until the beans are tender but still slightly resistant to the bite. Drain and run cold water over them to stop their cooking and set their color.

2. In the same pan, combine the *dashi,* sugar, ¼ teaspoon of salt, a sprinkle of MSG, 2 teaspoons of *sake* and ¼ teaspoon of soy sauce. Bring to a boil over moderate heat, add the string beans (or snow peas) and return to the boil. Then remove the pan from the heat and cool to room temperature.

3. Over high heat, heat 3 tablespoons of *sake* to lukewarm. Remove the pan from the heat and ignite the *sake* with a kitchen match, shaking the pan gently until the flame dies out. Pour the *sake* into a small bowl and cool to room temperature.

4. Add the *sake,* 2 teaspoons of sugar and 2 tablespoons of soy sauce to the previously prepared sesame paste, and mix together thoroughly.

TO ASSEMBLE AND SERVE: Pour the sesame dressing into a large bowl, add the drained string beans or snow peas and toss together until the vegetables are thoroughly coated. Taste for seasoning and add more salt if necessary. Serve at room temperature in small bowls, as a first course, salad or part of a Japanese meal *(page 198).*

Shira-ae 白和え

TOFU-AND-SESAME-SEED DRESSING WITH VEGETABLES

To serve 6

- 2 pieces canned *konnyaku* (gelatinous root vegetable), drained and shredded
- 1 loaf fresh, canned or instant *tofu* (soybean curd)
- 1 small (3- to 4-inch) carrot, scraped and shredded
- 1 teaspoon salt
- 1 teaspoon vegetable oil
- ½ cup *niban dashi (page 54)*
- 4 teaspoons sugar
- MSG
- ¼ teaspoon all-purpose soy sauce
- 3 tablespoons white sesame seeds

PREPARE AHEAD: 1. Bring 1 cup of water to a boil in a small saucepan and drop in the shredded *konnyaku*. Return to the boil, then drain immediately and cool to room temperature.

2. Bring another cup of water to a boil and drop in the loaf of *tofu*. Simmer uncovered over moderate heat for 5 minutes, drain, and cool to room temperature. Then wrap the *tofu* in a kitchen towel or napkin and squeeze it gently to rid it of its moisture. With the back of a wooden spoon, rub it through a sieve set over a bowl.

3. In another bowl, soak the shredded carrots in ¼ cup of cold water and ½ teaspoon of salt for about 30 minutes. Drain, squeeze dry, and set aside.

4. In a small saucepan heat 1 teaspoon of vegetable oil over high heat until a light haze forms above it. Stir in the *konnyaku, dashi,* 1 teaspoon of the sugar, the remaining ½ teaspoon of salt, a few sprinkles of MSG and ⅛ teaspoon of soy sauce, and bring to a boil. Boil uncovered until the liquid has reduced to about half. Cool to room temperature.

5. Heat a small frying pan over high heat until a drop of water flicked across its surface evaporates instantly. Add the sesame seeds and, shaking the pan almost constantly, warm them until lightly toasted. Grind them to a paste in a *suribachi* (serrated mixing bowl) or, more easily, pulverize them at high speed in an electric blender with ⅛ teaspoon of soy sauce. Transfer the sesame-seed paste to a mixing bowl and stir in the reserved *tofu.*

TO ASSEMBLE AND SERVE: Drain the *konnyaku* and its sauce through a sieve set over a small bowl. Stir 2 tablespoons of the sauce into the sesame-seed paste. Then stir in 1 tablespoon sugar, ¼ teaspoon salt, a few sprinkles of MSG, the drained *konnyaku,* and the reserved grated carrot.

Serve as a first course or part of a Japanese meal *(page 198).*

Sesame seeds, ground against the ribbed surface of a *suribachi* with a wooden pestle, quickly release their oil and turn into a paste.

Sambai-zu 三杯酢

RICE-VINEGAR-AND-SOY DIPPING SAUCE

To make about ½ cup

2½ tablespoons rice vinegar
2½ tablespoons *niban dashi (page 54)*
4 teaspoons sugar
2 teaspoons Japanese all-purpose soy sauce
⅛ teaspoon salt
MSG

TO PREPARE: Combine the rice vinegar, *niban dashi,* sugar, soy sauce and salt in a 1-quart enameled or stainless-steel saucepan and sprinkle lightly with MSG. Stirring constantly, bring the sauce to a boil, uncovered, over high heat. Then immediately remove the pan from the heat and set the sauce aside to cool to room temperature.

TO SERVE: Serve the *sambai-zu* in tiny individual cups or dishes, as a dipping sauce for *shime saba (opposite), kani kyuri ikomi (Recipe Index),* or *kani sunomono (Recipe Index).*

Suzuko Mizore-ae すすこ みぞれ和え

RED CAVIAR WITH "SLEET" DRESSING

The dressing of grated radish and lemon juice has a faintly iridescent sheen and reminds the Japanese of sleet. Its pungent flavor makes an excellent foil for the highly salted red caviar.

To serve 6

½ pound *daikon* (Japanese white radish), peeled and finely grated (about 1½ cups), or substitute ½ pound icicle radish or white turnips, peeled and grated
1 tablespoon fresh lemon juice
¼ teaspoon salt
MSG
6 ounces red caviar

GARNISH
6 sprigs parsley
6 thin slices lemon

ALTERNATE GARNISH
6 wedges of lemon
Japanese all-purpose soy sauce

TO ASSEMBLE AND SERVE: In a mixing bowl, combine the *daikon,* lemon juice, salt and a few sprinkles of MSG. Gently fold in the red caviar without crushing the eggs. Divide the mixture equally among 6 small bowls or dishes and garnish each serving with a sprig of parsley and a thin slice of lemon.

Serve *suzuko mizore-ae* at room temperature as a first course or part of a Japanese meal *(page 198).*

NOTE: In Japan, the ingredients in *suzuko mizore-ae* are often served separately rather than combined. In each bowl, place about ¼ cup of the *daikon* dressing and next to it, 2 tablespoons of red caviar. Garnish with a wedge of lemon and season with soy sauce to taste.

Namasu なます

DAIKON AND CARROT IN VINEGAR DRESSING

It is said that whenever lords and "daimyos" of an earlier era invited guests to dine with them for the first time, this simple salad was served as a first course—to indicate that the food to come was not poisonous in any way.

To serve 6

½ pound *daikon* (Japanese white radish), peeled and shredded, or substitute ½ pound icicle radish or white turnips, peeled and shredded
1 small carrot (about 3 inches), scraped and shredded
1 tablespoon salt
½ cup preflaked *katsuobushi* (dried bonito)
1 tablespoon rice vinegar, or substitute 1 tablespoon mild white vinegar
2 teaspoons sugar
MSG

PREPARE AHEAD: 1. In a small mixing bowl, combine the *daikon,* carrot, 1 cup of cold water and salt. Stir thoroughly, then soak the mixture for at least 30 minutes.

2. Meanwhile, place ¼ cup of *katsuobushi* in a small pan. Stirring constantly, cook uncovered over low heat, for 3 to 4 minutes, to dry the *katsuobushi* further and to release its flavor. Transfer the cooked *katsuobushi* to a *suribachi* (serrated mixing bowl) or to a mortar, and grind or pound the flakes to a fine powder. Shake the *katsuobushi* through a sieve onto a sheet of wax paper and set aside.

TO ASSEMBLE AND SERVE: Drain the *daikon* and carrot, squeeze them dry, and place in a mixing bowl. Add the vinegar, sugar and a few sprinkles of MSG, mix thoroughly, then stir in the powdered *katsuobushi.*

Serve at room temperature in individual bowls, either as a first or salad course or as an accompaniment to *shime saba (opposite).*

Shime Saba しめ鯖

MACKEREL IN VINEGAR DRESSING

To serve 4

1½ pounds Boston or Spanish mackerel, cleaned, scaled and filleted, but with skin left on
2 tablespoons salt
6 tablespoons rice vinegar, or ¼ cup mild white vinegar
¾ cup cold water
1½ tablespoons sugar

GARNISH

½ cup *namasu (opposite)*
4 sprigs parsley
1 teaspoon finely grated, scraped fresh ginger root

DIPPING SAUCE

½ cup *sambai-zu (opposite)*

PREPARE AHEAD: A day ahead, sprinkle the fish on both sides with salt and place the fillets in a deep glass, enameled or stainless-steel baking dish large enough to hold them in one layer. Cover with plastic wrap and refrigerate 8 hours or overnight. Then remove any remaining bones with tweezers.

In a small bowl, combine the vinegar, water and sugar, and pour over the fish. Marinate at room temperature for 15 minutes. Then place the fish on a cutting board and slice the fish diagonally into ½-inch-wide pieces.

TO SERVE: Divide the fish into 4 portions and arrange the slices side by side on individual plates or in small soup bowls. Garnish each portion with 2 tablespoons of *namasu* and a sprig of parsley. Sprinkle each serving of fish evenly with grated ginger and accompany with individual bowls of *sambai-zu.*

Shime saba will serve four as a first course or as part of a Japanese meal *(page 198)* or it will serve two as a main course for lunch.

Nameko Mizore-ae なめこ みぞれ和え

SLIPPERY MUSHROOMS WITH "SLEET" DRESSING

To serve 6

14 ounces canned *nameko* (slippery mushrooms)
1 to 2 inches *daikon* (Japanese white radish), peeled and finely grated (about ½ cup), or substitute ½ cup grated icicle radish or white turnips
1 teaspoon rice vinegar or lemon juice
⅛ teaspoon salt
1 teaspoon grated lime rind

PREPARE AHEAD: 1. In a small saucepan, bring 2 cups of water to a boil. Add the *nameko* and return to a boil. Drain in a sieve and plunge the sieve into cold water to cool the mushrooms quickly.

2. In a small mixing bowl, combine the *daikon,* rice vinegar and salt.

TO ASSEMBLE AND SERVE: Fold the mushrooms into the dressing and stir gently to coat them well. Divide the mushrooms among 6 small bowls, and sprinkle each serving with the grated lime rind. Serve at room temperature as a first course or part of a Japanese meal *(page 198).*

Silver-edged mackerel, flanked by *namasu* and grated ginger *(right)* is served with *sambai-zu* dipping sauce *(recipes opposite).*

To serve 4 to 6

- 2 cucumbers, about ½ pound each and about 2 inches in diameter
- 2 tablespoons salt
- 16 sprigs watercress or flat-leaf Italian parsley
- 2 ounces (¼ cup) canned crab meat, picked over to remove any bones or cartilage, then flaked
- 1 piece (¼ ounce) bottled *beni shoga* (red pickled ginger), shredded
- ¼ cup *sambai-zu (page 64)*

Kani Kyuri Ikomi 蟹胡瓜鋳込み

CUCUMBER STUFFED WITH CRAB MEAT AND PICKLED GINGER

PREPARE AHEAD: 1. With a rotary peeler or small, sharp knife, peel the cucumbers lengthwise but leave occasional ½-inch-wide green strips to add color to the finished dish.

Rub the cucumbers with 2 tablespoons of salt and set them aside in a bowl to marinate for 15 minutes. Then hold them under cold running water and wash them free of salt.

Pat them dry with paper towels. Trim the ends and, with a teaspoon or melon scoop, remove the pulp and seeds from the center of the cucumbers. The resulting tunnel in each cucumber should be about 1 inch in diameter.

2. Bring 1 cup of water to a boil in a small pan and drop in the watercress or parsley. Cook for 15 seconds, or only long enough to wilt the leaves. Then drain and run cold water over them.

TO ASSEMBLE: To measure correctly how much stuffing each cucumber will hold, place 1 cucumber at a time on a cutting board and lay half the crab meat in a straight line alongside it. Press the flakes of crab meat together with your fingers to make them adhere. Arrange half the watercress or parsley down the length of the crab meat and half the pickled ginger in a long strip beside it.

Slit the cucumber lengthwise along one side and, holding it open with your fingers, use tongs or chopsticks (or your hands) to insert the filling into the opening. Press the cucumber gently but firmly to seal it.

TO SERVE: Carefully slice the cucumbers into ½-inch-thick rounds, arrange them on individual serving dishes, and pour a little of the *sambai-zu* dipping sauce into each dish.

Serve the *kani kyuri ikomi* at room temperature as a first course, as part of a Japanese meal *(page 198)* or as accompaniments to cocktails.

Holding the slit cucumber open with one hand, use chopsticks or tongs to fill the hollowed-out shell with crab meat, watercress and red pickled ginger. Slice the stuffed cucumber *(right)* into ½-inch rounds and serve as an hors d'oeuvre or first course.

Neri Shiro Miso 練り白味噌

WHITE MISO DRESSING

Although 1 quart of "miso" dressing may seem a large amount to make at one time, it is used extensively in Japanese cooking and if tightly covered will keep as long as six months at room temperature.

To make about 1 quart

30 ounces packaged *shiro miso* (white soybean paste)
1¼ cups sugar
1 cup *sake* (rice wine)
2 egg yolks

TO COOK: Combine the *miso,* sugar and *sake* in a 1½- to 2-quart saucepan and, stirring constantly, bring to a boil over moderate heat. Lower the heat and simmer for 30 minutes, stirring from time to time to prevent the dressing from scorching.

Remove the pan from the heat and quickly beat in 2 egg yolks, 1 at a time. Immediately dip the bottom of the pan into a large bowl of iced water to cool the dressing rapidly. It may be used at once, at room temperature, in *nuta-ae (Recipe Index), nasu karashi sumiso-ae (Recipe Index)* and *kinome-ae (below),* or it may be poured into a tightly covered jar and stored at room temperature for future use.

Kinome-ae 木の芽和え

BAMBOO SHOOTS WITH GREEN SOY DRESSING

To serve 6

10 ounces whole or sliced canned *takenoko* (bamboo shoots), drained and scraped clean
1 cup *niban dashi (page 54)*
2 teaspoons sugar
2¼ teaspoons salt
MSG
2 tablespoons *sake* (rice wine)
A 2-inch square of *kombu* (dried kelp), cut with a sharp knife from a sheet of *kombu* and washed in cold running water
¼ pound fresh spinach leaves stripped from their stems
¼ cup white *miso* dressing *(above)*
¼ teaspoon *kona sansho* (Japanese pepper)

PREPARE AHEAD: 1. To prepare a whole bamboo shoot (superior to the sliced variety), place it on its side, cut off the base, then cut the base in half horizontally. Cut the tapered top lengthwise in quarters, then cut all of the pieces into ½-inch dice. Bring 1 cup of water to a boil, drop in the bamboo dice and return to the boil. Boil uncovered for about 10 minutes, or until the bamboo shoots show no resistance when pierced with the tip of a sharp knife. Drain and set aside.

Sliced bamboo shoots need only be cut into ½-inch dice, boiled for 2 to 3 minutes, then drained.

2. In a 1½- to 2-quart saucepan, combine the *niban dashi,* sugar, ¼ teaspoon of the salt, a few sprinkles of MSG, the *sake* and the *kombu.* Bring to a boil over high heat, stirring constantly, and add the bamboo shoots. Return to a boil and cook briskly, uncovered, until nearly all of the cooking liquid evaporates. Then cool to room temperature.

3. Wash the spinach leaves thoroughly and pat them dry with paper towels. In a *suribachi* (serrated mixing bowl) or with a mortar and pestle, grind or pound the leaves to a paste, adding the remaining 2 teaspoons of salt gradually as you proceed.

Or alternatively, chop the leaves fine with a large, sharp knife and mash them with the salt in a bowl.

4. No matter how you have made the spinach paste, stir into it 1 cup of cold water and transfer it to a 1-quart saucepan. Bring it to a boil over high heat, then pour the mixture into a sieve set over a mixing bowl and drain. Discard the liquid.

TO ASSEMBLE AND SERVE: Pour the *miso* dressing into a bowl and, with the back of a wooden spoon, rub the spinach paste through a sieve into the dressing. Then stir the mixture until it turns a soft, delicate green. Sprinkle with ¼ teaspoon of *kona sansho* powder, add the bamboo shoots, and stir together gently. Serve at room temperature in individual small bowls as a first course or part of a Japanese meal *(page 198).*

BENTO AND ZENSAI: The following recipes are "bento"—or picnic food—and "zensai"—Japanese hors d'oeuvre. Many of these recipes can be used for either purpose. The main point of picnic food, however, is that it can be served at room temperature and stand on its own, without a sauce. When used as "zensai," foods can, of course, be served hot, with a sauce.

Kamaboko 蒲鉾

STEAMED FISH LOAF

To make 24 *zensai*

- A 3-inch square *kombu* (dried kelp), washed under cold running water
- 1/3 cup flour
- 2/3 pound fluke or other white-meat fish fillet, without any skin or small bones
- 1 1/4 teaspoons salt
- 2 egg whites
- 1/4 cup *mirin* (sweet *sake),* or substitute 3 tablespoons pale dry sherry

GLAZE

- 1 egg yolk
- 1 teaspoon *mirin,* or substitute 1 teaspoon pale dry sherry

PREPARE AHEAD: 1. Cover the *kombu* with 1/2 cup of cold water and soak for 30 minutes in a small bowl. Add the flour, mix to a paste with a wooden spoon, and set aside.

2. Cut the fish into small pieces and purée them, a few at a time, in an electric blender. Then transfer the purée to a bowl and, with an electric beater or large spoon, beat into it the salt, egg whites, *mirin* and the flour-*kombu* liquid. Continue to beat until smooth.

3. With a pastry brush or paper towel, lightly oil a 3-cup cake pan or ovenproof baking dish and line the bottom of the pan or dish with a sheet of aluminum foil. Add the fish mixture and spread it evenly over the foil with a rubber spatula. Rap the pan on a table to remove any air pockets.

TO COOK: Preheat the oven to 250°. Place the pan of puréed fish in a shallow roasting pan and pour enough boiling water into the roasting pan to come halfway up its sides. Cook the fish loaf uncovered in the middle of the oven for 50 minutes, or until the fish is firm to the touch. Turn off the heat, keep the oven door closed, and let the fish cake rest for 10 minutes.

Preheat the broiler. In a small bowl, combine the egg yolk and *mirin* and, with a pastry brush, brush it evenly over the top of the fish. Slide the pan under the broiler and watch it closely as it browns lightly. Brush again with the glaze and broil again for another minute, repeating the process two more times until the fish becomes encrusted with a thick golden glaze. Cool to room temperature.

TO SERVE: Run a narrow spatula or knife around the inside of the pan. Cut the fish cake into slices 1/2 inch wide by 1 inch long, and transfer to a serving platter. *Kamaboko* is served at room temperature either as an hors d'oeuvre, part of a picnic box, or first course.

Kamo Sakamushi 鴨酒蒸

SAKE-STEAMED DUCK

To make about 24 *zensai*

- 2 whole boned duck or chicken breasts, with skin left on *(see pages 176-177)*
- 1 teaspoon salt
- 1 tablespoon *sake* (rice wine)

PREPARE AHEAD: Place the boned duck (or chicken) breasts skin side up on a flameproof dish or small platter and sprinkle them with 1 teaspoon of salt. Cover with plastic wrap, refrigerate and marinate for at least 3 hours.

TO COOK: Preheat the broiler to its highest point. Meanwhile, pour the *sake* over the duck and steam for 7 minutes either in an Oriental steamer or the steamer substitute described on page 180.

Remove the plate of duck from the steamer and slide it under the broiler about 3 inches from the heat. Broil for about 2 minutes, or until the breasts have turned a rich golden brown.

Cool to room temperature, then cut the breasts into 1/4-inch slices. Serve as an hors d'oeuvre or as a first course.

To prevent shrimp from curling as they cook, spear them along their inner curve with toothpicks or small skewers. After cooking, peel and devein the shrimp. Then cut three quarters of the way through along the inner curve and flatten the shrimp butterfly fashion.

Ebi Kimizushi 海老黄味ずし

SHRIMP SUSHI WITH EGG YOLK

To make 6 *zensai*

6 medium-sized raw shrimp in their shells (16 to 20 per pound)

MARINADE

¼ cup rice vinegar, or substitute ¼ cup mild white vinegar
⅓ cup water
1 teaspoon sugar
¼ teaspoon salt
MSG

FILLING

4 egg yolks
1½ teaspoons sugar
¼ teaspoon salt
1 tablespoon fresh lemon juice
MSG

TO COOK: Leaving the shells of the shrimp intact, insert toothpicks along their inside curves to prevent them from curling as they cook. Drop the shrimp into 2 cups of boiling water and cook briskly, uncovered, for 3 minutes, or until pink and firm. Drain in a sieve and cool quickly under cold running water.

Remove the toothpicks and peel the shrimp, leaving the last section of shell and the tail attached to each one.

Devein the shrimp by making a shallow incision across their tops with a small, sharp knife and lifting out the black or white intestinal vein with the point of the knife.

Butterfly the shrimp by cutting along their inner curves three quarters of the way through, spreading them open and flattening them lightly with the flat blade of a large knife or cleaver.

In a mixing bowl, combine the vinegar, water, sugar, salt and a few sprinkles of MSG, and stir together thoroughly. Add the shrimp, turn them about in the marinade to moisten them well, and marinate at room temperature for about 1 hour.

Drop the 4 egg yolks into a 1- to 1½-quart saucepan, and beat them lightly with a fork. Remove 1 tablespoon of the egg yolks, and set it aside in a small bowl.

Add 2 cups of water to the remaining yolks, stir thoroughly, and cook over moderate heat for about 10 to 15 minutes, or until the yolks are firm and hard-cooked. Drain them in a sieve, and mash them to a paste with a fork in a mixing bowl. Beat in the sugar, salt, lemon juice, a few sprinkles of MSG, and the remaining tablespoon of raw egg yolk and continue to beat until smooth. Then with the back of a spoon, rub the mixture through a fine sieve set over a bowl.

TO ASSEMBLE AND SERVE: Divide the seasoned egg filling into 6 equal parts and pack each part into the center of a butterflied shrimp. Seal the edges of each shrimp by pressing them firmly together. Serve *ebi kimizushi* at room temperature as an accompaniment to cocktails, part of a picnic box, or as a first course.

To make 10 to 12 *zensai*

6 slender young asparagus stalks, peeled
½ cup *shiro miso* (white soybean paste)
1 tablespoon powdered mustard

Karashi Zuke 辛子漬

MISO-MARINATED ASPARAGUS

TO COOK AND ASSEMBLE: 1. Snap the tips from the asparagus and save for future use. Slice the stalks lengthwise into strips ½ inch wide, then cut these into 1½-inch lengths. Over high heat, bring 2 cups of water to a boil. Add the asparagus, return to the boil, and drain immediately in a sieve. Run cold water over them to cool them quickly, and pat dry with paper towels.

In a small mixing bowl, combine the *miso* with the dry mustard and mix until smooth. Spread half the mixture in a shallow baking dish or casserole and cover with a double thickness of cheesecloth the size of the dish. Place the asparagus in one layer on the cheesecloth and cover with another double thickness of cheesecloth. Top with the remaining *miso* and mustard mixture. Marinate for about 3 hours at room temperature, or refrigerate overnight.

Discard the dressing before serving the asparagus.

To make 6 *zensai*

A 3-inch square *kombu* (dried kelp), cut from a sheet of packaged *kombu* and washed under cold running water
⅓ cup flour
24 large raw shrimp (10 to 15 per pound), shelled and deveined *(see page 168)*
¼ teaspoon salt
1 tablespoon *mirin* (sweet *sake*), or substitute 2 teaspoons pale dry sherry
1 egg white
6 small white turnips, peeled
3 ounces *somen* (Japanese noodle), or substitute any thin noodle, cut into 1-inch lengths (about 1½ cups)
Vegetable oil
6 *kuri fukume-ni (page 123)*

Igaguri いが栗

THORNY SHRIMP BALLS FILLED WITH SWEET CHESTNUTS

PREPARE AHEAD: 1. Soak the *kombu* in ½ cup of water for 30 minutes. Stir in ⅓ cup of flour, mix to a paste, and set aside.

2. Purée the shrimp, a few at a time, in an electric blender or put them twice through the finest blade of a meat grinder. Then, with an electric beater or large spoon, beat into the purée the salt, *mirin,* egg whites and 6 tablespoons of the flour-and-*kombu* liquid. Continue to beat until smooth.

3. With a small, sharp knife, trim the turnips into ½-inch balls. Divide the shrimp mixture into 6 parts and, moistening your hands with cold water, shape into 6 balls. Make an indentation in the top of each ball and force the turnip into it. Pat into shape again, enclosing the turnip.

4. Spread the cut noodles out on a sheet of wax paper. Then roll the shrimp balls about in them until they adhere and protrude like thorns.

TO COOK: Pour into a deep-fat fryer or deep skillet enough oil to come 3 inches up the sides. Set over high heat until the oil registers 375° on a deep-fat thermometer. Deep-fry the shrimp balls 3 or 4 at a time for 2 to 3 minutes, or until they are golden brown. Remove and drain on paper towels.

With a chopstick or the point of a knife, make a hole in the top of each ball and spread it open gently. One by one, remove the turnips and insert a sweet chestnut in its place. Serve at room temperature.

To make 6 chestnuts

6 peeled chestnuts *(page 123)*
1 tablespoon green Japanese tea leaves
5 teaspoons sugar
1 teaspoon Japanese all-purpose soy sauce

Shibu Kawa-ni 澁皮煮

CHESTNUTS COOKED IN GREEN TEA

TO COOK: In a 1-quart saucepan, cover the chestnuts with cold water and the tea leaves and bring to a boil. Lower the heat and simmer uncovered for 20 minutes, or until the chestnuts show no resistance when pierced with the tip of a sharp knife. Drain and wash under cold running water. Leave the brown membrane intact.

Combine 1 cup of cold water, the sugar and the chestnuts in a saucepan and bring to a boil. Reduce the heat and simmer 20 minutes, then stir in the soy sauce. Simmer another 5 minutes, remove from the heat and cool to room temperature before draining and serving.

Art Excels Nature in This Culinary Replica of a Thorny Wild Chestnut

Begin with a small ball of purèed, seasoned shrimp *(left)*. Make a dent in it and press in a trimmed ½-inch turnip ball. Pat into shape again *(right)*, enclosing the turnip.

Roll the shrimp ball about in bits of thin noodles until the noodles adhere to the purèed shrimp and stick out in all directions like thorns. Place in refrigerator until ready to cook.

Deep-fry the shrimp balls until they are a golden brown. Then with chopsticks or the point of a knife, make a hole in the top of each ball and spread it open gently. Pluck out the turnip *(above, left)* and in its place insert a sweetened chestnut *(above, right)*. The completed *igaguri (right)* now resembles a chestnut in its wild form, but its taste is highly sophisticated: first the diner encounters the crisp outer noodles, next the seasoned shrimp, and last the sweet-cooked chestnut.

A tempting array of *zensai,* small portions of food suitable as hors d'oeuvre or as first courses, can be made from the recipes on pages 68 to 73 and in the Recipe Booklet. They are, clockwise from upper right: shrimp wrapped in seaweed; rolled beef with scallions; fried fluke seasoned with vinegar sauce; *miso*-marinated asparagus; sliced squid topped with pickled cod roe; sliced abalone cooked in *sake* and soy sauce; soy-seasoned snails served in their shells and alone on a leaf.

Awabi Sakani 鮑酒煮

SWEET-COOKED ABALONE

To make 6 *zensai*

A 15-ounce can abalone, packed in water
3/4 cup cold water
3 tablespoons *sake* (rice wine)
2 tablespoons sugar
1 tablespoon Japanese all-purpose soy sauce

Empty the can of abalone into a 1-quart saucepan and add the water. Bring to a boil, then lower the heat and simmer uncovered 10 minutes. Add the *sake* and sugar and cook another 5 minutes, then stir in the soy sauce and cook 2 to 3 minutes longer. Cool to room temperature, then cut the abalone slices 1/2 inch thick and serve as an hors d'oeuvre or first course.

Hamaguri Shigure-ni 蛤しぐれ煮

SWEET-COOKED CLAMS

To make 24 *zensai*

1/4 cup *sake* (rice wine)
3 tablespoons sugar
24 small littleneck clams, shucked
3 tablespoons Japanese all-purpose soy sauce

TO COOK: Combine the *sake,* sugar and clams in a 10- to 12-inch skillet and stir together gently but thoroughly. Bring to a boil over high heat and cook about 3 minutes uncovered. Stir in the soy sauce and cook briskly for another minute. Then remove the clams and set them aside in a bowl.

Boil the liquid in the skillet over high heat for 10 minutes, or until it becomes syrupy. Add the clams and stir them gently in the sauce over high heat for about 1 minute, or until they are thoroughly glazed with the sauce.

Transfer the clams and their sauce to a deep bowl, and cool to room temperature. Serve cold, as part of a *bento,* or picnic box, or as hors d'oeuvre.

NOTE: Tiny shrimp, mussels or bits of fresh tuna may be substituted for the clams and prepared in precisely the same fashion described above.

Hamaguri Sakani 蛤酒煮

SAKE-SEASONED CLAMS

To make 12 *zensai*

12 littleneck clams
1 quart boiling water
1/4 cup *sake* (rice wine)
MSG
6 thin slices lemon, cut in half

PREPARE AHEAD: Have the clams shucked by your fish man and ask him to save the shells. Discard the shallower halves and scrub the deeper halves of the shells thoroughly. Drop them into boiling water, boil for 2 to 3 minutes, then drain. Rinse each shell under cold running water and pat dry.

TO COOK AND SERVE: Over high heat bring the *sake* to a boil in a 1-quart saucepan. Sprinkle with MSG, then drop in the clams, stir gently, and cover. Cook over moderately high heat for 3 to 4 minutes, remove the clams with tongs or chopsticks, and place one in each of the reserved shells. Garnish each clam with a half slice of lemon, and serve at room temperature.

Gyuniku Negimaki 牛肉葱巻

STEAK-AND-SCALLION ROLLS

To make 8 *zensai*

A 1/4-pound slice (about 1/4 inch thick) of sirloin steak
2 scallions, including 3 inches of the green stems, cut in half lengthwise, then cut into 4-inch pieces
1/4 cup *teriyaki* sauce *(page 175)*

PREPARE AHEAD: Place the steak between sheets of wax paper and, with a meat pounder or the flat of a cleaver, pound it to a 1/8-inch thickness. Cut the steak in half crosswise. Arrange a strip of scallions down the length of each piece of the meat, then, starting with the wide sides of the meat, roll the pieces into tight cylinders. Secure the seams with toothpicks.

TO COOK: Preheat the broiler (or light a charcoal grill or hibachi). With chopsticks or tongs, dip the rolls into the *teriyaki* sauce, and then broil them 3 inches from the heat for about 3 minutes. Dip them again into the sauce, and broil the other side for a minute. Remove the toothpicks, trim the ends of the rolls neatly with a sharp knife, and cut the rolls into 1-inch pieces. Stand each piece on end, to expose the scallions, and serve at once.

市 浜
濱

IV

The World's Greatest Seafood

Long strands of *kombu* (kelp) are tied in sheaves with straw by the grandmother of a fishing family that lives on the Inland Sea. The kelp, still damp after being washed up by the tide, is hung to dry. Eventually it will be used either to make a soup stock or be cooked as a vegetable to be eaten with fish.

The wealth that nature denied to the islands of Japan she seems to have lavished on the seas that surround them. No waters on earth are so generous as those that give Japan her astonishing variety of savory ocean fare.

As anyone who has eaten in Japan must have realized, if only vaguely, Japanese fish and shellfish taste better than the same species anywhere else. This is not just a matter of cookery, nor is it an illusion spun out of the bewitching color and design of exquisite presentation. The sea creatures themselves actually have a richer, deeper flavor—thanks to the Japan Current (similar to the Atlantic Gulf Stream), a mighty cornucopia of undersea life. Steep undersea escarpments outline this nation of 3,620 islands and create a roiling action as the tropical tide mingles with colder waters from the north; this turbulence prevents the nourishing ocean minerals from settling to the bottom. It is these suspended minerals, prime food for marine life, that make Japanese sea products the best tasting in the world.

Since ancient times the Japanese have known the sea and what is in it. Their ancestors were seafarers—they had to be to make their way to the islands in the first place—and the primitive attachment to the ocean has never been lost. Although hemmed into narrow coastal plains by rugged mountains, and lacking grazing lands, the Japanese are fortunate in their coastline, which is indented by thousands of shallow bays and sheltered inlets that make life easy for both fish and fishermen. So it was quite natural for the Japanese to forage seaward, first for sustenance, and then, as they discovered the extent of their marine treasure, to satisfy the craving for variety that distinguishes the civilized palate from the barbarian. Poor in many resources they may be, but no other people feasts more richly on the ocean's bounty.

Every man, woman and child in Japan eats something from the sea every day, if not at every meal; some sea products, like *dashi,* a soup or cooking stock, or *katsuobushi,* processed dried bonito, are in so many dishes that the Japanese diner may not be aware, unless he is a cook, that he is eating seafood. Japanese reliance on the sea has created something so much more fundamental than what the word "seafood" signifies to a Westerner that there is no Japanese equivalent of our seafood restaurants. In the great restaurants, a variety of seafood is essential to *every* carefully orchestrated meal, while smaller specialty houses produce symphonies with only one kind of fish, or one style of preparation. The gifts of the ocean are as basic to the Japanese diet as rice, and without them there would be no distinctive Japanese cuisine.

The ancient Shinto prayer, noted earlier, lists the ocean foodstuffs of the early Japanese: "... things that dwell in the blue sea-plain, the broad of fin and the narrow of fin, seaweed from the offing, seaweed from the shore. . . ." Broad fin and narrow, from shallow and deep, the Japanese have tried everything. There is probably nothing edible that swims or floats or scuttles across the ocean floor that they have not mastered. They eat whales that taste like beef and tiny clams that barely taste at all, pungent sea urchins and sweetish sea bream, tuna that fairly melts on the tongue and octopus tentacles that require good teeth. They have creamy sardines and juicy crabs and crisp squid and subtly flavored shrimp. There are aromas too delicate to name and flavors too rich to forget, globefish that could poison you if not properly cleaned, eels that hint at the murky fecundity of the ocean depths, and feathery-fleshed whitefish that suggest sunshine on a sparkling sea.

All told, the Japanese eat nine marine mammals, 63 species of sea fish, eight kinds of shellfish, three different crabs, two kinds of shrimp, plus half a dozen miscellaneous sea creatures. Six varieties of edible seaweed are plucked from the coastal waters, and 18 species of fresh-water fish (particularly carp and *ayu,* or sweetfish, a small river trout) find their places in the happy bellies of Japan. It adds up to 7,000 tons of seafood every day, or, to take a more palatable statistic, nearly one pound of fish per person per week.

To gather this harvest, Japan's commercial fishing boats scour every ocean of the world. The Pacific, of course, is virtually a lake for Japanese fishermen. But efficient Japanese tuna clippers roam the Atlantic and Indian Oceans, whale-killing fleets penetrate the Antarctic, and the Bering Sea is dragged for cod and halibut. Not even the Mediterranean is too far to roam for tuna. Equipped with loran navigation systems to guide them with precision to the best fishing grounds, with radar and sonar to locate the schools of fish, and with first-class canning, processing and deep-freeze devices, Japan's ocean-going fishermen take into their floating factories more fish than any other country—about one sixth of the world's total catch. Sometimes these vessels remain at sea for six months, return to Japan briefly to unload their haul at Tokyo's Tsukiji market, or the ports of Kobe or Hiroshima, and then are outward bound again without putting in at the small fishing towns the fishermen call home.

But for every humming trawler far at sea there must be a hundred put-putting wooden cockleshells no more than 20 feet long, trolling and seining and hand-lining the waters within sight of shore. They follow the tides and not the sun, and so, when the fish are running, I have often watched them as they leave at night, their yellow lanterns twinkling the surface of a bay like stars in a sky turned upside down.

In many places, women play a vital role in community fishing operations. When the boats come home to the coast of Chiba, near Tokyo, the wives and daughters of the fishermen turn out in force and plunge to their waists in the surf—even in the dead of winter—to haul the vessels onto the beach. In some Okinawa fishing communities the women take complete charge of the catch once it is landed, selling it, collecting the money, and paying their fishermen husbands' salaries.

But it is the *ama,* the strapping diving girls, who are the real queens of the seacoast, and who still provide most of the *awabi* (abalone, or sea-ear) and many other shellfish for the *sushi* counters of Japan. Baby oysters, called spat, can be grown in baskets, or can be raked up from sandy bottoms; clams can be dug up at low tide; octopus turn up regularly in fishnets and can be lured into earthenware pots on the sea floor and hauled out of the water before they know what's happening. But the *awabi,* single-shelled mollusks, live 40 feet down or deeper, and attach themselves like suction cups to the jagged undersea rocks. The only way to get them without destroying their young is to hack them off, one by one, with a heavy knife.

In Japan, diving for shellfish like *awabi* has always been women's work, a calling and a skill passed on from *ama* mother to *ama* daughter for generations. The Japanese say a woman can better withstand the prolonged cold of the deep than a man. In hundreds of bays along Japan's coast the peculiar periodic whistle of the *ama* surfacing and letting out her breath is as familiar a sound as the cry of a gull or the roar of the waves.

Nowadays, most *ama* wear white linen clothing from head to knee to protect them from the sun (during the moments they are on the surface), to frighten away sharks—and as a concession to modern ideas of modesty. But in out-of-the-way corners of the country sturdy, sun-bronzed *ama* in nothing but loincloth and belt (and perhaps a diving mask) still prowl through an undersea world that they know like the lanes of their village. Ordinary *ama* must go to the diving grounds in boatloads of a dozen or more, and surface and dive under their own power. But an expert *ama* has her own boatman—usually her husband or a male relative in whom she has utter faith. With a lead weight to pull her down, and her boatman to haul her up, she can go deeper than her less-skilled sisters, and spend more time and breath on the bottom where the shellfish are. During the season a champion *ama* may earn as much in a good day as the average Japanese factory girl makes in a month; not surprisingly, the *ama* rule matriarchal villages, and the best young divers can take their pick of husbands.

Nowadays the profession of *ama* is somehow considered feudal and degrading—though how it can be more degrading than working at a factory bench is difficult for me to understand—and fewer and fewer *ama* village girls are following their mothers down to the sea. Consequently *awabi* prices are steadily rising. No matter how expensive it gets, Japanese shellfish lovers are not likely to give it up; whether raw, semi-raw and pickled in vinegar, steamed, or even dried and made chewy, the firm, mellow flesh of the *awabi* will always be regarded by the Japanese as one of the prizes of the ocean.

Continued on page 80

魚

Beyond the gleaming tuna carcasses *(opposite)*, each identified by bold red numbers, brokers signal their bids at one of the many noisy auctions that start the day's business at Tokyo's Tsukiji Central Market. The brokers have previously inspected the tuna, noted their weights—some go as high as 450 pounds—and judged the flesh for quality. Tuna tails are slashed to reveal freshness and fattiness of the meat, important in determining price. When the auction begins, the rapid-fire barrage of bids reflects the brokers' appraisal of these factors. Lean tuna, brought all the way from the Indian Ocean, may sell for only 25 cents a pound; firm, fatty tuna from relatively nearby Pacific waters will bring up to a dollar a pound. Some 90 other kinds of fish—most of them unloaded only hours earlier—are sold at auctions. They include *(above)*: bonito *(1)*, *guji*, a type of sea bream *(2)*, whitebait *(3)*, squid *(4)*, small sea bream *(5)*, prawns *(6)*, clams *(7)*, sea bream *(8)*, lobsters *(9)*, a Japanese species of scorpion fish *(10)* and abalone *(11)*.

A Spectacular Market for Fresh Fish by the Ton

Fish is as important in the Japanese diet as meat is in the West. However, the watery harvest of river, lake and sea offers a far greater range of choices to the Japanese than do the farms of the West. Fish stores offer everything from whale steaks (whose taste is remarkably similar to beef) to tiny mollusks. Large and small, sweet and tangy, tons of fish are delivered daily to sprawling markets in every large city. At Tokyo's 50-acre Tsukiji Central Market alone, 2,000 tons of fish, most of it freshly caught, are traded each day. The process starts at 5:45 a.m. when fiercely competitive brokers bid at auction for a broad spectrum of finned and shelled products. These middlemen then display their wares in 1,500 market stalls at which they sell the fish to the city's clamoring shopkeepers and restaurateurs.

For a panoramic view of Japan's seafood empire, every visitor to the country should look in on Tokyo's Tsukiji fish market, any morning before dawn. Here, in a scene of incredible congestion and seeming chaos, a few blocks from the Ginza, more than 70,000 people buy and sell and cart away all the sea products that the 20 million Japanese of the Tokyo metropolitan area require every day—and most of the fish will have been eaten before the next day's turmoil begins. Some of the fish is unloaded at Tsukiji directly from ocean-going vessels just arrived from months at sea; most of it arrives in refrigerated freight cars from other ports. But all of it is laid out under glaring light bulbs to be carefully inspected before it is sold. Somehow, the market smells of the sea, not of fish.

On one quay, row on row of gleaming, bulky tuna, tails chopped off and stuffed into mouths, identifying numbers painted on sides, are laid out on wooden racks. Professional tuna buyers prod the carcasses, shine flashlights into the gills and examine the tail nubs to check the color and condition of the meat. And then they bid on them, in a dozen or more frantic, noisy auctions going on at once. Since much of the tuna will be eaten uncooked either as *sushi* or *sashimi,* the buyers are very fussy, not only about freshness but about ocean of origin. Tuna from the northern Pacific will fetch the highest prices because they will be fresher than Indian or Atlantic Ocean specimens and because they are fatter and contain more of the light pink, fatty *toro* flesh that *sashimi* fanciers prize.

From the auctions, hundreds of porters wheel the now-dismembered tuna to a vast maelstrom of activity where 1,500 wholesale stands display the full abundance of the sea. Here are silver sardines and mackerel, bright red *tai* (sea bream) with enormous, reproachful eyes, quivering squid and cuttlefish, blue-striped bonito, crates of pink Hokkaido crabs packed in ice, buckets of fresh oysters from Hiroshima on the Inland Sea, piles of iridescent *awabi,* boxes of prickly sea urchins—and fishes of all colors and sizes, some still flopping, some split, some already having lost their heads and tails.

To this heart of the market come the thousands of neighborhood fishmongers and restaurateurs, great and small, who insist on choosing everything fresh themselves. They look, they prod, they sniff and they buy, and then they cart their glistening purchases through clogged aisles to a seething traffic jam. As the sun rises, the flood of fish spreads out by truck, motorcycle and bicycle, to every cranny of the world's biggest city and its suburbs.

Some of the best of the sea produce does not go far, for the finest fish eating in Japan is to be had in the environs of Tsukiji and in nearby Ginza. This is especially true of *sashimi* and *sushi,* the two basic raw-fish dishes. In the days before refrigeration and fast transport, restaurants serving uncooked fish naturally set up near the docks to assure freshness. Nowadays delicious raw seafood is available far inland, but the excellent Tsukiji restaurants survive, supported by thousands of people who know their fish.

Eating uncooked fish strikes many Westerners as barbaric and somehow indecent, but this attitude usually disappears with the first brave bite. Part of the instinctive Western uneasiness is due to the ugly word "raw," with its misleading suggestion of something coarse and tough. To overcome the initial reluctance of my friends, I remind them that *sashimi* is sometimes the first solid food served by Japanese hospitals to patients who have been on a liq-

uid diet. The fact is that raw fish as the Japanese eat it does not taste or smell fishy. In a blindfold test the skeptic would not have the faintest idea he was eating fish; he would probably assume that his chunk of raw tuna was a cube of refrigerated rare roast beef.

Sashimi is the Japanese umbrella term for raw fillets of fish eaten by itself, usually dipped in soy sauce and a special pungent horseradish. *Sushi* (of which more will be said in Chapter 7) consists of balls of vinegared rice garnished either with a strip of raw seafood or with cooked shrimp, cooked fish, vegetables, seaweed or egg.

Both *sashimi* and *sushi* are extremely popular. No formal menu in a good Japanese restaurant ever omits the *sashimi* course; but *sushi,* which is a meal in itself (as it includes rice) does not appear at formal dinners, though there are more *sushi* restaurants in Japan than any other kind. *Sashimi* may also make up a meal by itself, and some restaurants serve nothing else, offering a dozen or more varieties of fish for a full dinner. Because so many sea animals can be eaten this way, an all-*sashimi* menu is never monotonous: it's more like a glorious binge. Of all their foods, I think the Japanese love *sashimi* best; certainly it is what they long for most when they are traveling abroad and can't eat as they do at home.

Everything concerned with the handling and preparation of *sashimi* is carried out with elaborate care. Not only must the fish be fresh—ideally between

Attracted by the flames of burning pine boughs, tasty, troutlike fish called *ayu* swim close to this skiff. There they are easy prey for trained cormorants, fish-catching birds that a boatman holds on 12-foot-long leashes. A ring around the cormorant's neck keeps it from swallowing, and when the bird is taken aboard, it surrenders its catch. *Ukai* (cormorant fishing) is more than 1,200 years old but flourishes today mainly on the Nagara River in Gifu Prefecture, where it has become a tourist attraction. The captured *ayu* are transferred to a restaurant boat where they are served raw or salt-broiled to the diners on board.

four and 12 hours out of the water, and refrigerated all the way from ship to lip —but never frozen, for the drip of thawing leaches out all the flavor. The chef who cuts the *sashimi* into chunks just big enough for chopsticks to handle uses his knife to pick up the pieces so the heat of his fingers won't be transferred to the fish. Nor is fish skinned, or shellfish opened, until the moment of serving, for their natural "envelopes" preserve the flavor. Occasionally, to vary the taste and make a prettier presentation, the Japanese take their *sashimi* with the skin on. But fish skins are hard to chew when raw, so they have to be treated lightly with heat, either by pouring hot water over the skin through cheesecloth or by broiling the skin side for a few seconds.

By far the most popular *sashimi* fish is *maguro,* tuna, both the fatty pink meat and the red lean, and the Japanese prefer it in spring or early summer. It appears before you in a shallow porcelain bowl, five or six juicy-looking, square-cut little red slabs, leaning on each other like fallen dominoes and decorated with slivers of green cabbage or white radish. Alongside, bedded on a tiny slice of radish, you find a dab of *wasabi,* the hot, green horseradish paste. A separate small dipping bowl and a bottle of soy sauce complete the ensemble. Soy sauce goes into the dipping bowl, and *wasabi* is added with chopsticks. With chopsticks pick up a chunk, dip it in the sauce and pop the whole bit in your mouth. Chew slowly and roll it on your tongue: it is tender, meaty and succulent, a taste that can be compared to no other.

In winter, the Japanese are partial to white-meat *sashimi,* such as yellowtail, *tai* (sea bream), flounder and squid. Squid is served in slabs, just like the red tuna, for squid is a rugged meat in spite of its color. But the other white-meat *sashimi* usually arrives in slices so thin that you can see right through them to the pattern of the dish beneath. In this case, a dipping sauce called *ponzu,* half soy sauce and half a sour juice like our lime, imparts a slight tang, but the sea-sweet flavor of the fish always comes whispering through.

The Japanese hold that any fish or shellfish that can be eaten cooked is also edible raw, but that doesn't mean that they consume raw seafood indiscriminately. For one thing, some fish just taste better raw than others. And fish that are excellent in one season may lack flavor at another; many are too fat just before the spawning period, for instance, and too lean right after it. Nor are all parts of the creature good raw; the thickest parts of the fish fillet are best; and only the main flesh of shellfish, crustaceans and mollusks qualifies for *sashimi.* Another consideration is the degree of freshness. This is especially important for anyone buying fish for *sashimi* in the United States, where standards of freshness fall far short of the Japanese.

The Japanese dine gloriously on raw carp and other fresh-water *sashimi.* Americans preparing a *sashimi* meal would also be wise to stick to fresh-water species. Although parasites causing the troublesome infection, *Anisakiasis,* are sometimes found in fresh-water fish, more are hosted by salt-water fish. It is therefore safer, when eating raw fish in the U.S., to eat fresh-water species. Exceptions are pike and pickerel in the Northeast, which contain other parasites. Lobsters and crabs must be bought alive to be eaten raw.

For many Japanese gourmets, all this attention to freshness and season and cut is not enough. They insist quite simply that a dead fish is not a fresh fish, and they prefer to eat them alive. The victim usually selected for this sacrifice is the shrimp, and the eating ritual is called *odori. Odori* means dance,

Raw Fish and the Risk of Anisakiasis

As Americans in growing numbers dine on raw fish, they should be aware that they are exposing themselves to a possible gastrointestinal parasitic infection, Anisakiasis. Several thousand cases of this infection, first discovered in the 1950s, have been diagnosed, most of them in Japan and The Netherlands. Symptoms range from short, mild gastrointestinal discomfort to severe attacks lasting months. The infection is generally not fatal, but if the parasite dies in the tissues, causing a lesion, surgery may be necessary. Frequently mimicking other illnesses, Anisakiasis has been variously misdiagnosed as roundworm, gastric tumor, appendicitis, cancer, gall bladder inflammation, tuberculosis, peritonitis, cancer of the colon and diverticulitis. Parasites causing Anisakiasis have been found in one species of squid and some 50 types of fish, mostly salt-water species. These include: mackerel, tuna, salmon, "rock" or red fish, Alaskan pollock, haddock, cod, pike, herring, bonito, red snapper, white sea bass, and aweoweo —a fish traditionally eaten raw in Hawaii. The increasing incidence of cases is due to improved diagnosis as well as the growing popularity of sashimi. Considering the numbers of people eating raw fish, however, the risk is fairly small.

and that's what the flesh is doing as it is picked up, chewed and swallowed.

A Japanese doctor I know introduced me to *odori* at an excellent but unpretentious restaurant in the Shinjuku section of Tokyo. We sat at a counter and sipped *sake*. Then my host said something to the chef. Before my eyes the chef grabbed a live shrimp from a squirming tankful, gutted and beheaded it with two quick flicks of his knife, stripped off the shell and rinsed the flesh, and placed the dancing shrimp in front of me—all in about five seconds. Before I could react he did the same with another for my friend, who immediately captured it by the wriggling tail, dipped it in a sauce, and swallowed it down, adding appreciative sounds.

Determined not to be outfaced I summoned all my resolve and reached for mine, but it squirmed violently—in agony, I was sure—and escaped from my trembling fingers. That was enough for this adventurous American. I waited patiently until the performance was over and then gingerly tasted the shrimp. It was delicious, of course, although my host told me I had missed the best part. He insisted that the flavor is several times better while the *odori* is in progress—and I am willing to take his word for it.

Later I learned that most Japanese react to the experience much as I did. My friend is in a minority in his passion for *odori;* perhaps his being a surgeon has something to do with his tastes. But there is a restaurant in Tsukiji that cuts all its *sashimi* fillets out of living fish, and it is so busy that advance reservations are suggested.

A seafood even more dramatic than *odori,* at least potentially, is *fugu,* the blowfish or globefish. This intriguing little creature, which can puff itself up to beachball size when threatened, is actually poisonous. That is, the liver and ovaries of the *fugu* contain a deadly toxin that spreads through the rest of the fish in an instant unless deftly removed in the first step of cleaning. To the untrained eye, however, the liver looks just like the male fish's testes, a special delicacy highly prized by Japanese men as a virility builder.

Dozens of times a year some cocksure fisherman in Japan finds a mess of *fugu* in his nets, decides he knows how to clean them—and drops dead, chopsticks clattering from paralyzed fingers. Duly reported in the Japanese press, these tragedies give the *fugu* connoisseur the heady feeling that he is playing a kind of Russian roulette—and winning. The danger of *fugu* has in fact inspired a homily on all kinds of risk. "Fugu wa kuitashii, inochi wa oshishii," says the Japanese who can't quite make up his mind on a bold course of action: "I would like to eat *fugu,* but I would like to live."

In fact, eating *fugu* prepared by a licensed *fugu* chef is perfectly safe. The chef has to pass oral, written and practical examinations in the techniques of cleaning, and must demonstrate an infallible ability to distinguish testes from liver; his license, with photo attached, is displayed prominently.

Thus safeguarded, the gourmets of Japan happily pay out eight dollars or more for a two-ounce portion of delicate "tiger" *fugu sashimi,* without doubt Japan's costliest food. In the best *fugu* restaurants they get it arranged in intricate patterns simulating chrysanthemum blossoms or birds in flight, and sliced so thin that the colors and design on the dish are visible through it. They eat it with almost ritual awe, dipping the transparent slices in a special *ponzu* supercharged with chopped scallions and radish, and welcoming the slight numbness of lips and tongue that results, it is said, from minute

Continued on page 86

White, nearly transparent slices of raw *fugu* are often fashioned into fragile designs such as the sacred flying crane, Japan's noblest bird *(above)*, garnished with a pine twig. The dark areas and the beak are made from broiled *fugu* skin, which is also edible, and the crest is grated *daikon* radish mixed with hot red pepper.

"*Fugu*" Eating: A Thrill in Every Bite

From October 1 to March 31 each season, millions of Japanese bet their lives —some 200 lose—by eating *fugu,* a kind of blowfish with a lethal poison in its liver and ovaries. But besides being esteemed by Japanese as the most delicious of fish, carefully cleaned *fugu* is perfectly safe to eat. So restaurants whose chefs must be specially licensed serve it and customers devour it.

A family trustingly dips into a beautifully designed crane fashioned from raw and broiled *fugu.* At Fukugen, a renowned Tokyo restaurant devoted to serving "tiger" *fugu,* which is the tastiest and also the deadliest variety of the fish, the skilled and dedicated chefs reduce the chances of accidental poisoning to zero.

traces of the poison. Sophisticated *fugu* enthusiasts prefer the "noble" and "philosophical" flesh of *fugu* to all other *sashimi,* and they grow fretful during the summer months when it is not available; but unbelievers claim that the only thing they can taste is the sauce. To my taste buds, *fugu* does have a distinctive tang that is not present when the same sauce is applied to other fishes; but strangely, the tang is not always there when the *fugu* is tasted without the sauce. It seems to be another example of the Japanese genius for enhancing the natural flavor of their foods.

Fugu restaurants also produce a strong, pungent *fugu* stew served piping hot. And, of course, for hundreds of thousands of adventurous Japanese the high point of a *fugu* meal comes when the chef, with a comradely leer, offers them a cup of hot *sake* mixed with *fugu* testes. *Fugu* chefs and aging businessmen swear by it, but what effect it may have I cannot say. Undoubtedly the theoretical danger in *fugu* enhances its popularity. Certainly the esthetic and symbolic presentation of all foods makes them taste better to the Japanese. In the same way the very sounds of the names of certain fish increase their value in Japan.

The best example of this is the *tai,* a flat, bright-pink fish. The *tai* has a distinguished flavor, and its red skin is considered lucky in itself, but it is the very name *tai* that ranks it as the finest fish in the sea. *Tai* sounds like *medetai,* meaning "felicitous," the root word for "congratulations," and so the *tai* has become the ceremonial fish served at weddings and other happy occasions. Sending a boxed fish to a friend for a New Year's greeting may not sound like a good idea to us, but if the friend is Japanese and the fish is a *tai,* he will be delighted. The idea that *tai* is a noble fish has become so ingrained in Japanese minds that there is even a proverb that depends on the notion: "Kusattemo tai," meaning, "Even if it stinks, it's *tai,*" conveys the thought that neither poverty nor age can destroy real quality.

This kind of symbolic pun, which may seem superstitious to Westerners, helps the Japanese in their eternal quest for harmony with nature. To the Japanese, nothing on earth, not even a common fish, can exist in isolation; everything must be accorded its rightful place in the universal scheme of things. All aspects of a creature, its soul, its color and character, even its name, are duly honored. Take the carp: the Japanese admire its courage and perseverance in struggling upstream to spawn, and they make it a symbol of masculine strength, ambition and stick-to-itiveness. On Children's Day, early in May, every household with a son flies one or more gaily colored wind-sock streamers, in the shape of a carp. When carp is eaten it is not just the flesh that is absorbed but in some way the noble attributes as well.

Through the centuries, water, fish and crabs have figured prominently in Japanese folklore and art. Fish are considered to be among the most beautiful of nature's creatures, for they have grace and suppleness. A swimming fish is a favorite subject for picture scrolls to hang in the *tokonoma,* especially when these alcoves are in restaurants. In Buddhist temples the little gong that the priests beat while chanting their prayers most often turns out to be a hollow, carved wooden fish nestling on a silken pillow.

The Japanese respect for fish that is manifest in the way they catch, prepare and eat it even leads to solemn religious ceremonies. Every year, at the great temple of Sojiji, near Tokyo, priests chant their prayers to comfort the souls of fish that have died to feed the nation. On the following day the priests go out in boats to the middle of Tokyo Bay to perform the same service for fish that have died of natural causes. At Shimonoseki, on the straits between Honshu and Kyushu Islands where most of the *fugu* is caught, still another ceremony honors the spirits of *fugu,* specifically. And throughout Japan fishermen toss a basketful of eels back into the sea once a year to atone for all the eels they have caught.

One of the most respected and symbolic fish products of all is *katsuobushi,* dried bonito, an essential ingredient of all Japanese cookery. The ideographs for *katsuobushi* simply mean "bonito knot" *(katsuo* is bonito), but another set of ideographs pronounced the same way means "victorious warrior." Hence a stick of *katsuobushi* is a perfect gift on all congratulatory occasions, and it has become the most common and appropriate wedding present, meaningful, traditional and lucky.

But in a sense the real beauty of a *katsuobushi* wedding gift is that it is also eminently practical. The giver never is concerned whether his gift will be duplicated by others; every bride knows that the larger her army of victorious warriors, the better off she is: *katsuobushi* never spoils and it is used in almost everything. In fact, I think it is the most remarkable food product of Japan, a superb example of the adroit and sophisticated methods that the Japanese have devised for processing their ocean harvest.

From fresh bonito to finished *katsuobushi* is a transformation as complete as turning milk into cheese. The ancient, lengthy process is complex and scientifically sound, involving drying, smoking and mold fermentation. The result looks and feels like a mahogany boomerang, and it can be shaved into flakes only with a very sharp tool. (Every Japanese kitchen is equipped with a special plane for doing this but it is available in the U.S. pre-flaked.) Although *katsuobushi* preserves all the protein value of the bonito, it doesn't even taste fishy—but it *is* delicious.

The Japanese love to sprinkle *katsuobushi* flakes on cooked vegetables, particularly spinach, on *tofu* dishes and even on rice; but the most important use for it is as a base for *dashi (Chapter 3),* the remarkable soup stock that I consider to be the most sophisticated Japanese recipe of all.

The versatile *katsuobushi* represents only one of the many ways that the Japanese process their seafood. Seventy-six per cent of the 7.8-million-ton annual catch is preserved somehow: canned, frozen, salted, dried, preserved in soy sauce, or turned into sausage. Many of these methods are unique to Japan. For instance, a smooth, jellylike fish paste, *kamaboko,* has been part of the Japanese diet for more than 400 years, and a fish sausage, developed as a result of the food shortages of World War II, tastes like traditional sausage and is consumed at the rate of 150,000 tons a year. A mixture of tiny fishes and slivers of kelp is preserved by simmering in a salted, seasoned soy sauce until all the liquid is boiled away. The result, called *tsukudani,* makes a fine garnish for plain rice and other foods and is also served up to customers at *sake* shops and bars to keep them thirsty. Like peanuts or potato chips, these sticky, insidious little snacks are difficult to resist once you've had a taste. Oriental food stores in the United States sell several kinds of *tsukudani,* packaged in pliofilm, but I don't advise anyone to start on a packet unless he's prepared to finish it.

Looking like spiders squatting in a giant web, workers collect carefully cultivated *nori* (laver seaweed) while the tide is out. The vitamin-rich *nori* is picked off the hemp nets, then spread on coarse reed matting to sun-dry. Sold in bundles of 10 sheets, the paper-thin *nori* is used for wrapping around rice or as a garnish.

Many Japanese get most of their high-quality protein from dried fish and shrimp. One method of semidrying fish that I have never encountered elsewhere keeps it for about eight or 10 days without refrigeration and is very convenient for the housewife's lunch. Broiled, it tastes like a fresh fish though somewhat saltier. Its smell while cooking is marvelous, like unleavened bread baking just at the moment before it burns. As you walk along crowded residential streets at lunchtime this delectable aroma wafts from many houses—and sends me scurrying to the nearest restaurant.

Of all the marine miracles to which the Japanese can guide us, none so insults our prejudices and offers so much for the future as the murky world of undersea vegetables. Again our English vocabulary leads us astray, and I do not know which word is worse: "seaweed," with its explicit meaning of uselessness and its dank evocation of sunken ships and drowned sailors, or "algae," the correct scientific term, which suggests to most Americans the green scum on stagnant ponds. When you think about it, of course, there is no reason why kelp or laver should be considered less appetizing than asparagus—in fact they are delicious—but the prejudice remains. Many Westerners in Japan go queasy at the thought of seaweed but happily gobble up crisp sheets of pressed *nori* (laver) without a moment's hesitation.

In Japanese, the words for most seaweeds are as commonplace and respectable as "cabbage," and one of them even provides another of those homonymic symbols. Kelp *(katsuobushi's* partner in *dashi)* is *kombu* and it sounds like *yorokobu,* the word for "happiness." Japanese department stores therefore offer vast arrays of elegantly packaged *kombu* assortments that Japanese guests bring to their hostess as one might offer a box of chocolates. Wise foreign residents have discovered that a gift of *kombu* is the quickest passport to acceptance by a Japanese, for it indicates that the giver really understands and appreciates Japan.

The six kinds of algae that the Japanese use account for about 10 per cent of their total food intake. Some of these sea vegetables are found wild in the ocean, but *nori* is painstakingly cultivated in sheltered inlets along the coast. Tokyo Bay itself produces excellent *nori.*

All of these products are rich sources of minerals and vitamins, all easily and quickly digestible. The basic good health of the Japanese people, despite their low consumption of foods like milk and meat and eggs that Westerners consider essential, is generally credited to the seaweed as well as the fish in their diet. Most delightful of all, the seaweeds, especially *kombu* and *nori,* open up a whole new world of seasoning possibilities that have been fully exploited by the Japanese for centuries. And since all of the principal Japanese seaweeds are available at Oriental food stores in the United States, there is no reason not to explore these novel ingredients.

Nori, particularly rich in vitamins A, B_{12} and D, is pressed into paper-thin sheets and sun-dried on a smooth surface. Toasted to crispness and rolled neatly around rice and other ingredients, these purplish-black sheets make one standard kind of *sushi;* a clump of rice wrapped less elegantly in *nori* becomes *onigiri,* a plebeian snack that can be eaten by hand. Crumbled as a garnish over rice or *ochazuke,* the farmer's common mixture of rice and tea, *nori* imparts a salty flavor.

Besides its vital role in *dashi, kombu* (which is rich in iodine and vitamin C) shows up as a seasoning for root vegetables, as a peppy garnish for rice and as another kind of *tsukudani.* Sometimes *kombu* is cut into tiny, oily strips and woven into miniature baskets about an inch high. Deep-fat-fried until crisp, these baskets are loaded with minute amounts of cooked vegetables and served on a tray; you eat the vegetables and then munch on the nourishing basket—which some say is the best part.

Wakame and *hijiki,* the other important sea vegetables, are used principally as salad material and in soups. Sold dried, they are restored to a fresh state by a brief soaking.

Population experts have predicted that as man exhausts the earth's resources, he will have to farm the sea for sustenance. We need only to taste the seemingly infinite delights of Japanese seafood to discover how exciting this otherwise dismal future could be. Some doctors feel that such a diet would be good for others as well. Japanese suffer fewer heart attacks and have far less cholesterol in their veins than Americans; comparative studies on Japanese-Americans have shown that this is not a racial quirk. It may be partly due to diet, to the fact that the Japanese people still take most of their protein from the animal and vegetable dwellers in the blue sea plain. However, if seafood is to be important in the human diet of the future, the seas off Japan, as well as elsewhere, will have to be protected from pollution.

RECIPES

Sashimi: SLICED RAW FISH
Sushi: VINEGARED RICE DISHES
Agemono: FRIED FOODS

SASHIMI: Many Westerners who are disconcerted by the Japanese delight in eating raw fish themselves think nothing of eating raw clams and oysters. Interestingly, "sashimi" neither tastes nor smells "fishy" and moreover, certain types of "sashimi," notably tuna, have the texture and the flavor of tender, rare beef.

Sashimi

鮨

SLICED RAW FISH

The most important factor in the preparation of "sashimi" is the absolute freshness of the fish. Frozen fish cannot be used. It is best to avoid salt-water fish since they are more likely to carry parasites. Keep the fish refrigerated, wrapped in cheesecloth until ready to use. Handle the fish as little as possible; the warmth of your hands can spoil its freshness.

To serve 4 to 6

1 pound fresh filleted porgy, sea bass, striped bass, red snapper, squid, abalone or tuna, in one piece

DIPPING SAUCE

4 to 6 tablespoons Japanese soy sauce, *chirizu (page 94)* or *tosa joyu* and its garnish *(page 94)*

GARNISH

A 2-inch section of *daikon* (Japanese white radish) or large icicle radish or white turnip, peeled, shredded and soaked in cold water until ready to use

1 carrot, peeled, shredded and soaked in cold water until ready to use

1 stalk celery, cut in half lengthwise, shredded and soaked in cold water until ready to use

CUTTING THE FISH: There are four basic fish-cutting methods for *sashimi* and a very sharp, heavy knife is indispensable to them all. *(See pages 92-93 for pictures and diagrams.)*

1. *Hira giri* (flat cut): This is the most popular shape, suitable for any filleted fish. Holding the fish firmly, cut straight down in slices about 1/4 to 1/2 inch thick and 1 inch wide, depending on the size of the fillet.

2. *Kaku giri* (cubic cut): This style of cutting is more often used for tuna. Cut the tuna as above (flat cut), then cut the slices into 1/2-inch cubes.

3. *Ito zukuri* (thread shape): Although this technique may be used with any small fish, it is especially suitable for squid. Cut the squid straight down into 1/4-inch slices, then cut lengthwise into 1/4-inch-wide strips.

4. *Usu zukuri* (paper-thin slices): Place a fillet of bass or porgy on a flat surface and, holding the fish firmly with one hand, slice it on an angle into almost transparent sheets.

TO SERVE: *Sashimi* may be composed of one fish or a variety of fish. To serve as part of a meal, arrange the fish attractively on individual serving plates. Garnish each plate with about 1/2 teaspoon of *wasabi (see "tosa joyu" garnish, page 94)*, and decorate with strips of *daikon*, carrot and/or celery. Cover with plastic wrap and refrigerate for no more than 1 hour before serving.

Pour the dipping sauce of your choice into tiny individual dishes and accompany each serving of *sashimi* with its own dipping sauce. The *wasabi* may be mixed into the soy sauce or *tosa joyu* to taste.

NOTE: To serve as an hors d'oeuvre, arrange two or more varieties or cuts of *sashimi* on a serving platter and accompany with dipping sauce.

The "petals" of this *sashimi* flower are of striped bass, sliced transparently thin. In the center is red tuna, topped by a mound of *wasabi*. Alongside the soy sauce *(left)* is a garnish of *some oroshi (page 94)* in *ponzu*.

Here is an assortment of the most popular cuts and types of fish served as *sashimi*. At top left is squid, for which cutting directions are given below. The dark red fish is tuna—sliced horizontally, straight and in cubes *(directions opposite, bottom)*. The white-meat fish is striped bass, cut straight, paper thin, and mounded in strips *(opposite, center)*.

Transforming a Whole Fish or Fillets into "Sashimi"

Properly prepared *sashimi*—sliced raw fish—is one of the glories of the Japanese cuisine, and is steadily gaining in popularity throughout the Western world. To make *sashimi* takes little effort, but one rule must be remembered: always use fresh—never frozen—fish.

Sashimi is made from porgy, sea bass, striped bass, red snapper, squid, abalone or tuna fillets. While most of these fish are available throughout the United States, their absolute freshness is another matter and may be dictated by region and season.

Directions for cutting the various kinds of fillets are given at right and opposite. You may, however, want to begin with a whole fish—either because you have caught one yourself, or because you plan to use the head and trimmings for fish stock. In that event, see the drawings *(top, opposite)* for filleting a whole fish. Instructions for serving *sashimi* are on pages 90 and 94.

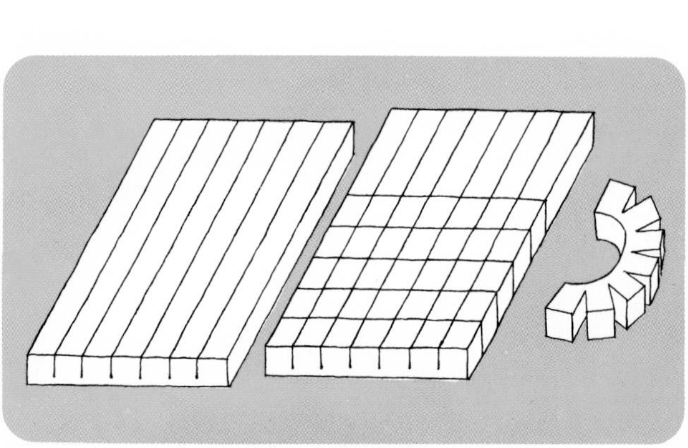

A DECORATIVE CUT FOR SQUID: With a sharp, heavy knife, make shallow cuts down the length of the fillet to within 1/8 inch of the other side. Then cut through the fillet crosswise, at 1/4-inch intervals. Bend the ends of the strips inward slightly to reveal the slits.

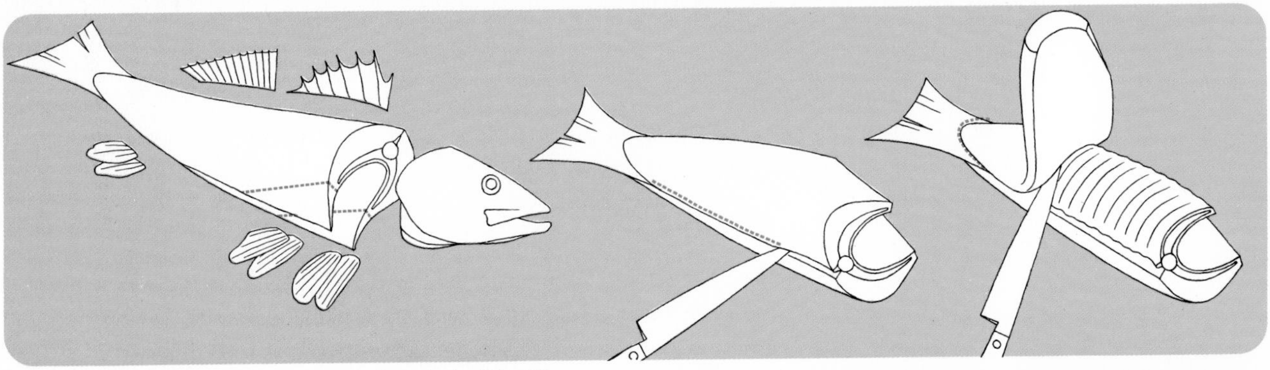

TO FILLET A FISH: First scale and wash the whole fish. Slit the fish open along its belly to gut it, then *(above, left)* cut off the fins, head and hard flaps near the head. Starting at the head, cut along back *(above, center)*, freeing the top from the spine and radiating bones *(above, right)*. Continue cutting until you reach the tail. Turn over and repeat the same procedure on the other side, starting from the tail. Discard the spinal bones.

To skin *(right)*, insert the tip of the knife at the pointed end of the fillet; holding firmly onto the skin, cut and push the flesh away with the side of the knife.

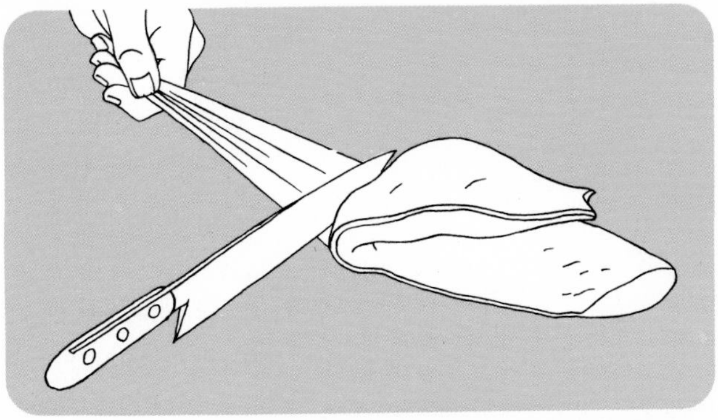

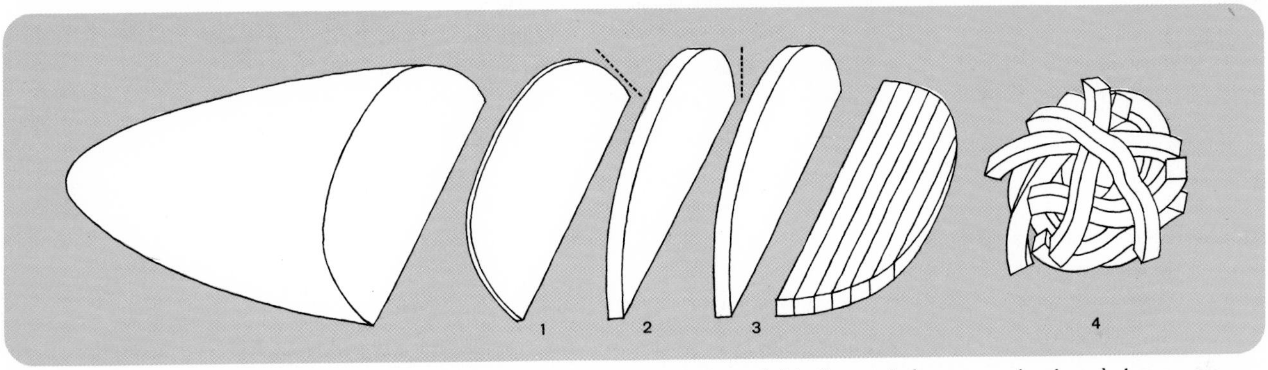

SLICING WHITE-MEAT FISH: Place the fish fillet (bass or porgy) on a cutting surface and cut *usu zukuri* style into paper-thin slices *(1)*. Or, cut any filleted fish straight down *hira giri* style into ¼-inch-thick slices *(2)*. A variation of this flat cut is known as the thread shape *(ito zukuri)*, and is suitable for white-meat fish or squid: cut the ¼-inch-thick slices lengthwise into ¼-inch-wide strips *(3)* and mound these *(4)* one atop the other.

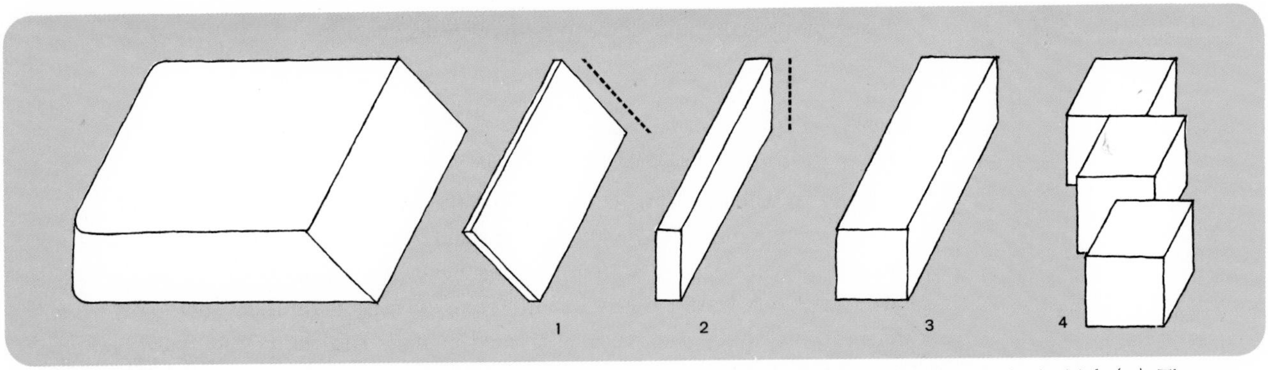

SLICING A TUNA FILLET: Begin with a section of tuna fillet, trimmed by you or your fishman into a rectangular loaf shape. The tuna can be sliced *usu zukuri* style at an angle into paper-thin slices *(1)*. Or it can be sliced in the *hira giri* style, suitable for any fish fillet, in which you cut straight down into slices ¼ inch thick *(2)*. The cubic cut *(kaku giri)* is a style of cutting used almost exclusively for tuna because of its firmness. First cut straight down, into slices ½ inch thick *(3)*. Then cut these slices into ½-inch-wide cubes *(4)*.

Isobe Zukuri 磯辺づくり

SASHIMI WRAPPED IN NORI

To serve 6 to 8

6 sheets of packaged *nori* (dried laver)
1 pound fresh fish fillet *(see sashimi, page 90)*

DIPPING SAUCE
½ cup *chirizu* or *tosa joyu (below)*

PREPARE AHEAD: 1. Select the fish according to directions on page 90. Cut the fillet into slices ½ inch thick and 6 or 7 inches long or as long as the sheet of *nori.*

TO ASSEMBLE AND SERVE: To intensify its flavor and color, pass the *nori,* a sheet at a time—and on one side only—over a gas flame or candle. Lay the *nori* flat on a hard surface—the Japanese use a bamboo mat to facilitate the rolling—with the wide side of the mat facing toward you. Place a long slice of fish along the length of the *nori* and roll the *nori* into a long, thick, tight cylinder. With a sharp knife cut it crosswise into 1½-inch slices. Roll and cut the remaining fish and *nori* in similar fashion. Serve with a dipping sauce, as part of a Japanese meal *(page 198)* or first course.

Chirizu ちり酢

SPICY DIPPING SAUCE FOR SASHIMI

To make about ½ cup

2 tablespoons *sake* (rice wine)
A ¼-pound section *daikon* (Japanese white radish), peeled and finely grated (¼ cup), or substitute ¼ cup grated icicle radish or white turnips
2 scallions, including the trimmed green stems, sliced thin into rounds
¼ cup Japanese all-purpose soy sauce
¼ cup fresh lemon juice
MSG
⅛ teaspoon *hichimi togarashi* (seven-pepper spice)

PREPARE AHEAD: 1. Warm the *sake* in a small saucepan. Then, off the heat, ignite it with a match and shake the pan gently until the flame dies out. Pour the *sake* into a small dish and cool.

2. In a small mixing bowl, combine the *sake* with the grated *daikon,* sliced scallions, soy sauce, lemon juice, a sprinkle of MSG and ⅛ teaspoon of seven-pepper spice. Mix well.

TO SERVE: Pour the dipping sauce into tiny individual dishes and serve with bass, striped bass, porgy or fluke *sashimi.*

Tosa Joyu 土佐醤油

DELICATE SOY-BASED DIPPING SAUCE FOR SASHIMI

To make about ½ cup

¼ cup Japanese all-purpose soy sauce
1 tablespoon *sake* (rice wine)
2 tablespoons preflaked *katsuobushi* (dried bonito)
MSG

GARNISH
1 tablespoon *wasabi* (green horseradish) powder, mixed with just enough cold water to make a thick paste and set aside to rest for 15 minutes

Combine the soy sauce, *sake, katsuobushi* and a sprinkle of MSG in a small saucepan and bring to a boil uncovered, stirring constantly. Strain through a fine sieve set over a small bowl and cool to room temperature.

Divide the dipping sauce among 6 tiny individual dishes, and serve it with *sashimi* of any kind.

Garnish each plate of *sashimi* with about ½ teaspoon of *wasabi,* this to be mixed into the dipping sauce to individual taste.

Some Oroshi 漢字

WHITE RADISH AND RED PEPPER GARNISH

To make ½ cup

A 3-inch round section of *daikon* (white radish), peeled
4 *takano tjume* (dried whole red peppers)
½ cup *ponzu* (equal parts soy sauce and lemon or lime juice)
2 scallions, including 3 inches of the green stems, sliced thin into rounds

PREPARE AHEAD: With chopsticks or the tip of a sharp, pointed knife, make four openings in the flat side of the *daikon.* Insert a dried red pepper deep into each opening, so that its tip is level with the surface of the *daikon.* Set aside for at least 4 hours, or refrigerate overnight. By then, the *daikon's* moisture will have reconstituted the red peppers and the pepper will have spiced the *daikon.*

Grate the pepper-stuffed *daikon,* divide into 6 equal parts, and roll each part into a small ball.

TO SERVE: Pour the *ponzu* into 6 tiny dishes and add a grated *daikon*-and-pepper ball to each dish. Garnish with sliced scallions and serve with *sashimi.*

"SUSHI"—vinegared rice dishes—appears in many forms. All are based on vinegared rice, accompanied by slices of raw fish with or without omelet strips, sliced vegetables, "nori" seaweed, and a variety of colorful garnishes. These Japanese "sandwiches" may be prepared simply, by topping an oblong of vinegared rice with a dab of prepared horseradish and slice of fish, or elaborately, by topping the rice with a wide variety of delicately seasoned ingredients, rolling them all in "nori," and cutting them into 1-inch-thick slices. The "sushi" recipes on the following pages can make unusual hors d'oeuvre first courses, or satisfying lunches for a Westerner.

Sushi 鮨

RICE IN VINEGAR DRESSING

To make about 6 cups

VINEGAR DRESSING
- 1/4 cup rice vinegar, or substitute 3 tablespoons mild white vinegar
- 3 1/2 tablespoons sugar
- 2 1/2 teaspoons salt
- 1 1/2 tablespoons *mirin* (sweet *sake*), or substitute 1 tablespoon pale dry sherry
- 1/2 teaspoon MSG

- 2 cups Japanese or unconverted white rice, washed thoroughly in cold running water and drained
- A 2-inch square of *kombu* (dried kelp), cut with a heavy knife from a sheet of packaged *kombu* and washed under cold running water

DRESSING: Combine the rice vinegar, sugar, salt and *mirin* in a 1- to 1 1/2-quart enameled or stainless-steel saucepan. Bring to a boil uncovered and stir in the MSG. Cool to room temperature.

NOTE: This dressing can be made in large quantities and stored unrefrigerated in a tightly covered jar for as long as 1 year.

RICE: Combine 2 1/2 cups of cold water and the rice in a 1 1/2- to 2-quart stainless-steel or enameled saucepan and let the rice soak for 30 minutes. Then add the square of *kombu* and bring to a boil over high heat. Cover the pan, reduce the heat to moderate, and cook for about 10 minutes, or until the rice has absorbed all of the water. Reduce the heat to its lowest point and simmer another 5 minutes. Let the rice rest off the heat for an additional 5 minutes before removing the cover and discarding the *kombu*.

Transfer the hot rice to a large nonmetallic platter or tray—made of wood, enamel, ceramic, glass or plastic. Immediately pour on the vinegar dressing and mix thoroughly with a fork. The rice is ready to use when it has cooled to room temperature. Or it may be covered and left at room temperature for as long as 5 hours before serving.

Temarizushi 手鞠ずし

VINEGARED RICE-AND-FISH BALLS

To make 10 balls

- 3 ounces fluke or other white-meat fish fillet, cut crosswise into paper-thin slices
- 1 tablespoon salt
- MSG
- 1/4 teaspoon black sesame seeds
- 1 1/2 tablespoons rice vinegar or mild white vinegar
- 1 teaspoon sugar
- 1/4 cup *sushi* rice *(above)*

PREPARE AHEAD: 1. Sprinkle the fish liberally on both sides with salt and sparingly with MSG, and marinate at room temperature for 3 hours (or cover and refrigerate for 6 hours).

2. Heat a small skillet over high heat until a drop of water flicked across its surface instantly evaporates. Add the sesame seeds. Shaking the pan almost constantly, toast the seeds for 2 to 3 minutes, or until they are lightly and evenly colored. Set aside.

TO ASSEMBLE: Combine the vinegar, sugar and 3 tablespoons of cold water in a mixing bowl. Dip the fish, a slice at a time, in the mixture, moistening it well.

Lay a slice of fish in the center of a strip of cheesecloth about 3 inches long and 2 inches wide. Place 1 teaspoon of *sushi* rice on the fish, then fold the ends of the fillet over it, enclosing the rice. Bring up the ends of the cheesecloth, and twist them tightly to squeeze the fish into a ball. Unwrap and repeat this process with the remaining fish and rice, until all the balls are made. Sprinkle each ball with a few toasted sesame seeds and serve as hors d'oeuvre or a first course.

To serve 6

6 cups *sushi* rice *(page 95)*

2 rounds of canned sliced *renkon* (lotus root)
1⅓ cups *niban dashi (page 54)*
1 teaspoon rice vinegar, or substitute 1 teaspoon mild white vinegar
3 tablespoons plus 1½ teaspoons sugar
½ teaspoon salt
MSG
1 medium-sized carrot, scraped and sliced thin
1 whole canned *takenoko* (bamboo shoot), scraped, quartered and sliced thin
2 teaspoons *sake* (rice wine)
1 ounce (about 2 tablespoons) shelled green peas
4 *shiitake* (dried Japanese mushrooms)
Vegetable oil
A 2-ounce piece *gobo* (burdock), shredded and soaked in cold water
3 tablespoons Japanese all-purpose soy sauce
3 eggs
6 medium-sized shrimp (16 to 20 per pound)
3 ounces canned crab meat, picked over to remove any bones or cartilage, then flaked

GARNISH
1 sheet *nori* (dried laver)
1 to 2 pieces bottled *beni shoga* (red pickled ginger)

Mazezushi まぜずし

VINEGARED RICE MIXED WITH VEGETABLES AND SEAFOOD

PREPARE AHEAD: 1. Peel the lotus root rounds and cut them in half horizontally. Slice them crosswise into ⅛-inch-thick slices. In a 1-quart saucepan, bring 1 cup of water to a boil. Drop in the sliced lotus root, boil for 10 seconds, then transfer the lotus root to a sieve and drain.

Combine ⅓ cup of the *niban dashi,* 1 teaspoon vinegar, ½ teaspoon sugar, ⅛ teaspoon salt and a few sprinkles of MSG in the saucepan. Bring to a boil over high heat and add the lotus root. Boil for 1 minute, stirring constantly, then drain again and set the lotus root aside.

2. Bring 1 cup of water to a boil, add the thinly sliced carrot and bamboo shoot and boil briskly, uncovered, for 3 minutes. Transfer to a sieve and drain thoroughly.

Combine ½ cup of the *niban dashi,* 1 teaspoon sugar, ⅛ teaspoon salt, a few sprinkles of MSG and 2 teaspoons of *sake* in the saucepan. Bring to a boil over high heat and add the bamboo shoots and carrots. Boil uncovered for 3 minutes, and drain through a small sieve set over a mixing bowl. Set the bamboo shoot and carrot aside in a bowl. Reserve the cooking liquid.

3. Bring 1 cup of lightly salted water to a boil and drop in the green peas. Boil for about 20 seconds, then drain in a sieve and add the peas to the reserved bamboo-and-carrot cooking liquid.

4. Place the *shiitake* in a bowl and cover with 2 cups of cold water. Soak for at least 1 hour. Remove the *shiitake* from their soaking water, and reserve the water. Trim and discard the hard mushroom stems, squeeze the mushrooms dry and chop them fine.

In a small skillet, heat 1 tablespoon of vegetable oil over moderately high heat. Add the drained, shredded *gobo* and stir for about 1 minute, then add the mushrooms, ½ cup of their soaking liquid, ½ cup of the *niban dashi* and 3 tablespoons of sugar. Cook for 5 minutes, stirring frequently, then stir in 3 tablespoons of soy sauce. Reduce the heat to moderate and cook for about 15 minutes, or until all of the liquid in the pan evaporates. Remove the pan from the heat and cool to room temperature.

5. The omelets: In a mixing bowl, beat 3 eggs thoroughly with ⅛ teaspoon salt and a few sprinkles of MSG. With a pastry brush or a paper towel, lightly coat the bottom and sides of a 8- or 9-inch skillet with oil. Heat the pan over moderate heat until a drop of water flicked across its surface instantly evaporates. Pour in just enough of the eggs to coat the bottom of the pan lightly. Cook for about 30 seconds, then turn the omelet over—with chopsticks, a spatula or the tips of your fingers—and cook for another 10 seconds, or until firm.

Slide the omelet onto a flat dish and cook 5 or 6 more omelets in the same fashion, lightly oiling the pan each time. As the omelets are done, pile them one on top of another. Then with a large, sharp knife, slice the omelets into the thinnest possible shreds.

6. Shell the shrimp and devein them by making a shallow incision along the top with a small, sharp knife and lifting out the white or black intestinal vein with the tip of the knife. Wash the shrimp quickly under cold running water and pat them dry with paper towels.

Bring 1 cup of lightly salted water to a boil and drop in the shrimp. Bring back to a boil, and boil uncovered for 3 minutes. Drain and set aside.

7. Pass the sheet of *nori* over a flame (or candle) on one side only, to intensify its color and flavor, then slice into fine shreds.

8. Have the previously prepared *sushi* rice, *shiitake, gobo,* bamboo shoot, carrot, lotus root, shredded omelets, peas, shrimp, crab meat, pickled ginger and *nori* within easy reach.

TO ASSEMBLE AND SERVE: With a wooden spoon or a fork, gently but thoroughly stir the *shiitake, gobo,* carrot, lotus root, bamboo shoot and crab meat into the *sushi* rice. Divide the mixed *sushi* into 6 equal portions. Firmly pack them into 6 small, round bowls or small, square tins just large enough to hold them. Unmold onto individual plates, and garnish each portion with strips of the egg pancake, a whole shrimp, a few peas, a few slivers of *beni shoga,* and shredded *nori.*

TO MAKE FUKUSA ZUSHI, a variation of *mazezushi:* Chop all the shrimp coarse and add them, along with the peas, to the ingredients as described in the previous paragraph. Instead of shredding the omelets, however, place them on a cutting board. Trim the omelets into squares, and place a mound of the mixed *sushi* in the middle of each. Lift up the sides of each omelet and fold them into the middle to make a neat package. Then carefully turn the package over to conceal the seams. Lay a thin strip of the *nori* across the middle of each, thus decoratively "tying" the package, and decorate with small circles of *beni shoga.*

Serve *mazezushi* or the more elaborately presented *fukusa zushi* as a one-dish meal—for lunch or a light supper—perhaps with *misoshiru* soup *(Recipe Index)* and pickles.

Fukusa zushi, a "package" of vinegared rice, shrimp, crab meat and vegetables, is made by first combining the ingredients in a bowl, then shaping the mixture in a small square or round mold. The mixed *sushi* is then wrapped in a thin, trimmed omelet. Tie the package with a strip of *nori,* and garnish with circles of red pickled ginger.

Colorful Variations on the Theme of "Sushi"

Sushi is, simply, vinegared rice plus, but the *sushi* devotee is faced with a difficult choice among the additions—the multitude of toppings and fillings. Above are *sushi* that have been rolled in *nori*—dried laver—and cut into rounds *(see sample recipe and pictures, page 100)*. The *sushi* in the foreground is rice that is rolled up with strips of omelet, watercress, mushrooms and gourd shavings. Behind these are *sushi* filled with red tuna, and in the back, *sushi* filled with pickled yellow radish. To the right are *sushi* with mushrooms *(top)* and cucumbers. All are accompanied by soy dipping sauce and strips of pickled ginger.

Another type of *sushi* is *nigiri zushi,* in which an oblong of rice is topped with fish *(page 101).* In the foreground the topping is of cooked, butterflied shrimp. Behind these are alternate rows of striped bass, partially surrounding a mound of *sushi* rice topped with red caviar and encircled by *nori.* Behind the leaf fence on the right is oily tuna; in front of the fence to the left is the lean dark-meat tuna. The toppings in the back row are of omelet and squid, the omelet decorated with a strip of *nori.* The cucumber *makizushi (above, right)* is a refreshing change of pace, and the pickled ginger at bottom left adds a touch of sharpness.

To serve 6

6 cups *sushi* rice *(page 95)*

5 *shiitake* (dried Japanese mushrooms)
¼ cup sugar
2 tablespoons Japanese all-purpose soy sauce
1 ounce *kanpyo* (dried gourd shavings)
1 cup *niban dashi (page 54)*
1⅛ teaspoons salt
2 eggs
MSG
6 sheets packaged *nori* (dried laver)
12 sprigs watercress or Italian parsley or 12 young spinach leaves
18 very thin slices *beni shoga* (red pickled ginger)

Makizushi 巻ずし

VINEGARED RICE AND VEGETABLES ROLLED IN SEAWEED

PREPARE AHEAD: 1. In a large mixing bowl, soak the mushrooms in 2 cups of cold water for 30 minutes. Then cut off and discard the stems and slice the mushrooms into ½-inch-wide strips. Place them in a small saucepan with 1 cup of their soaking liquid, 2 tablespoons of the sugar, and the soy sauce. Stir thoroughly and bring to a boil over high heat. Then remove the mushrooms and continue to boil the liquid until it has reduced to ¼ cup. Replace the mushrooms in the liquid, and cool to room temperature.

2. Soak the *kanpyo* in cold water to cover for about 30 minutes, or until very soft. Bring to a boil over high heat, boil 3 minutes and drain.

In another small pan, combine the *kanpyo, niban dashi,* 2 tablespoons of the sugar and 1 teaspoon salt, and bring to a boil. Reduce the heat to moderate and cook uncovered until almost all the liquid evaporates. Be careful not to let it burn.

3. In a small mixing bowl, beat 2 eggs with ⅛ teaspoon of salt and sprinkle lightly with MSG. With a pastry brush, lightly coat the bottom and sides of a heavy 10- to 12-inch skillet with vegetable oil. Heat the pan over moderate heat until a drop of water flicked onto its surface instantly evaporates. Pour in the eggs and tip the pan back and forth to spread them evenly. Cook for a few seconds, or until the omelet is firm but still moist. Then tilt the pan above the heat. With chopsticks or a fork, roll the omelet into a compact cylinder and flip it onto the edge of a bamboo mat. Roll the omelet in the mat with one or two turns, and squeeze gently to make the roll firmer. Let it rest in the mat for 5 minutes, then unroll the omelet and cut it lengthwise into 6 narrow strips.

TO ASSEMBLE AND SERVE: Pass the sheets of *nori* over a flame, on one side only, to intensify their color and flavor. Place a sheet of *nori* on a bamboo mat or heavy cloth napkin. Divide the *sushi* rice into 6 portions and spread one portion over most of the *nori* sheet, leaving a 2-inch edge of the *nori* exposed. Place the *kanpyo* strips in a row across the middle of the rice, and lay

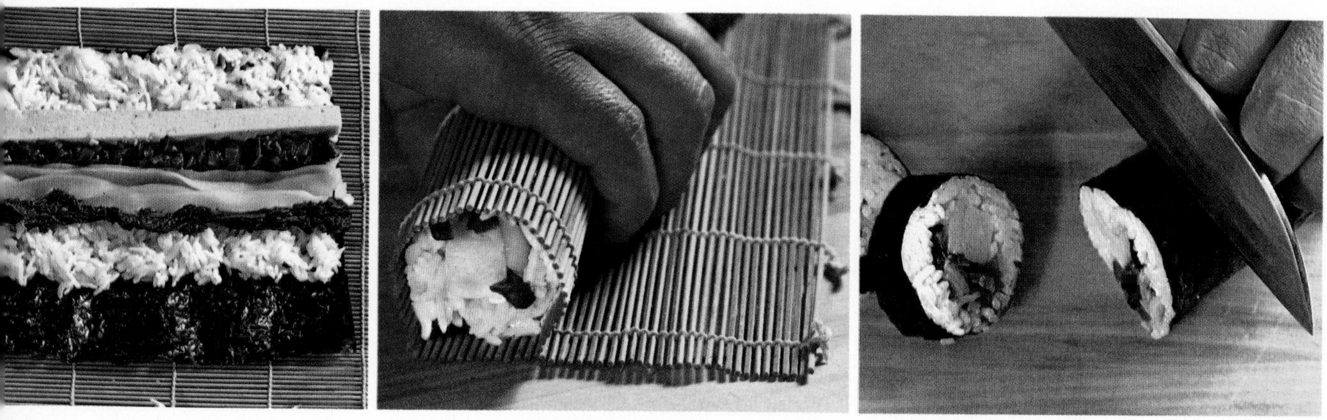

For *makizushi,* place a sheet of *nori* on a bamboo mat or cloth napkin and spread it within 2 inches of the edge with vinegared rice. Lay watercress and strips of *kanpyo,* mushrooms and omelet in rows across the middle of the rice *(left).* Use the mat to help roll the *nori* up, then roll in the mat one or two turns and squeeze gently *(center)* to make firmer. Unroll and slice *(right)* into 1-inch-wide rounds.

a row of mushrooms, watercress and a strip of egg along both sides. Roll the mixture up in the mat following the procedure described above. Let the *makizushi* rest 5 minutes, then unroll it and cut it into 1- to 1½-inch rounds. Assemble, roll and cut the remaining ingredients similarly.

Serve the *makizushi,* garnished with slices of pickled ginger, as cocktail accompaniments, a first course, or as a main luncheon course.

Nigiri Zushi にぎり鮨

VINEGARED RICE-AND-FISH "SANDWICHES"

To make about 4 dozen

3 cups *sushi* rice *(page 95)*

6 medium-sized raw shrimp (16 to 20 per pound) in their shells
3 tablespoons *sushi* dressing *(page 95)*
2 pounds filleted porgy, sea bass, striped bass, red snapper, squid, abalone or tuna, in one piece *(see sashimi, page 90)*
1 tablespoon *wasabi* (green horseradish) powder, mixed to a paste with 1 tablespoon of cold water and set aside to rest for 15 minutes

TEKKA AND KAPPA MAKI
2 sheets *nori* (dried laver)
1 cucumber, about 4 inches long, peeled, halved, seeded and cut lengthwise into ¼-inch-wide strips

Japanese all-purpose soy sauce

PREPARE AHEAD: 1. To prevent the shrimp from curling when cooked, insert a toothpick lengthwise along their inner curves. Bring 1 cup of water to a boil in a small saucepan and drop in the shrimp. Cook for 3 minutes, then drain, remove the toothpicks and peel the shrimp. Devein them by making a shallow incision along the top of each shrimp and removing the white or black intestinal vein with the point of a knife. Then cut the shrimp three quarters of the way through along their inner curves and gently spread them open, butterfly fashion. Flatten them slightly with the side of a cleaver or knife.

In a mixing bowl, combine ⅓ cup of cold water and 2 tablespoons of the *sushi* dressing. Add the shrimp, turn them about to coat them well, and marinate for 15 to 30 minutes.

2. With a sharp knife, cut the filleted fish crosswise at an angle, into slices ¼ inch thick. (The thicker tuna fillet should be cut crosswise into ½-inch-thick slices.) Arrange the fish on a platter and serve, or cover with plastic wrap and keep in a cool place (not the refrigerator) for no longer than ½ hour.

TO ASSEMBLE: In a small bowl, combine the remaining tablespoon of *sushi* dressing with 3 tablespoons of cold water. Called *tezu,* this mixture is used to moisten the hands to prevent the rice from becoming sticky. Dip your fingers in the *tezu* and lift up about 1 tablespoon of the rice. Shape it into an oblong. Smear a bit of the *wasabi* paste down the center of a piece of fish and holding the rice in one hand and the fish in the other, press the two together. The fish should completely cover the top of the rice.

TO MAKE TEKKA MAKI, a variation of *nigiri zushi:* 1. Prepare the *sushi* rice, raw fish and shrimp as directed above.

2. Pass the *nori* over a gas flame or candle on one side only to intensify the flavor and color. Cut the *nori* in half and lay ½ sheet on the edge of a bamboo mat or sturdy cloth napkin. Spread about ¼ cup of rice over most of the *nori* sheet, leaving a 1-inch border of the *nori* exposed. Spread a streak of the *wasabi* paste crosswise through the middle of the rice and top with a row of raw fish. Use the mat or napkin to help you roll the *nori* up tightly. Then roll up in the mat or napkin one or two turns, and let it rest 5 minutes. Remove the mat and slice crosswise into 1- to 1½-inch pieces. Make similar rolls with the remaining ingredients.

TO MAKE KAPPA MAKI, another variation: Substitute narrow strips of cucumber for the fish on one of the sheets of *nori,* omitting the *wasabi.*

TO SERVE: *Sushi* may be served, with soy sauce accompanying it, in many ways: on a large platter as cocktail food; 3 to 4 per person at the beginning of an elaborate Japanese dinner; 6 to 8 per person as a main luncheon course or presented on a large tray at the end of a Japanese meal to accompany *misoshiru (Recipe Index).*

To make a rice-and-fish "sandwich," hold an oblong of vinegared rice in one hand and a slice of raw fish (tuna, here) dabbed with horseradish in the other. Top the rice with the fish, and it is ready to eat.

Seafood and vegetables await immersion in batter and oil *(below, right)* and emerge *(left)* as delicately coated *tempura*.

AGEMONO: The following recipes are called "agemono," literally, "fried things." Japanese frying techniques are similar to those of the West, but because of the close attention paid to the batter with which the food is often coated and to the condition and temperature of the oil, Japanese fried foods are especially notable for their delicacy.

To deep-fry, fill a deep-fat fryer or heavy 10- to 12-inch skillet or casserole to a depth of 3 inches with vegetable oil (or a combination of vegetable and sesame-seed oil). Heat the oil until it registers 375° on a deep-fat-frying thermometer.

To keep the oil clean during the frying, use a mesh skimmer or metal spatula to remove food particles from the oil as they appear.

Tempura 天麩羅

DEEP-FRIED SHRIMP AND VEGETABLES IN BATTER

The "tempura" recipe below by no means encompasses all the ingredients that may be used. In addition to the ones listed at right, substitutions or additions might include 1/4-inch-thick slices of fish fillets; 1/4-inch-wide strips of carrot; blanched, quartered bamboo shoot; blanched string beans; 1/4-inch-wide strips of lotus root; skewered sections of scallions; or small asparagus stalks.

To serve 6

1 small eggplant (about 1/2 pound)
18 canned *ginnan* (ginkgo nuts), drained
1 pound raw shrimp (16 to 20 per pound), shelled and deveined *(see page 168)*
12 snow peas, fresh or frozen and defrosted
6 white mushrooms, cut in half
1 medium-sized sweet potato (about 1/2 pound) peeled and sliced into 1/4-inch-thick rounds
Vegetable oil
1/2 cup flour

BATTER (to make about 3 cups)
1 egg yolk
2 cups ice-cold water
1/8 teaspoon baking soda
1 2/3 cups flour

DIPPING SAUCE
1 1/2 cups *soba tsuyu (page 104)* or 1/4 cup *ajishio (page 104)*

PREPARE AHEAD: 1. Peel the eggplant, but leave occasional 1/2-inch-wide strips of purple skin to add color to the finished dish. Cut the eggplant in half lengthwise, then cut into 1/4-inch-thick slices. Wash in cold water, pat thoroughly dry with paper towels, and set aside.

2. Skewer 3 ginkgo nuts on each of 6 toothpicks.

3. Dip the shrimp in the flour, and vigorously shake off the excess.

4. To prepare the batter, combine 1 egg yolk with 2 cups of ice-cold water and 1/8 teaspoon of baking soda in a large mixing bowl. Sift in the flour and mix well with a wooden spoon. The batter should be somewhat thin and watery, and run easily off the spoon. If it is too thick, thin it with drops of cold water. Ideally, the batter should be used shortly after being made, but it may wait if necessary for no longer than 10 minutes.

TO COOK: Preheat the oven to 250°. Since *tempura* must be served hot, the most practical way to cook *tempura* is to divide the ingredients into individual portions, placing them on separate sheets of wax paper so that a complete serving—composed of 3 shrimp, 2 snow peas, 2 mushroom halves, 3 ginkgo nuts, or slice of sweet potato—can be fried at a time and kept warm in the oven while the remaining portions are being fried.

Heat the oil as described in the introduction above, until it registers 375° on a deep-fat thermometer.

Dip one piece of food at a time into the batter, twirling it around to coat it, then drop it into the pan. Fry only 6 or 8 pieces of food at a time. Turn the pieces with chopsticks or tongs after one minute, and fry another minute, or until they are a light gold. Drain on paper towels, arrange a serving of food on an individual plate or in a basket and keep warm in the oven for no longer than 5 minutes. Skim the oil, check the temperature of the oil, and fry the remaining portions.

TO SERVE: Each serving of *tempura* should be accompanied by a small dish of one of the *tempura* dipping sauces *(page 104)*. Although this recipe will serve 6 as a main course, smaller amounts of *tempura* are often served as part of a 5-course Japanese dinner or as a first course.

Ajishio 味鹽

LEMON AND SALT DIP

To serve 8

3 tablespoons salt
2 teaspoons MSG
16 thin wedges of lemon

TO ASSEMBLE AND SERVE: Mix the 3 tablespoons of salt and 2 teaspoons of MSG together in a small bowl, then divide it into equal mounds in the centers of 8 very small plates. Garnish each portion with 2 thin lemon wedges.

Serve *ajishio* with *tempura (Recipe Index)* or *domyoji age (opposite)*. A little lemon juice is squeezed over the fish or shellfish, which is then dipped into the salt-and-MSG mixture. Traditionally the mixture is half and half, but that requires more MSG per serving than this book recommends.

Kaki Age かき揚

MIXED DEEP-FRIED PANCAKES

To serve 4 to 6

1 small carrot, scraped and cut into fine shreds (about 1/4 cup)
A 2-inch piece *gobo* (burdock), cut into fine shreds (about 1/4 cup)
2 tablespoons scraped fresh ginger root, cut into fine shreds
6 ounces fresh or frozen scallops or shelled shrimp, cut in 1/4-inch dice
1/2 cup shelled green peas or 1/2 cup frozen, defrosted peas
1 cup *tempura* batter *(page 103)*
1/4 cup flour
Vegetable oil

DIPPING SAUCE
1 cup *soba tsuyu (below)*

PREPARE AHEAD: In a large bowl, mix together the shredded carrot, *gobo,* ginger, seafood and peas. Add the previously prepared *tempura* batter, sift the 1/4 cup of flour over it, and vigorously mix with a large spoon until the ingredients are well combined.

TO COOK: Place about 2 tablespoons of the pancake mixture on a wide, flat metal spatula and flatten it into 2 1/2- to 3-inch rounds with the palm of your hand. With the aid of chopsticks or the side of a knife, carefully slide the pancake into the pan of hot oil and quickly repeat the procedure with 2 more pancakes. Fry the *kaki age* for about 1 minute on each side, or until they are a golden brown, turning the pancakes carefully with chopsticks or tongs. Remove from the oil with a spatula.

Drain the pancakes on paper towels. With the metal spatula or a skimmer, carefully remove any food particles from the cooking oil, and shape and fry the remaining pancakes as described above, skimming the oil of food particles after each batch is fried.

TO SERVE: Place 3 or 4 pancakes on individual plates and serve, accompanied by the *soba tsuyu* dipping sauce, as part of a Japanese meal *(page 198)*, for lunch or as a light supper.

A popular way of serving *kaki age* in Japan is as *domburi*—that is, a one-course meal: 2 pancakes are placed on top of individual servings of steamed rice *(Recipe Index)*, and the dipping sauce is poured over them.

Soba Tsuyu そばつゆ

MIRIN-AND-SOY DIPPING SAUCE FOR TEMPURA AND NOODLES

To make 1 1/2 cups

1/4 cup *mirin* (sweet *sake),* or 3 tablespoons pale dry sherry
1/4 cup Japanese all-purpose soy sauce
1 cup *niban dashi (page 54)*
2 tablespoons preflaked *katsuobushi* (dried bonito)
Salt
MSG

TEN TSUYU
1/4 cup *usukuchi* soy sauce, or substitute 3 tablespoons Japanese all-purpose soy sauce
1/4 cup *mirin* (sweet *sake),* or 3 tablespoons pale dry sherry
1 cup *niban dashi (page 54)*
1/8 teaspoon salt
MSG
1/4 cup preflaked *katsuobushi* (dried bonito)

GARNISH
3 tablespoons grated *daikon* (Japanese white radish), or substitute 3 tablespoons grated icicle radish or white turnip
1 tablespoon scraped, grated fresh ginger root

TO COOK: Heat the *mirin* in a 1-quart saucepan over moderate heat until lukewarm. Turn off the heat, ignite the *mirin* with a match, and shake the pan gently back and forth until the flame dies out. Add soy sauce, *niban dashi, katsuobushi,* a pinch of salt, and sprinkle lightly with MSG. Bring to a boil over high heat, then strain the sauce through a fine sieve set over a small bowl. Cool to room temperature and taste for seasoning (adding a little salt if necessary).

TO SERVE: Serve *soba tsuyu* or *ten tsuyu*, a variation, with *tempura (Recipe Index), kaki age (above)* or *tatsuta age (Recipe Index)*. The garnish of grated *daikon* and grated ginger root should be divided into separate portions and placed on the individual servings of food. Customarily, the garnish is mixed into the dipping sauce to individual taste.

Lacy *tempura* pancakes are made from morsels of seafood and vegetables. The food is twirled in batter, then scooped out with a flat spoon or spatula. Chopsticks or the side of a knife are used to slide the food into the hot oil, where it instantly turns golden brown.

Domyoji Age 道明寺揚

DEEP-FRIED SHRIMP COATED WITH RICE

To serve 6

¼ cup *domyoji* (precooked dried rice)
12 medium-sized raw shrimp (16 to 20 per pound), shelled and deveined *(see page 168)*
½ cup flour
2 egg whites, lightly beaten
1 medium-sized green pepper, seeded, deribbed and cut into strips 2 inches long and ½ inch wide
Vegetable oil

DIPPING SAUCE
¼ cup *ajishio (opposite)*

PREPARE AHEAD: 1. Wash the rice in a strainer or colander under cold running water until its draining water runs clear. Then transfer it to a large mixing bowl, cover with cold water, and soak for 4 hours at room temperature. Drain and steam for 30 minutes in an Oriental steamer, or steam the rice in an improvised steamer as described on page 180.

Spread the steamed rice out on a tray or large flat platter and cool to room temperature. Separate the grains by rubbing them gently through your fingers; then with a cleaver or large, sharp knife, chop the rice coarsely.

2. Make 3 cuts at ½-inch intervals across the inner curve of the shrimp to prevent them from curling when fried.

3. Coat the shrimp with flour and shake off any excess. Dip them into the bowl of egg whites, and roll them in the rice until the grains firmly adhere. Lay the shrimp side by side on wax paper and set aside.

TO COOK: Heat the oil in a deep-fat fryer, casserole or skillet, as described on page 103, until the oil registers 350° on a deep-fat thermometer. Fry the shrimp 6 at a time for about 1 minute and drain on paper towels. Drop the green pepper into the oil and fry for 1 minute, until they are a delicate brown.

TO SERVE: Place 2 shrimp and a strip or 2 of green pepper on each of 6 serving plates, and accompany with a small, individual dish of *ajishio.* Serve as part of a Japanese meal *(page 198),* or as a first course.

Agedashi 揚げ出し

DEEP-FRIED TOFU IN SOY-SEASONED SAUCE

To serve 6

4 cakes *tofu* (soybean curd), fresh, canned or instant, each cake cut into 6 equal parts
Vegetable oil
6 tablespoons *soba tsuyu (opposite)*
6 tablespoons Japanese all-purpose soy sauce
6 tablespoons grated *daikon* (Japanese white radish), or substitute 6 tablespoons grated icicle radish or white turnip
2 tablespoons scraped, grated fresh ginger root
1 tablespoon preflaked *katsuobushi* (dried bonito)

TO COOK: Pat the *tofu* dry with paper towels and deep-fry them in the pan of hot oil for 3 to 4 minutes, or until they have turned a golden brown. Remove with a slotted spoon and drain on paper towels.

TO SERVE: In a small mixing bowl, combine the *soba tsuyu* and the soy sauce and divide this dipping sauce among 6 individual serving bowls. Place 4 cubes of the fried *tofu* in each bowl and garnish each serving with 1 tablespoon of grated *daikon,* 1 teaspoon of grated ginger and ½ teaspoon of *katsuobushi.* Customarily each garnish is mixed into the sauce to taste.

V

Simple, Satisfying Foods of Home

A steaming pot over a glowing hearth—ancient symbol of home—contains boiling bamboo shoots that will be part of the meal Mrs. Fuji Horie *(background)* will serve her family. In her farmhouse about 100 miles southwest of Tokyo, this industrious housewife turns out a never-ending stream of meals with the aid of the jointed iron rod, said to be 500 years old, from which the pot is suspended.

One aspect of Japanese cuisine that remains a mystery to the foreign visitor is home cooking. Even Westerners who have lived in Japan for years complain that "we have never been invited to a Japanese home." The simple explanation for this seeming standoffishness is that Japanese do far less home entertaining than Americans. For that matter, in the traditional Japanese manner, only a conceited husband would say that he thinks his home and his table are fit for an important guest (a category that includes many foreign visitors). Even if he is secretly proud of his house and of his wife's cooking, a well-bred man will assert, if pressed, that his home is too humble and his wife too unworldly to entertain—and will therefore honor his guest by taking him to the best restaurant he can afford.

Neither a broad hint that the visitor honestly wants to "see how the Japanese really eat and live" nor insistence on informality is likely to carry much weight in these circumstances: the former might seem patronizing—and there is no such thing as informality where an important guest is concerned. Not only would it be rude to give a guest anything but the best the host can manage, but it would be a blow to the host's pride because it would suggest that he did not know the proper way to do things.

The only Westerners who eat with any frequency in Japanese homes are the few who have built up long friendships with individual Japanese and those, more numerous, who have married Japanese. But even such privileged foreigners are not likely to have dined at homes other than those of their intimate friends or their spouses' relatives. If the foreign gourmet tries very hard, he may be able to convince his Japanese acquaintance that he is truly in-

Japanese-English Glossary

AEMONO: *mixed foods in dressing*
DAIKON: *giant radish*
MIZUTAKI: *simmered chicken dish*
MOCHI: *rice cake*
NABE: *pot or saucepan*
SASHIMI: *slices of raw fish*
SHABU SHABU: *simmered beef dish*
SUKIYAKI: *simmered beef dish*
SUNOMONO: *vinegared salad*
SUSHI: *vinegared rice topped with raw fish or wrapped in laver*
TOFU: *soybean curd*
WASABI: *green horseradish*
YUZU: *citrus fruit similar to lime*

terested in eating Japanese food; then, if he is lucky and if his host is daring, he will get to a Japanese restaurant instead of a Western one.

When the Japanese insist that they can't entertain under their own roofs they do have a point. Many Japanese houses *are* small and crowded, especially in the cities, and the kitchens are tiny and poorly equipped. Only fairly wealthy Japanese can afford to have one uncluttered room with a *tokonoma*—or to own tasteful objects suitable for display in this alcove—and even possessors of mansions who still entertain find it hard these days to obtain the squads of maids who formerly took care of the kitchen work and serving. A tremendous amount of work is implicit in the artistic and seasonally harmonious meals that constitute Japanese *grande cuisine* and that a guest deserves; nowadays only a fine restaurant is prepared to do this properly.

There is, finally, one more reason why so few outsiders, even Japanese, sit down at the family dinner table. Japanese men and women to a considerable extent still lead separate social lives. A woman has her circle of neighbors and friends whom she will occasionally invite in for lunch when husband and children are away—but in all likelihood she will never meet their husbands. A man's social life is centered around the people he works with; he will play golf and relax in bars, cabarets and restaurants with his colleagues and customers and never dream of including the wives in a party. On these bibulous occasions feminine companionship is provided by professional entertainers—geisha and bar hostesses; they are better trained in the witty and risqué repartee that is required for Japanese masculine enjoyment than are the proper housewives of Japan, whose traditional job is simply to take care of home and children, not to amuse their menfolk.

Consequently a Japanese husband rarely brings home casual acquaintances or important guests. When a Japanese family does entertain, the visitors are apt to be relatives, or very old and long-standing friends (classmates, perhaps) whose tastes and preferences are known and who can be fed without undue fuss. Even when an old friend comes for a visit, he is likely to leave his wife at home unless she happens to be a good friend of his host's wife.

Despite the fact that the Japanese housewife has little audience for her culinary skill, the meals she provides her family are delectable, various and nourishing. For one thing, she has probably studied home economics in school and then attended cooking classes (as well as lessons in flower arranging and the tea ceremony) in that period after finishing her schooling when a Japanese girl is formally prepared for marriage. Even after marriage she is likely to be enrolled in one of the many flourishing cooking schools that can be found in every town and city in Japan. Some of these schools are so successful that they own big buildings on downtown streets, publish exquisitely illustrated cookbooks, run their own TV programs, teach Chinese and Western cooking as well as Japanese, and even sponsor correspondence courses.

Many housewives belong to cooking clubs that invite a different chef to lecture and demonstrate every week, and still others eagerly take note of the recipes and cooking hints that come to them regularly in a steady barrage, from women's magazines, TV and radio, and neighborhood ladies' organizations. It is safe to say that the Japanese *ok'san* ("honorable interior one," i.e., housewife) spends more time and thought on food than does her American counterpart. Part of this is necessity; her kitchen and refrigerator are so small that she must shop every day. And part springs from the ready availability of fresh foods in season.

The more sophisticated Japanese housewife strives toward the same artful presentation of food in season that the great chefs have mastered and keeps to the same basic principle of emphasizing natural tastes. But she knows she has neither the equipment nor the many hands needed to achieve perfection, and so she readily compromises. Her cooking reflects the pragmatic, rather than the artistic, side of the Japanese character, which can be summed up in the Japanese proverb, "hana yori dango," which means, roughly, that dumplings are better than flowers when you are hungry.

Certainly there is nothing very artistic or refined about *umeboshi,* the first item on the traditional morning menu. *Umeboshi* is a tiny red pickled plum so sour that just one nibble will lift your scalp, shoot lightning down your spine, and shrivel your toes—an inner cold shower that will wake you up if it doesn't knock you out. Those Japanese who start their day with *umeboshi*—nature's own mouthwash—find that it clears the fuzzy night tastes from their tongues. Rural families, and even some city households, still pickle their own *umeboshi* and keep them in tubs for years. *Umeboshi* is not only a family standby; it is served with morning tea at all Japanese inns, so beware!

Umeboshi also turns up in Japanese *bento* (the little lunch boxes sometimes put up by housewives, but more frequently sold to railroad passengers, picnickers and theater audiences), where it fulfills a double purpose: set in the middle of a field of white rice the little red plum provides a pretty representation of the Japanese flag and it helps preserve the rice as well.

The classic breakfast dish at home is rice, a heaping bowl of it often sprinkled with flakes of *nori* (dried laver) or other garnishes. Mama or the maid will have set out the *nori* in a pile of toasted, crispy sheets, giving everyone a choice of crumbling it over his bowl or constructing an impromptu *makizushi* by rolling a wad of rice in a sheet of *nori* and eating it by hand.

The rice bowl with *nori* can be considered the Japanese approximation of eggs, buttered toast, cornflakes, and pancakes—all of which are gaining popularity in Japan. But the nourishing soup called *misoshiru (Recipe Index)* is the equivalent of bacon and eggs. *Misoshiru* is also eaten at other meals, and is encountered in many varieties in all kinds of restaurants, but at the first meal of the day it seems to be required fare. To a majority of Japanese, breakfast is not breakfast without this thick, aromatic soup.

Essentially, *misoshiru* is merely *dashi,* the soup stock, plus about a tablespoonful per serving of *miso,* the fermented paste of soybeans and rice that has so many uses in Japan. To these basics are added a few cubes of *tofu* and possibly some *wakame* (seaweed) and sliced or chopped vegetables such as scallions or *daikon.* Often, particularly in farm households where everyone eats every meal at home, a huge pot of *misoshiru* will be cooked in the morning and reheated for each meal, and it seems to get better as the day goes on. In large families *ok'san* keeps the *misoshiru* pot beside her at the table, next to the tub of rice, and ladles out refills to her hungry brood.

You never use a spoon for *misoshiru*—or for any Japanese soup. You pick up the lacquered wooden bowl, pluck out the *tofu* and chunks of vegetable with your chopsticks, and then sip down the steamy liquid.

Misoshiru comes in a bowl with a lid to keep it warm until you are ready for it. But unlike the exquisite color combinations and symbolic patterns of *suimono,* a clear soup, *misoshiru* makes about as much appeal to the eye as a bowl of porridge. All it offers is filling, low-calorie warmth, tremendous nourishment and a distinctive mellow-pungent flavor. It is not a taste that makes new friends right away, especially when *wakame* is included, but once you've adjusted to it, you can't get enough. One American I know, a long-time Tokyo resident who always stayed at Japanese-style inns when traveling through Japan, says it took him many months of exposure before he could face *misoshiru* on an empty stomach. At length he found it tastier than the cold fried eggs (sometimes cooked the night before) that a good many inns inflict on foreign guests at breakfast. Now, back home in the States, he insists that his Japanese wife give him *misoshiru* every morning. She Americanizes it occasionally by dropping in an egg, and when they've run out of *tofu* he substitutes cottage cheese, but the taste of *misoshiru* remains pure.

Japanese who can afford it eat eggs for breakfast, too, but not usually in their bean-paste soup. One favorite dish is a frothy whip of raw egg poured over hot rice (which cooks the egg) sprinkled with *nori.* Then there is *tamago dashimaki (Recipe Index),* the sweetened, flaky, many-layered omelet described in Chapter 3; however this dish requires considerable time to make and is often bought already prepared. A similar egg concoction turns up, with vinegared rice, as one kind of *sushi.*

With husband and children gone for the day, and assuming that no neighbors or relatives are expected to drop in, frugal *ok'san* will probably put together a lunch from leftovers. The first step will be to reheat the breakfast rice in a rice cooker. Unheard of a generation ago, the electric rice cooker is now standard equipment in just about every Japanese kitchen, and it is such an amazing appliance that it has become one of Japan's most successful exports to rice-eating nations all over Asia. Anyone who can measure cupfuls of rice and water can cook rice to perfection with this thinking kitchen machine. Provided the measurements are accurate, the rice cooker will turn itself off when the rice is done and will keep it hot until served. And for making cold rice seem like new, the cooker is ideal.

Although the Japanese love their white rice plain after other foods, when they are making a meal of rice itself they usually combine it with something else or garnish it before serving. The housewife preparing her noonday meal of rice that has already been cooked by itself can choose from a variety of methods to dress it up for taste and added nourishment.

The simplest of these is to sprinkle *furikake* over the heated rice. Years ago, housewives made their own mixtures, but now *furikake* comes bottled with a sprinkler top. In every bottle is a combination of two or more contrasting ingredients, dried and chopped into tiny bits that expand and develop their taste when they come into contact with the hot, moist rice. There are dozens of combinations: *katsuobushi* (dried bonito) flakes, sesame and seaweed; or seaweed, egg, fish, sesame, salt, tea and monosodium glutamate (a taste enhancer familiar to American housewives under the brand name of Ac'cent, and to Japanese as Aji-no-moto); or dried sea bream, ground sesame seed, toasted *nori* and salt. *Furikake* is always somewhat on the salty side.

If cooked fish or meat or vegetables are left over from the previous evening, the housewife may reheat these, with dipping sauces, and pour the

Opposite: The Japanese belief that "man eats with his eyes as well as his mouth" is demonstrated by the place setting of a typical five-course family dinner. The portions are delicate, and the colors, shapes and textures are as carefully balanced as the flavors. On the black lacquer tray is a bowl of *botan wan,* a clear soup with sea bass, wild vegetables and lime. Above it is a light second course, *kani kyuri ikomi*—cucumber rounds encircling crab meat, watercress and red pickled ginger. The third course, presented on the folded napkin on the red tray at upper right, is a fried dish —*domyoji age*—deep-fried shrimp encrusted with dried rice and served with green pepper, eggplant and lemon. Below it, in the round ceramic bowl, are *nimono,* or simmered dishes—taro potatoes, duck and chrysanthemum leaves. The pickled vegetables on the square plate below traditionally close the meal, providing a refreshing, palate-cleansing taste. With the pickles comes rice, at left on the black tray. The tea service at upper left—like the hot *oshibori* (the folded napkin in a basket) at bottom right—is an integral part of a Japanese meal. Recipes for all the dishes pictured may be found in the Recipe Index.

Although the best Japanese cooking is found in the great restaurants, there are a number of fine amateur chefs. One of them is Mitsugoro Bando, a leading actor who has enjoyed cooking since he was 16 years old. In the two pictures at the right Mr. Bando prepares a meal and then plays host to his daughter and son-in-law, Mr. and Mrs. Masaki Sano. At near right, he is dipping pieces of pork, which will be broiled, into a sauce of his own concoction that includes soy sauce, vinegar, sweet rice wine, called *mirin,* and seasoned salt. On the table in the foreground are a steamed lobster and raw *sayori* (snipe fish).

whole thing over her rice bowl. This is a casual version of *domburi* (the word merely means bowl), a cheap but delicious dish found in ordinary restaurants with many different kinds of ingredients. Probably one of the most popular is *oyako domburi (Recipe Index). Oyako* means mother and child; in *oyako domburi* the word is a poetic reference to the chicken and egg spread over the rice.

Still another common rice lunch is *chazuke,* literally, "soaked in tea." A long time ago, *chazuke* was simply the quickest way to finish a bowl of rice: you poured a little tea in the bowl and drank it down, tea and rice grains together. This is still done at home, although it is considered bad manners in public. A more elaborate *chazuke* ranks as an interesting dish in its own right; there are many restaurants well known for their *chazuke* recipes and every housewife has her favorite formula. Generally, slices of *sashimi,* slivers of salted fish, plus *nori, katsuobushi* or pickles of various kinds are placed on top of the rice, and boiling tea is poured over it and allowed to soak for a few minutes. It is eaten with chopsticks, not drunk. Frequently the tea is omitted and replaced by *dashi,* opening up another whole realm of flavor.

The family evening meal is much more complicated. For one thing, the Japanese housewife is often uncertain as to when her husband will arrive home,

or whether he will show up tiddly or sober, well-fed or famished. (In working-class households this often depends on how long it has been since payday and whether Papa still has cash to splurge. But on the expense-account level, *ok'san* has no such guide to her husband's probable condition.) Nevertheless, it is considered her wifely duty to wait up for him with a hot meal at the ready, no matter how late he returns. Some modern wives balk at this vestige of feudalism and insist that one's husband at least inform his wife of his plans; but the loyal wife who sits patiently until the wee hours, with her pots simmering instead of her temper, is still an ideal of connubial virtue, and believe it or not, she still exists.

The task of patient *ok'san* is further complicated by the fact that the Japanese distinguish between children's and adults' tastes to a greater extent than we do. The recipes in this book are designed for the adult palate, but many of the dishes also come in a children's version, and so Mama must prepare both. For example, the *tare* sauce (a kind of Japanese barbecue sauce) used by adults is considered too "hot" for children; they will get a sweeter edition. In *kushizashi*—brochette grilling of meats, fowl and vegetables—adults will find hot peppers on their bamboo skewers while children get milder scal-

lions instead. Even *sushi* mellows a bit for young taste buds: no hot *wasabi* in the rice, more bland items like egg instead of the pungent sea urchin, a greater number of pretty, bright-colored attractions. On the other hand—and this is a contradiction I cannot explain—Tokyo children love the strong-smelling cheesy *natto,* fermented soybean, which, frankly, repels every adult Westerner I have ever asked about it—and is not sought after by many Japanese from other parts of the country either.

To cope with both of these problems at once, the Japanese housewife is more than likely to feed her children first. When *danna-san* (master) arrives, he will then be able to take a leisurely bath and change to kimono without having to feel guilty about delaying the children's supper; then he may join his wife over a relaxing bottle of hot *sake* before proceeding to dine.

All the courses of the meal probably will be served at the same time, enabling a diner to pick and choose from each dish as he pleases. What we would call the main course (the Japanese don't think of it that way) will vary, but there are three additional dishes that are absolutely indispensable: rice, soup (clear or *misoshiru*) and *tsukemono.*

Tsukemono (soaked things) are lightly pickled and slightly sour *daikon,* cucumber, miniature eggplant, melon, and other vegetables, which the Japanese eat with their plain rice toward the end of a meal. This rice-and-pickles combination is basic to the traditional Japanese diet. Regardless of what else is on the menu, many Japanese still crave their rice and *tsukemono*—and some poor people eat nothing else. The most common type is *takuan,* which is *daikon* pickled for months in rice bran and salt, and the phrase "rice and *takuan*" is an everyday metaphor for a frugal meal, though even the wealthy also eat *takuan* and other pickles following other dishes.

City dwellers now buy their *tsukemono* ready-made, but in the old days (and this is still true in some rural areas) the most important test for a bride was her skill at making *tsukemono.* Of the many varieties of *tsukemono* my favorites are *nara zuke* (melons pickled in the residue of *sake* manufacture) and *wasabi zuke,* vegetables, such as miniature eggplant, pickled in *wasabi* and mustard—a kind of unsweetened Japanese piccalilli.

Although a dish of rice and pickles is the most important part of the meal to many Japanese, it usually follows what we would regard as the main course. Generally that consists of fish or shellfish, either broiled, steamed or deep-fried as *tempura.*

For *ok'san,* steaming (see Recipe Index for *mushimono)* is the easiest of these methods, for she simply puts such ingredients as fish, mushrooms, onions, ginkgo nuts and slivered carrots into a covered pot. This is a popular technique, and delicious enough, but not one to tempt a husband who is already overly fond of eating out. As these steamed dishes include many foods, the only side dish served with them is *sunomono,* the Japanese version of salad, already discussed in Chapter 3.

With a little more effort and essentially the same ingredients, the housewife can probably offer her family more taste and variety by broiling her fish; then she fills out the menu with other dishes besides *sunomono,* particularly *aemono (Recipe Index).* At this point, with broiled fish, *sunomono, aemono,* soup, rice, pickles and tea, our cozy home dinner begins to look like a modest feast, and *danna-san* may decide to enjoy home cooking more often.

Opposite: The Watanabe family enjoys a very special picnic under a cherry tree in the garden of Kyoto's famed Heian Shrine. Prepared by a caterer, their repast is far more elaborate than the lunch most housewives would put up. In each of the individual half-moon boxes, called *hangetsu,* there is a selection of appetizing morsels and a ball of rice. The contents of the three round bowls in the foreground, which fit together to become a lidded box called a *koban,* consists mainly of pieces of roast duck and various kinds of fish.

If *ok'san* is really eager to please her family she may produce a dinner of *tempura (Recipe Index).* The diners dip the cooked *tempura* into salt or perhaps the mother has made a special sauce to mark the occasion. Afterwards, of course, comes the soup, rice and pickles.

On those happy evenings when a housewife knows for certain that the whole family will be able to eat together, with perhaps some relatives or old friends contributing to the festive mood, she might plan a dinner where everyone does his own cooking, right at the table. This technique, called *nabemono,* not only saves work for the housewife but it gives her the rare chance to sit down with everyone else and enjoy the party, instead of spending most of the mealtime shuttling between stove and table.

Among the popular *nabemono* dishes are the already described *sukiyaki* and *mizutaki.* In *nabe* cooking *(Recipe Index)* the ingredients are all precut into bite-sized pieces and cooked in a broth that is bubbling in a pot on a brazier or hot plate in the center of the table. The diners either pick up the raw ingredients from a plate with their chopsticks and hold them in the broth until cooked (as in *shabu shabu*), or they simply pluck the tidbits from the communal broth, one by one. The broth may be *dashi* alone, or *dashi* seasoned with soy sauce and *sake;* it may also be a "self-stock" made from the meat to be used—chicken broth (with fat removed) for chicken, beef broth for beef, fish stock (made from heads and bones) for seafood *nabe.* More often than not this broth is eaten as a soup at the end of the meal.

One of the most common *nabe* dishes is *yosenabe (Recipe Index),* a Japanese bouillabaisse of many kinds of fishes cooked with vegetables, kelp and *dashi.* (It can also be prepared in the kitchen and brought to the table when ready.) Most *nabe* cooking is not strongly seasoned, and *yosenabe,* no exception, is rather bland in taste, but a dipping sauce based on *yuzu* juice, soy sauce and *sake* imparts a tangy flavor to the juicy chunks of tender fish.

Another, even simpler, communal dish is *yudofu (Recipe Index),* steaming *tofu.* The cubes of *tofu* are boiled at the table in a pan of water often with *kombu* added, and dipped with chopsticks into a mixture of soy sauce, chopped scallions and *katsuobushi* flakes. Since *tofu* retains a remarkable amount of heat (like melted cheese in a fondue), it is easy to burn one's lips on it, so everyone gently waves his cube in the air to cool it before gobbling it down. *Yudofu* is a very homespun dish, superb on a cold winter's night.

No one, least of all *ok'san,* pretends that on-table cookery is a high-level gourmet cuisine. But for the Japanese there is some special magic about it. Perhaps the sight and aroma of the steaming cauldron stimulates the appetite, perhaps it is the conviviality and spirit of togetherness that automatically springs up when a group of people eat from the same pot, perhaps it is merely the warmth of the fire or the rare presence of both parents enjoying themselves at the same table at the same time—whatever it is, almost every Japanese cherishes poignant childhood memories of the bubbling pot.

On an ordinary day, Mama might put almost anything into the pot so long as it will taste good and is nourishing. But on occasions of special significance, such as holidays, weddings, funerals and baby's first visit to a shrine, the menu is fixed by tradition and not even a modern young housewife would ignore the culinary requirements of each particular ceremony.

In their devotion to ritual and form the Japanese have invented dozens of

Continued on page 120

Shinto Rituals for Marital Vows

Japanese marriages are seldom made in heaven. Most often, the parents of the young people arrange the union with the aid of a go-between, usually a trusted family friend. No religious sanction is required; formerly the ceremony was conducted in the home of the bridegroom. In recent years, however, an increasing number of weddings, such as the one seen below, have been held in Shinto shrines, the centers of the ancient and still-venerated worship of nature and ancestors. In contrast to home weddings, where the only outsiders were serving girls, the shrine ceremony includes white-robed priests and black-hatted musicians who play archaic music composed centuries ago for the imperial court.

A solemn moment of the Shinto wedding occurs when the groom promises the gods to assume the responsibility of marriage. In this ceremony at the Toshogu Shrine in Nikko, the demure bride kneels beside her husband before an altar laden with offerings. She is resplendent in a costly silk robe; over her heavy wig, a white silk *tsunokakushi* (horn concealer) symbolizes her promise to avoid jealousy.

The high point of the ceremony is called the *sansankudo,* literally "three, three, nine times." The custom requires that the bride and groom take three sips of cold *sake* from each of three lacquered cups. A smiling attendant *(above)* pours *sake* into the first cup. The bride downs the *sake* in three sips; the cup is refilled and passed to the bridegroom, who does the same. When the second cup is offered, it is the groom who sips before the bride. But the bride again drinks first from the third cup. Since three is considered a lucky number and nine the luckiest, the felicitous combination helps explain why, with this rite, the marriage is finally solemnized. Shortly after the ceremony, the wedding party joins relatives and friends at a banquet *(above, right)* that includes entertainment. Bride and groom *(behind the dancers)* are flanked by the go-between and his wife, then by their parents, relatives and guests.

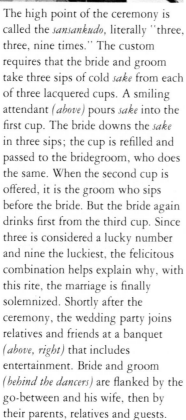

For the banquet, the bride *(center)* exchanges her bridal robe for a vivid kimono and dons a different wig that indicates matronly status. The bride accepts warm *sake* from a geisha, one of many cups that will flow freely. The lavish meal includes a clam soup, *hamaguri,* whose coupled shells symbolize the union. To make it clear who the principal characters are, the lettered napkins in front of the red lacquered trays mean bride and groom.

新婦

This type of candy, called *kyogashi,* which is made to order for special events such as birthdays and weddings, varies in colors and themes according to the seasons. The flowery blossom shapes and the predominantly pastel coloring of this assortment from Kyoto mark the candies as springtime confections. The octagonal box at top left was designed to commemorate the birth of the Emperor's grandson.

these special ceremonial dishes. Each one symbolizes in some way the meaning of the event. I have already mentioned (Chapter 4) that *tai* (sea bream) and *kombu* (kelp) are considered felicitous foods because of their names; they are eaten on almost all happy days. Another happy food is *sekihan,* red rice *(Recipe Index),* made by steaming a glutinous species of rice together with *azuki,* red beans; it comes out a bright pinkish red, and, for the simple reason that red is considered a joyous and lucky color, *sekihan* is required fare at shrine and children's festivals, and at every wedding in Japan.

For a reason that seems strange to us, the lobster is also a necessary food for festive days, particularly birthdays. The lobster's body is bent, like those of many old people in Japan, and the Japanese regard it not as a reminder of infirmity, as we might, but as a symbol of the ripe old age that those who partake of lobster will hopefully achieve.

On Children's Day (May 5), a sweet cake wrapped in oak leaves is offered; oak leaves stand for a long life and family continuity as they do not fall until new leaves come out in the spring. Girls' Day (March 3), also known as the Doll Festival, invariably brings out a green cake called *kusamochi,* probably because the green suggests the new innocent buds of springtime, and therefore girlhood. There is even a special funeral cake, impressed with a design of the leaf of the lotus, a plant sacred to Buddhism.

Tai, sekihan and *kombu* are of course essential to the traditional wedding feast. *Kombu* in this case carries a double meaning: the word can mean a fertile woman as well as being a pun on happiness. And the wedding *tai* is always served whole, because there is joy and hope in wholeness and to cut it implies separation. Then there is sure to be *kazunoko,* herring roe, which sounds like the words for "many children," and *mame* beans, which also can mean good health. The wedding *suimono* will usually contain a clam in the shell, the two shells of the clam signifying the two partners in marriage.

At the New Year, Japan's biggest holiday, families gather happily at the ancestral home and partake of the most elaborately symbolic menu of all. Many of the foods considered felicitous the year round are included in the feast, but in addition there is a long list of special foods and eating customs varying from region to region. *Mirin,* the sweet *sake,* for example, is used only for cooking during the rest of the year, but on the four or five days of the New Year holiday it is lightly flavored with pepper and other spices and sipped by family members and visitors, from a set of three ritual cups.

The main New Year's meal, traditionally served from a special four-tiered set of nesting boxes, includes *kombu,* lobster, *mame,* slices of *kamaboko* (fish loaf) and *tai,* plus *daidai* (a Japanese orange), which also means "generation after generation"; leaves of chrysanthemum, the imperial flower; chestnuts, from a pun on part of the written character meaning "mastery"; carp, for its indomitable spirit; and a good-luck fern called *urajiro,* which is white on its underside and therefore stands for honesty and purity of motive.

The most important New Year food is *mochi,* a rice cake made by pounding hot, steamed rice into a sticky dough. *Mochi-tsuki,* the rice-pounding ceremony, takes place a few days before the New Year and is a festive occasion at the rural homes that still observe it. Only men, working in pairs, are permitted to wield the big mallets that pulverize the mass of steamed rice in a wooden tub, while the agile housewife, ducking in between the blows, turns the hot paste. When finished, the dough is formed into round cakes (symbolizing a mirror, one of the three ancient imperial treasures) which are placed as offerings on the Shinto god-shelves, and into square cakes for eating.

Mochi can also mean "to have," so it symbolizes wealth. The cakes are very practical as well: they can be kept for days and prepared for eating merely by toasting over a fire, so during the New Year season, which is supposed to be a time of rest for all, *ok'san* never has to bother to cook rice for her family. This enables *ok'san* to accompany the family to the shrine on New Year's morning and to enjoy the holiday with her husband and children.

The fun and emotional satisfaction that the Japanese get out of the appearance and symbolism of their ceremonial foods is difficult to translate into other cultures. Some years back the Japanese chef of an American family in Tokyo was confronted, one December day, with unexpected guests for lunch. His larder was nearly bare and he had no time to shop, but he did his best. One side dish he produced puzzled the lady of the house: on dainty saucers he spread a thin layer of ketchup on which he placed a few green peas, arranged in an asymmetrical pattern. "Like Christmas?" he later asked his employer, hopefully. "No," she thought, keeping silent, "like Japan."

Nimono: FOODS COOKED IN SEASONED LIQUIDS

Gohan: RICE

Menrui: NOODLES

Nabemono: ONE-POT COOKERY

NIMONO: The following recipes are for "nimono"—foods simmered in liquids. Although a few "nimono" dishes serve as main courses, for the most part they are delicately seasoned small dishes, usually meant to accompany other courses in a meal.

Kimini 黄身煮

SAKE-SEASONED SHRIMP WITH EGG-YOLK GLAZE

To serve 6

- 18 medium-sized raw shrimp (16 to 20 per pound), shelled and deveined *(see page 168)*
- Cornstarch
- 1/4 cup *sake* (rice wine)
- 6 tablespoons *niban dashi (page 54)*
- 1 teaspoon sugar
- 1/2 teaspoon salt
- 1/2 teaspoon MSG
- 4 egg yolks, well beaten

GARNISH

- 1 pound string beans, trimmed and cut into 1/2-inch pieces, or fresh or frozen snow peas
- Salt
- 1 cup *niban dashi (page 54)*
- 1 teaspoon sugar
- 1/4 teaspoon salt
- 2 teaspoons *sake* (rice wine)
- 1/4 teaspoon Japanese all-purpose soy sauce

PREPARE AHEAD: 1. Salt the shrimp lightly and dip them into cornstarch to coat them well on all sides, then shake off any excess. Bring 2 cups of water to a boil in a 1-quart saucepan and add the shrimp. Boil for about 10 seconds, remove with a slotted spoon, and rinse under cold running water. Drain and set aside.

2. Sprinkle the beans or snow peas liberally with salt before dropping them into 2 cups of boiling water. Boil briskly, uncovered, for about 8 to 10 minutes, until tender but still slightly resistant to the bite. Drain the beans in a sieve and cool them quickly under cold running water.

3. In a 1-quart saucepan, combine 1 cup *niban dashi,* 1 teaspoon sugar, 1/4 teaspoon salt, 2 teaspoons *sake,* 1/4 teaspoon soy sauce. Bring to a boil over moderate heat and add the green vegetables. When the liquid returns to the boil remove the pan from the heat and set aside to cool.

TO COOK AND ASSEMBLE: In a 1 1/2- to 2-quart saucepan, combine 1/4 cup *sake,* 6 tablespoons *niban dashi,* 1 teaspoon sugar, 1/2 teaspoon of salt and 1/2 teaspoon of MSG. Bring to a boil, drop in the shrimp and return to the boil. Slowly pour the beaten egg yolks over the shrimp, do not stir, but cover the pan immediately. Then lower the heat and simmer for 2 minutes. Turn off the heat and let the shrimp rest still covered for a minute before serving.

Drain the cooled string beans or snow peas and serve with *kimini* as part of a Japanese dinner *(page 198).*

Nitsuke 煮付け

FRESH SARDINES COOKED IN SAKE-FLAVORED SAUCE

To serve 6

- 2/3 cup *sake* (rice wine)
- 1/4 cup sugar
- 1/3 cup Japanese all-purpose soy sauce
- 2 1/2 teaspoons scraped, finely sliced fresh ginger root
- 2 to 2 1/2 pounds fresh sardines, or substitute 2 1/2 pounds Spanish mackerel or porgy, cleaned and with head removed

TO COOK: Combine the *sake,* sugar and soy sauce in a 4-quart saucepan, add the ginger and bring to a boil over high heat. Drop in the fish, return to a boil, then reduce the heat to its lowest point. Set a small, heavy pot lid inside the pan directly on top of the fish to keep them intact. Simmer for 20 to 30 minutes, until the liquid has almost completely evaporated.

TO SERVE: *Nitsuke* may be served either hot or at room temperature, with any remaining sauce poured over the fish. Serve as part of a Japanese dinner *(page 198)* or as a luncheon dish.

Nitsuke may be refrigerated and kept for two or three days. When ready to serve, reheat, moistened with a tablespoon or so of *sake*.

Kuri Fukume-ni 栗ふくめ煮

SWEET CHESTNUTS

To serve 4 to 6

20 chestnuts
5 tablespoons sugar

PREPARE AHEAD: With a small, sharp knife, cut a long gash in the flat, softer side of each of the 20 chestnuts. Put the chestnuts in a 1½- to 2-quart saucepan, cover them completely with cold water and bring to a boil. Cook briskly for 2 or 3 minutes, then remove the chestnuts from the pan and peel off their shells.

TO COOK AND SERVE: Bring 2 cups of water to a boil in a 1-quart saucepan and drop in the peeled chestnuts. Simmer uncovered for about 20 minutes, then drain and set aside.

Combine 1 cup of cold water and 3 tablespoons of sugar in a 1-quart saucepan. Bring to a boil, add the chestnuts, and cook uncovered over moderate heat for 20 minutes, or until the chestnuts are tender but not falling apart. Stir in 2 more tablespoons of sugar and cook for another 5 minutes. Cool to room temperature in the cooking liquid.

Drain the chestnuts and serve as a sweet course, toward the end of a Japanese meal or as the filling for *igaguri (Recipe Index)*.

Umani うま煮

CHICKEN AND VEGETABLES SIMMERED IN SEASONED BROTH

To serve 6

2 *gobo* (burdock), washed and cut into 1-inch-long pieces
3 *shiitake* (Japanese dried mushrooms)
⅓ cup fresh or thoroughly defrosted shelled green peas
2 tablespoons vegetable oil
1 whole chicken breast, boned but with skin left on *(see page 168)*, and cut into strips ½ inch wide by 1 inch long
1 canned *konnyaku* (gelatinous root vegetable), cut into ½-inch dice
2 carrots, scraped and cut into ½-inch pieces
2 whole canned *takenoko* (bamboo shoots), cut into ½-inch pieces
1 cup *niban dashi (page 54)*, or substitute 1 cup chicken broth, fresh or canned
3 tablespoons sugar
1½ teaspoons salt
1 teaspoon Japanese all-purpose soy sauce
MSG

PREPARE AHEAD: 1. Bring 2 cups of water to a boil in a 1-quart saucepan, drop in the *gobo* and boil briskly, uncovered, for 5 minutes. Drain and set them aside.

2. Soak the mushrooms in cold water for 2 hours. Then cut off and discard their stems, and slice the mushrooms into ½-inch pieces. Discard their soaking liquid.

3. Bring 1 cup of water to a boil in a 1-quart saucepan, drop in the peas, and cook briskly for 2 minutes. Drain the peas in a sieve and cool them quickly under cold running water.

TO COOK: In a heavy 10- to 12-inch skillet, heat 2 tablespoons of oil over high heat until a light haze forms above it. Add the strips of chicken and, stirring frequently, cook for 2 to 3 minutes, or until the chicken is golden brown. Add the *konnyaku,* carrots, bamboo shoots and *gobo,* and stir thoroughly. Then pour in the *dashi* or chicken stock, and 3 tablespoons of sugar. Stir again, cover the pan and cook for 5 minutes over moderately high heat.

Now add the mushrooms, salt, soy sauce and a few sprinkles of MSG and re-cover the pan. Lower the heat and simmer an additional 8 to 10 minutes. Stir in the fresh or defrosted frozen green peas, and simmer another 2 to 3 minutes, or only long enough to heat them through.

TO SERVE: Serve hot or at room temperature as part of a Japanese meal *(page 198)* or as a luncheon dish.

RICE is so essential to Japan—as it is to all of Asia—that it has come to have a symbolic meaning: a bowl of steamed unadorned rice always appears at the end of even the most sumptuous dinner, so that the host can ensure that the diner has indeed had enough to eat. Of course, rice is also served more elaborately—in a bowl as a one-dish meal topped or mixed with fish, meat, poultry, eggs or vegetables.

Gohan 御飯

STEAMED RICE

To make 3 cups

1 cup Japanese rice, or substitute 1 cup unconverted long-grain white rice
1½ cups cold water

TO COOK: Pour the rice into a sieve. Stirring with a large spoon, run cold water over the rice until the draining water is clear. Drain thoroughly and transfer the rice to a heavy 2- to 3-quart saucepan. Add 1½ cups of cold water and let the rice soak undisturbed for 30 minutes. Then bring to a boil over moderate heat, cover the pan tightly and cook for about 10 minutes, or until all the water has been absorbed. Reduce the heat to its lowest point and simmer the rice undisturbed for 5 minutes. Remove from the heat and let the rice rest, still in its covered pan, for 5 more minutes. Remove the lid from the pan and fluff the rice gently with chopsticks or a fork to separate the grains. Serve the hot rice at once.

To reheat leftover rice, place it in a colander and set the colander over 1½ inches of boiling water in a large, heavy pot. Cover the pot tightly, and steam the rice for about 5 minutes.

Oyako Domburi 親子丼

CHICKEN OMELET OVER RICE

To serve 2

½ chicken breast (about 4 ounces), skinned and boned *(see pages 176-177)*, cut into ¼-inch dice
2 scallions, including about 2 inches of the green stems, cut in half lengthwise, then into 1½-inch-long pieces
½ cup *domburi ni shiru (opposite)*
3 cups *gohan* (steamed rice, *above)*
4 eggs
A dash of *kona sansho* (Japanese pepper)
1 sheet *nori* (dried laver), crumbled

PREPARE AHEAD: 1. Divide the chicken and scallions in half and place them in separate bowls. Mix ¼ of a cup of *domburi ni shiru* into each bowl, and have the bowls within easy reach of the stove.

2. Place 1½ cups of hot steamed rice in each of 2 serving bowls, cover, and keep warm in a 250° oven while you prepare the omelets.

TO COOK AND SERVE: Pour the entire contents of one of the bowls of chicken, scallions and sauce into a 5- or 6-inch skillet or crêpe pan. Bring to a boil over high heat, reduce the heat to moderate, and cover the pan. Cook for 2 minutes.

Meanwhile, break 2 eggs in a small bowl and, with chopsticks or a spoon, stir together only long enough to combine the yolks and whites. Stir in the *kona sansho* and pour the eggs into the pan. Cover the pan again and cook another 2 to 3 minutes, or until the eggs are lightly set.

Slide the omelet on top of one of the bowls of rice and garnish with the crumbled *nori.* Quickly make the second omelet with the remaining ingredients and serve at once.

VARIATIONS ON OYAKO DOMBURI: To make *tanin domburi,* follow the procedure above precisely, but substitute 6 ounces of very thinly sliced beef for the chicken. In other variations, the omelet is omitted. Instead, 4 or 6 shrimp *tempura (Recipe Index)* are placed over the rice in a bowl and served with ¼ cup *domburi ni shiru* poured over the top *(tendon domburi).* Similarly, to make *yakitori domburi,* prepare chicken and scallions as for *yakitori (Recipe Index),* then, after arranging a serving on the cup of steamed rice, pour ¼ cup *domburi ni shiru* over it. Sprinkle with *kona sansho.*

Domburi Ni Shiru どんぶり煮汁

DIPPING SAUCE FOR DOMBURI

To make about 1½ cups

- ⅓ cup *mirin* (sweet *sake),* or substitute ¼ cup pale dry sherry
- ⅓ cup Japanese all-purpose soy sauce
- 1 cup *niban dashi (page 54)*
- MSG

TO COOK: Over moderate heat, bring the *mirin* to a boil in a 1-quart saucepan. Remove the pan from the heat and set the *mirin* alight with a match. Shake the pan gently until the flame dies out, then stir in the soy sauce and *dashi,* and sprinkle lightly with MSG. Bring to a boil over high heat, then cool to room temperature.

Serve with *oyako domburi, tendon domburi* and *tanin domburi (Recipe Index).*

Tori Gohan 鶏御飯

CHICKEN AND RICE WITH MUSHROOMS

To serve 4

- 1 whole chicken breast (about ½ pound), skinned and boned *(see pages 176-177)*
- 4 medium-sized *shiitake* (dried Japanese mushrooms)
- 1½ cups white Japanese rice, or substitute 1½ cups unconverted long-grain rice, washed and soaked in water to cover for 3 hours
- 4 cups *niban dashi (page 54),* or substitute 4 cups chicken broth, fresh or canned
- 4 teaspoons *mirin* (sweet *sake),* or substitute 1 tablespoon pale dry sherry
- 1 teaspoon salt
- MSG
- 1 teaspoon Japanese all-purpose soy sauce
- 2 ounces (about 4 inches) *gobo* (burdock), washed and very thinly slivered
- 1 tablespoon finely chopped parsley

PREPARE AHEAD: 1. Cut the chicken breast into shreds approximately 1 inch long and ⅛ inch wide.

2. Steam the *shiitake* for 1 minute in an Oriental steamer or in the improvised steamer described on page 180. Remove from the pot and shred the mushrooms as fine as possible while they are still hot.

TO COOK: Drain the rice and combine it with the *dashi, mirin,* salt, a few sprinkles of MSG and the soy sauce in a 3- to 4-quart pot. Add the *gobo* and *shiitake,* then the chicken. Bring to a boil over high heat, stir once or twice and cover tightly. Reduce the heat to moderate and cook for 3 minutes, then lower the heat again and simmer about 4 minutes longer. Turn off the heat, and let the *tori gohan* rest covered for 2 minutes before serving.

TO SERVE: Divide equally among 4 serving bowls and garnish each portion with a sprinkling of the chopped parsley. Serve as a luncheon dish, accompanied perhaps by *miso* soup *(Recipe Index)* and bottled Japanese pickles; or serve in smaller portions at the end of a 5- or 7-course Japanese dinner *(page 198).* Shredded uncooked shrimp, clams or lobster may be substituted for the chicken and cooked in precisely the same fashion.

The automatic electric rice cooker is a comparatively recent Japanese invention that can insure perfectly steamed rice every time. It works on the principle of the double boiler. Thermostatic controls reduce the heat at precisely the right moment, and then keep the rice warm until needed. The cooker is available in the United States *(page 207).*

Sekihan 赤飯

RED-COOKED FESTIVAL RICE

To serve 6

- 2 cups *azuki* (red beans)
- 1 pound *mochi gome* (Japanese sweet rice)
- 1 teaspoon black sesame seeds
- 1 teaspoon salt
- 1/4 teaspoon MSG

PREPARE AHEAD: 1. A day before you plan to serve *sekihan,* place the beans in a colander or sieve and wash them under cold running water. Then transfer them to a 2-quart pan, cover them with 4 cups of cold water, and bring to a boil over high heat. Reduce the heat to its lowest point and simmer the beans uncovered for 45 minutes, until they are tender but still intact.

Drain the beans through a large sieve or colander set over a large mixing bowl. Reserve the bean liquid and cover the beans with cold water in another bowl. Cool to room temperature.

2. Stirring with a large spoon, wash the rice in a large colander or strainer under cold running water until the draining water runs clear. Drain thoroughly and add the rice to the bowl of bean liquid. Soak for 8 hours or overnight, covered, in the refrigerator.

3. Drain the rice, discard the soaking liquid and combine the rice and 1 cup of the beans in a bowl.

NOTE: The remaining beans, which were used to give added flavor to the *sekihan,* can be drained and refrigerated in plastic bags, then cooked with sugar as a dessert *(mizuyokan, Recipe Index).*

Steam the rice and beans in an Oriental steamer, or place them in a colander and set the colander in a large pot filled with 1½ inches of water. Bring the water to a boil over high heat, cover the pan tightly, and steam for 40 minutes, replenishing the water in the pot if it boils away.

4. Meanwhile, heat a small skillet over high heat until a drop of water flicked across its surface evaporates instantly. Add the sesame seeds and, shaking the pan gently, cook 2 to 3 minutes, until the seeds are lightly toasted. Transfer the seeds to a small bowl and toss with 1 teaspoon of salt and 1/4 teaspoon of MSG.

TO SERVE: Transfer the steamed rice and beans to a large serving bowl or individual bowls. Serve either hot or at room temperature with baked fish or as a sweet course with *kuri fukume-ni (Recipe Index).* In either case sprinkle the *sekihan* with the sesame seeds before serving.

In Japan *sekihan* is a festive dish, served at weddings or birthdays.

Maze Gohan まぜ御飯

MIXED RICE AND VEGETABLES

To serve 3

- 1 *shiitake* (dried Japanese mushroom)
- A 4-ounce loaf of canned *konnyaku* (gelatinous root vegetable), sliced thin and shredded
- 3 cups *niban dashi (page 54)*
- 2 tablespoons *mirin* (sweet *sake*), or substitute 5 teaspoons pale dry sherry
- 1¼ teaspoons salt
- 1 teaspoon Japanese all-purpose soy sauce
- 1 cup Japanese rice, or substitute 1 cup unconverted long-grain white rice, soaked 3 hours in water to cover
- 1 carrot, scraped, cut in half lengthwise and shredded fine
- 12 canned *ginnan* (ginkgo) nuts
- A 3-ounce piece of canned *kamaboko* (fish cake), sliced thin
- ½ cup fresh or thoroughly defrosted frozen green peas

PREPARE AHEAD: 1. Soften the *shiitake* by steaming it for 1 minute in an Oriental steamer or the substitute described on page 180. While the mushroom is still hot, cut off and discard its hard stem, and shred the cap fine.

2. In a small saucepan, bring 1 cup of water to a boil. Add the shredded *konnyaku* and return the water to the boil. Drain the *konnyaku* in a sieve and run cold water over it to cool it quickly. Drain again and set aside.

3. In a large mixing bowl, combine the *dashi, mirin,* salt and soy sauce.

TO COOK: In a 2- to 3-quart saucepan, combine the rice, *dashi* mixture, *shiitake, konnyaku,* carrot, nuts and fish cake. Stir together gently, and bring to a boil over high heat. Then reduce the heat to low, cover the pan, and simmer undisturbed for 4 to 6 minutes, or until the liquid is completely absorbed by the rice. Stir in the green peas, cover again and simmer for 2 minutes. Serve as a main course for lunch or supper, accompanied perhaps by soup.

MENRUI—almost as important an element in the Japanese cuisine as rice—are available as thin noodles, wide noodles and buckwheat noodles. They are served simply—with a dipping sauce—or are combined with other ingredients in a broth as a one-dish meal. The following recipes include not only hot noodle dishes but also those served ice cold as delicate summer meals.

Kitsune Udon きつねうどん

FOX NOODLES

Because it is reputed in legend that the Japanese fox has a passion for fried "tofu"—how he managed to first taste it is never explained—this slightly sweet "tofu"-and-noodle dish is fancifully called "kitsune udon," or fox noodles.

To serve 6

A 6-ounce cake of *tofu* (soybean curd), fresh, canned or instant, sliced in 1/4-inch-thick pieces
Vegetable oil
A 14-ounce package Futonaga *udon* (wide noodles), or substitute 1 pound No. 2 spaghetti
Salt
1 cup *niban dashi (page 54)*
3 tablespoons sugar
2 tablespoons Japanese all-purpose soy sauce
MSG
6 cups *ichiban dashi (page 54)*
2 scallions, including at least 3 inches of the green stems, sliced into thin rounds

PREPARE AHEAD: 1. If you want to rid the *tofu* of excess moisture, thus making it firmer, place the slices side by side on a flat plate. Cover with foil and place a 1-pound pan, casserole or small cutting board on top. Tilt the plate so that the water drains off. Set aside for at least 30 minutes, then pour off the accumulated water and pat the *tofu* dry with paper towels.

2. Pour enough vegetable oil into a heavy 10- to 12-inch skillet to come about 1½ inches up the sides of the pan. Set over high heat until the oil registers 350° on a deep-fat thermometer. Drop in 6 or 8 slices of *tofu* at a time and fry them for about 1 minute, turning them over with tongs or chopsticks until they are brown on all sides.

Drain the fried *tofu* on paper towels. Then with the tongs or chopsticks, dip them one at a time in a bowl of hot water to rid them of any remaining oil, and drain again on paper towels.

3. In a 3- to 4-quart pot, bring 2 quarts of water to a boil. Drop in the noodles, return the water to a boil, and cook them uncovered for about 20 minutes, stirring occasionally, until they are very soft. Stir in 1 tablespoon of salt, cover the pot, and turn off the heat. Let the noodles rest covered for 5 minutes, then drain them in a colander, and run cold water over them for 5 minutes. Drain again and set aside.

4. In a 1-quart saucepan, combine 1 cup of *niban dashi* with 2 tablespoons of the sugar and 1 tablespoon of the soy sauce. Stir thoroughly and bring to a boil over high heat. Then add 1/8 teaspoon of salt and a sprinkle of MSG. Drop in the *tofu* and boil over high heat for 5 to 8 minutes, or until the liquid has cooked down to about 1/3 of a cup. Set the *tofu* and its liquid aside off the heat.

TO COOK AND SERVE: In a 2-quart saucepan, combine 6 cups of *ichiban dashi* with 1 tablespoon sugar, 2½ teaspoons salt and 1 tablespoon soy sauce. Stir thoroughly, bring to a boil, and add the noodles. Return to the boil and serve at once. Pour the broth and noodles into 6 serving bowls, top each serving with a few pieces of the sweetened *tofu* and garnish with the sliced scallions.

NOTE: If you prefer subtler flavor, omit cooking the *tofu* in the sweet sauce *(step 4)*. Instead, cut both the *tofu* and scallions lengthwise into long, narrow strips. After the noodles have been reheated in the broth, transfer them to serving bowls, and leave the broth in the pan. Add the scallions and *tofu* and bring back to the boil, then divide the contents of the pan equally among the bowls of noodles.

To make 1½ cups

¼ cup *mirin* (sweet *sake)*, or substitute 3 tablespoons pale dry sherry
¼ cup Japanese all-purpose soy sauce
1 cup *niban dashi (page 54)*
2 tablespoons preflaked *katsuobushi* (dried bonito)
½ teaspoon salt
MSG

Menrui No Dashi 麵類のつけ汁

DIPPING SAUCE FOR NOODLES

TO COOK: Quickly heat the *mirin* to lukewarm in a 1-quart saucepan, then remove the pan from the heat and set the *mirin* alight with a match. Shake the pan gently until the flame dies out.

Stir in the soy sauce, the *dashi, katsuobushi,* salt and a few sprinkles of MSG. Bring to a boil over high heat, and strain the sauce into a bowl. Let it cool to room temperature.

Serve as the dipping sauce for *hiyamugi (below), zarusoba (Recipe Index)* or *hiyashi somen (Recipe Index).*

To serve 6

6 medium-sized shrimp in their shells (16 to 20 per pound)
12 sprigs watercress or young spinach leaves
3 *shiitake* (dried Japanese mushrooms)
½ teaspoon sugar
1 tablespoon Japanese all-purpose soy sauce
Vegetable oil
2 eggs, well beaten
A 16-ounce package of *hiyamugi* (thin Japanese noodles), or substitute 1 pound Italian vermicelli

DIPPING SAUCE
1½ cups *menrui no dashi (above)*
1½ teaspoons grated lime rind

Hiyamugi ひやむぎ

COLD NOODLES WITH SHRIMP AND MUSHROOMS

PREPARE AHEAD: 1. Drop the shrimp into 2 cups of boiling water and boil for 3 minutes, or until they turn pink and are firm to the touch. Drain in a colander and run cold water over them.

Peel the shrimp and devein them by making a shallow incision down their backs with a small, sharp knife and lifting out the black or white intestinal veins with the point of the knife.

2. Blanch the watercress or spinach by plunging it into a small pan of boiling water for 10 seconds, then drain it. Let it rest in a bowl of cold water until ready to use.

3. Soak the *shiitake* in 4 cups of cold water for 1 hour, then transfer the mushrooms and their soaking liquid to a 2-quart saucepan and bring to a boil over high heat. Add ½ teaspoon of sugar and 1 tablespoon of soy sauce, lower the heat to moderate, and cook the *shiitake* uncovered for 20 minutes, or until the liquid is a rich brown and has reduced to about ⅓ cup. Set the pan aside off the heat.

4. With a pastry brush or paper towel, lightly coat a 10- to 12-inch skillet or omelet pan with vegetable oil. Heat the pan over moderate heat until a drop of cold water flicked on its surface evaporates instantly. Pour in the eggs and cook without stirring for about 20 seconds, or until the omelet is set, then turn it out on a platter in one piece.

Trim the rounded edges of the omelet with a knife to form a rectangle, and cut into 1-inch squares. Holding the squares with chopsticks or tongs, dip them one at a time into a bowl of hot water for 1 second to remove any remaining oil, and drain on paper towels.

TO COOK AND SERVE: In a 3- to 4-quart pot, bring 2 quarts of water to a boil. Drop in the noodles, return to a boil and, stirring occasionally, cook uncovered for about 10 minutes, or until they are very soft. Drain the noodles in a colander, run cold water over them for 5 minutes, and drain them thoroughly again.

Divide the noodles among 6 individual serving bowls and place 2 or 3 ice cubes in each bowl. Garnish the servings with 1 shrimp, 2 sprigs of watercress or spinach, ½ *shiitake,* and a few squares of the egg. Accompany with the dipping sauce flavored with grated lime rind.

A light summer meal of *hiyamugi*—cold noodles topped with shrimp, mushrooms, eggs and watercress—is encircled by green bamboo and accompanied by a delicate dipping sauce *(top right)* and warm *sake.*

To serve 6

A 14-ounce package Futonaga *udon* (wide noodles), or substitute 1 pound No. 2 spaghetti
5½ teaspoons salt
1 whole ½-pound chicken breast or duck breast, skinned and boned *(pages 176-177)*
6 cups *ichiban dashi (page 54)*
1 tablespoon sugar
1 tablespoon Japanese all-purpose soy sauce
2 scallions, including at least 3 inches of the green stems, halved and sliced thin lengthwise

Tori Nanban とりなんばん

HOT NOODLES AND CHICKEN IN BROTH

PREPARE AHEAD: 1. In a 3- to 4-quart pot, bring 2 quarts of water to a boil. Drop in the noodles, return to a boil and, stirring occasionally, cook uncovered for about 20 minutes, until the noodles are very soft. Stir in 1 tablespoon of the salt, cover the pan tightly, and turn off the heat. Let the noodles rest covered for 5 minutes. Then drain them in a colander, and run cold water over them for 5 minutes. Drain again and set aside.

2. Cut each boned chicken breast in half horizontally, then into strips about ¼ inch wide by 2 inches long.

TO COOK AND SERVE: In a 2- to 3-quart saucepan, combine the *dashi,* sugar, the remaining 2½ teaspoons of salt and the soy sauce, stir and bring to a boil, uncovered. Add the noodles, return to a boil, and remove from the heat. With chopsticks, pasta tongs or your hands, remove the noodles from the soup and divide them among 6 deep bowls.

The delicate flavor of noodles, served in broth with duck and scallions, is accented by *suzuko mizore-ae*—red caviar and radish *(page 64)*.

Drop the strips of chicken and the scallions into the soup. Bring the soup to a boil again over high heat, boil for 2 minutes, then pour the contents of the pan over the noodles and serve at once.

Zarusoba ざるそば

BUCKWHEAT NOODLES WITH LAVER

To serve 6

A 16-ounce package *soba* (buckwheat noodles)
3 sheets packaged *nori* (dried laver), passed over a flame on one side only and coarsely crumbled
2 scallions, including at least 3 inches of the green stems, sliced into thin rounds
4 teaspoons *wasabi* (horseradish) powder, mixed with just enough cold water to make a thick paste, then set aside to rest for 15 minutes

DIPPING SAUCE
1½ cups *soba tsuyu* *(page 104)*

In a 3- to 4-quart pot, bring 2 quarts of water to a boil. Add the *soba* and, stirring occasionally, cook for 6 to 7 minutes, until very soft. Drain the noodles in a colander and quickly run cold water over them. Drain again and divide the noodles among 6 serving bowls (the Japanese would use *zaru,* which are round, curved bamboo baskets), and top with crumbled *nori.* Garnish each bowl with scallions and a teaspoon of *wasabi* paste. Serve the dipping sauce separately, in individual small bowls or dishes. Traditionally, the *wasabi* and scallions are mixed into the dipping sauce to the individual diner's taste.

Buckwheat noodles, topped with bits of *nori,* are shown with dipping sauce *(top right)* and hot water to make soup from leftover noodles.

IN ALL "NABE"—one-pot, do-it-yourself—cooking, the actual cooking is done at the dinner table, although the uncooked food is sliced and arranged in advance. An electric skillet or casserole is most effective in preparing "nabemono," but a heavy, shallow casserole or skillet set over an alcohol burner, charcoal-burning hibachi, or gas table burner does almost as well.

Set the heating unit and its cooking pot in the center of the dining table and preheat, or bring the specified liquid to a boil. Adjust the heat so that the liquid simmers throughout the cooking. Provide each diner with a plate, a small dish of dipping sauce (where applicable) and chopsticks or a long-handled fork with heatproof handle (such as a fondue fork). Traditionally, each diner selects his own food from the platter of ingredients and cooks it himself in the simmering cooking liquid.

Yosenabe 寄鍋

SEAFOOD AND VEGETABLES IN BROTH

To serve 6

- A 1½-pound live lobster, cut into serving pieces, or substitute 12 large raw shrimp (10 to 15 per pound), peeled and deveined *(see page 168)*
- 2 medium-sized carrots, scraped
- 3 ounces *harusame* (cellophane or transparent noodles)
- ½ pound fillet of porgy or any other white-meat fish, cut into 1-inch pieces
- 12 cherrystone clams, shucked
- 8 scallions, including at least 3 inches of the green stems, cut into 2-inch pieces
- 3 cups chicken broth, fresh or canned, or 3 cups *ichiban dashi (page 54)*
- A 4-inch piece *kombu* (dried kelp), cut with a heavy knife from a sheet of packaged *kombu* and washed under cold water

DIPPING SAUCE

- 1 recipe *chirizu (page 94)*

"Yosenabe" means "a gathering of everything," and as in all "nabe" cooking, other vegetables than those specified may be used—among them cabbage rolls (see "tori mizutaki," and "shabu shabu," pages 134-135), bamboo shoots, and mushrooms.

PREPARE AHEAD: 1. With a cleaver or large, heavy knife, chop off the tail section of the lobster at the point where it joins the body. Twist or cut off the large claws. Split the body of the lobster in half and remove and discard the gelatinous sac (stomach) in the head and the long intestinal vein attached to it. Cut the tail crosswise into 1-inch-wide slices and chop the lobster halves crosswise into quarters.

2. Cut the carrots obliquely, by making a diagonal slice, then rolling the carrot a quarter turn and slicing again.

Bring 1 cup of water to a boil in a small saucepan, drop in the carrots and return to the boil. Drain the carrots in a sieve and run cold water over them. Set aside.

3. Soak the *harusame* in a bowl of cold water for about 30 minutes, or until soft. Drain and cut into 4-inch lengths.

4. Bring 1 cup of water to a boil in a small saucepan and drop in the fish. Cook briskly for about 10 seconds, drain in a sieve and run cold water over the fish to cool it quickly.

5. Arrange the clams, lobster or shrimp, carrots, scallions, noodles and fish chunks attractively on a large platter.

TO COOK: Following the directions in the introduction *(above)*, place 3 cups of chicken broth and the piece of *kombu* in the cooking utensil and bring to a boil. Lower the heat so that the broth simmers constantly throughout the meal. Traditionally, each diner selects and cooks his own food to taste. None of the ingredients in *yosenabe* needs be cooked longer than a moment, two at the most. Serve with small dishes of dipping sauce.

Yudofu 湯豆腐

BUBBLING TOFU

To serve 4

- 6 cups cold water
- A 4-inch square *kombu* (dried kelp), cut with a heavy knife from a sheet of packaged *kombu* and washed under cold running water
- 4 cakes *tofu* (soybean curd), fresh or canned

DIPPING SAUCE

- ½ cup Japanese all-purpose soy sauce
- 2 tablespoons *mirin* (sweet *sake*), or substitute 5 teaspoons pale dry sherry
- MSG

PREPARE AHEAD: 1. In a small saucepan, combine ½ cup soy sauce with 2 tablespoons of *mirin* (or the dry sherry) and sprinkle lightly with MSG. Bring to a boil, stirring constantly, then pour into individual serving bowls.

A colorful *yosenabe*—"gathering of everything"—includes lobster, shrimp, red snapper, carrots, scallions, *tofu* and fine noodles.

2. Slice the 4 scallions crosswise into very thin rounds.

3. Garnish the sauce with the scallions, ginger, *hanakatsuo* and *nori,* and then set it aside.

4. Cut the 4 cakes of *tofu* into 1-inch cubes.

5. Pass the sheet of *nori* over a flame on one side only and cut it into ½-inch-square pieces.

TO COOK AND SERVE: Following the *nabe* procedure described in the introduction on the opposite page, place the cooking pot of your choice on the dining table. Pour in the 6 cups of cold water, add the square of *kombu,* and bring to a boil.

Drop in the *tofu* and simmer gently for 2 to 3 minutes—if cooked too rapidly or too long, the *tofu* will harden.

Scoop the *tofu* out of the broth with a slotted spatula or spoon and place in individual bowls. Ladle a little of the broth into each bowl, and serve with the dipping sauce and garnishes.

GARNISH

4 scallions, including 3 inches of the green stems
1 tablespoon grated, scraped fresh ginger
1 tablespoon *hanakatsuo* (fine flaked dried bonito)
1 sheet packaged *nori* (dried laver)

Sukiyaki すき焼

BEEF AND VEGETABLES SIMMERED IN SOY SAUCE AND SAKE

To serve 4

1 pound boneless lean beef, preferably tenderloin or sirloin
An 8-ounce can *shirataki* (long noodlelike threads), drained
1 whole canned *takenoko* (bamboo shoot)
A 2-inch-long strip of beef fat, folded into a square packet
6 scallions, including 3 inches of the stem, cut into 1½-inch pieces
1 medium-sized yellow onion, peeled and sliced ½ inch thick
4 to 6 small white mushrooms, cut into ¼-inch-thick slices
2 cakes *tofu* (soybean curd), fresh, canned or instant, cut into 1-inch cubes
2 ounces Chinese chrysanthemum leaves, watercress or Chinese cabbage

SAUCE

¼ to ¾ cup Japanese all-purpose soy sauce
3 to 6 tablespoons sugar
¼ to ¾ cup *sake* (rice wine)

PREPARE AHEAD: 1. Place the beef in your freezer for about 30 minutes, or only long enough to stiffen it slightly for easier slicing. Then, with a heavy, sharp knife, cut the beef against the grain into slices ⅛ inch thick, and cut the slices in half crosswise.

2. Bring 1 cup of water to a boil and drop in the *shirataki;* return to the boil. Drain and cut the noodles into thirds.

3. Scrape the bamboo shoot at the base, cut it in half lengthwise, and slice it thin crosswise. Run cold running water over the slices and drain.

4. Arrange the meat, *shirataki* and vegetables attractively in separate rows on a large platter.

TO COOK AND SERVE: If you are using an electric skillet, preheat to 425°. If not, substitute a 10- to 12-inch skillet set over a table burner and preheat for several minutes.

Hold the folded strip of fat with chopsticks or tongs and rub it over the bottom of the hot skillet. Add 6 to 8 slices of meat to the skillet, pour in ¼ cup of soy sauce, and sprinkle the meat with 3 tablespoons of sugar. Cook for a minute, stir, and turn the meat over. Push the meat to one side of the skillet. Add about ⅓ of the scallions, onion, mushrooms, *tofu, shirataki,* greens and bamboo shoot in more or less equal amounts, sprinkle them with ¼ cup *sake* and cook for an additional 4 to 5 minutes.

With chopsticks or long-handled forks (such as fondue forks), transfer the contents of the pan to individual plates and serve. Continue cooking the remaining *sukiyaki* batch by batch as described above, checking the temperature of the pan from time to time. If it seems too hot and the food begins to stick or burn, lower the heat or cool the pan more quickly by adding a drop or two of cold water to the sauce.

Tori Mizutaki 鶏水炒

CHICKEN AND VEGETABLES COOKED IN BROTH WITH PONZU DIPPING SAUCE

To serve 6

2 whole chicken breasts, boned *(see pages 176-177)* and cut into 1-inch pieces
2 pounds Chinese cabbage
2 tablespoons salt
4 large scraped carrots, cut lengthwise into ¼-inch-wide strips
8 scallions, including 3 inches of the green stems, cut lengthwise into narrow strips
2 cakes *tofu* (soybean curd), fresh, canned or instant, cut into 1-inch cubes
12 small white mushrooms
12 to 14 sprigs watercress
1 quart chicken stock, fresh or canned
A 4-inch square of *kombu* (dried kelp), cut with a heavy knife from a sheet of packaged *kombu* and washed under cold running water

PREPARE AHEAD: 1. In a 1-quart saucepan, bring 2 cups of water to a boil. Drop in the pieces of chicken and boil briskly for about 10 seconds, then drain and rinse under cold running water.

2. Cut off the base of the cabbage and separate the leaves. Discard the inner core.

In a 2-quart saucepan, bring 2 cups of water to a boil with 2 tablespoons of salt. Drop in the cabbage and boil for 1 minute, or until the leaves wilt and shrink. Then cover the pan and boil 1 minute longer. Drain in a colander and cool the cabbage under cold running water. Drain again.

Arrange the cabbage leaves one on top of another in the center of a bamboo mat or heavy cloth napkin. Starting with the wide end, use the mat or napkin to roll the cabbage into a tight cylinder. Unwrap and cut the roll crosswise into sections 1 inch wide.

3. Bring 1 cup of water to a boil in a small saucepan and drop in the carrot strips. Return to the boil, drain, and cool under cold running water.

4. Arrange the chicken, cabbage rolls, carrots, scallions, *tofu,* mushrooms and watercress in concentric circles or long rows on a large platter.

5. To make the sauce and garnish, combine the lemon or lime juice and

soy sauce in a mixing bowl, then pour into individual small bowls. In other small, separate bowls or dishes place the grated *daikon* and sliced scallions. Set a bowl of sauce and garnish beside each serving plate. Traditionally they are then mixed together to the taste of each diner.

TO COOK AND SERVE: Following the procedures described on page 132, prepare the cooking pot of your choice at the table and pour in the chicken stock. Add the *kombu* and bring the stock to a boil. Then lower the heat so that the stock keeps simmering throughout the meal. Instruct each diner to dip the food of his choice into the broth, cook it for 2 or 3 minutes, then drop it into the sauce.

When all the food has been consumed, remove and discard the *kombu*. Ladle the broth into individual bowls and serve as a soup course.

NOTE: Warm *sake* is particularly suitable for this winter *nabe*. In Japan, for an intimate home dinner, the ceramic *sake* bottle is often placed directly in the broth to keep it warm during the meal.

TO MAKE CHIRINABE: Substitute white-meat fish chunks for the chicken. In this case, use water instead of chicken stock and serve with *chirizu* dipping sauce *(Recipe Index)*.

PONZU DIPPING SAUCE

6 tablespoons fresh lemon or lime juice
6 tablespoons Japanese all-purpose soy sauce

GARNISH

3 tablespoons finely grated *daikon* (Japanese white radish), or substitute 3 tablespoons peeled, grated icicle radish or white turnip
2 scallions, including 3 inches of the green stems, sliced into thin rounds

Shabu Shabu しゃぶしゃぶ

BEEF AND VEGETABLES COOKED IN BROTH WITH DIPPING SAUCE

To serve 6

1½ pounds boneless shell or sirloin steak, sliced ⅛ inch thick
2 pounds Chinese cabbage
2 tablespoons salt
12 to 14 young spinach leaves, stripped from their stems
8 carrots, scraped and cut lengthwise into strips ¼ inch wide by 2 inches long
8 scallions, including at least 3 inches of the green stems, cut lengthwise into narrow strips
2 cakes *tofu* (soybean curd), fresh, canned or instant, cut into 1-inch cubes
12 small white mushrooms
6 cups chicken broth, fresh or canned
A 4-inch square of *kombu* (dried kelp), cut with a heavy knife from a sheet of packaged *kombu* and washed under cold running water

DIPPING SAUCE

1 cup *goma joyu* dressing *(page 62)* or *ponzu* (equal parts soy sauce and lemon or lime juice)

PREPARE AHEAD: 1. Cut each slice of meat in half crosswise.

2. Trim the base of the cabbage and separate the leaves. Discard the inner core. In a 1-quart saucepan, bring 2 cups of water to a boil with 2 tablespoons of salt. Drop in the cabbage and boil for a minute, or until the leaves wilt and shrink. Then cover the pan and boil 1 minute longer. Drain in a colander and run cold water over the cabbage to cool it quickly.

3. Bring 1 cup of water to a boil in a small saucepan and drop in the spinach. Return to a boil, drain and cool under cold water. Bring another cup of water to a boil and add the carrot strips. Return to a boil, then drain and cool similarly.

4. Arrange the cabbage leaves one on top of another in the center of a bamboo mat or heavy cloth napkin. Lay the spinach leaves in a neat row down the center of the top leaf. Starting with the wide side of the mat or napkin, use it to roll the cabbage into a tight cylinder. Unwrap and cut the roll into 1-inch-long sections.

5. Arrange the beef, cabbage rolls, carrots, scallions, *tofu* and mushrooms in concentric circles or rows on a large serving platter.

TO COOK AND SERVE: Following the directions on page 132, pour the chicken broth into the cooking pot of your choice and add the square of *kombu*. Bring to a boil, then adjust the heat so that the stock simmers throughout the meal. Each guest selects a piece of food from the platter with chopsticks or a fork and swishes it about in the simmering broth until it is cooked to taste. It is this swishing that sounds to the Japanese like *shabu shabu,* hence the name of the dish.

The cooking procedure is as follows: First cook the meat in the broth for 2 to 3 seconds, then add the vegetables. Simmer another minute and remove the food with chopsticks or a fork. When all the food has been cooked, the *kombu* is removed and the broth is ladled into bowls and drunk as soup.

VI

A Ceremony That Sired a Cuisine

A Japanese hostess conducting the unique social and artistic function called the tea ceremony, graciously offers a bowl of tea to a guest. Evolved by Zen Buddhist monks centuries ago as an esthetic experience, the ceremony strongly influenced Japan's culture and gave rise to a highly refined cuisine.

The best food in Japan goes by the name of *kaiseki,* a word that comes from a curious and beautiful Japanese social custom called the tea ceremony. The tea ceremony, in simplest terms, is a way of getting the most out of drinking tea—not tea as we know it or even as the Japanese know it everyday, but a very special kind of tea made from green tea leaves ground to a fine powder, then reverentially served according to rules laid down centuries ago and still faithfully followed. The food that accompanies the tea is special too: *kaiseki ryori,* "tea cooking," is food prepared and eaten under the most refined circumstances possible. Many of the best restaurants in Japan call their cooking *kaiseki,* and the dishes they offer may indeed be identical to those one would find at a tea ceremony. But unless the food is served as an accompaniment to the tea ceremony it will not add up to the complete esthetic experience that Japanese know and love. No one can understand Japan and its food without having *kaiseki,* and no one can appreciate the nuances and rituals of *kaiseki* without some understanding of the origins of the tea ceremony. It is unique in all the world.

The roots of these rituals go back to the 13th Century, when Zen Buddhist monks in China drank tea ceremonially during their devotions—partly to keep themselves alert, partly as a gesture of fraternity, like the passing of a loving cup. In the 15th and 16th Centuries, these rituals were raised to a fine art by Japanese tea masters, men appointed to prepare the ceremonial teas of Japanese rulers and their court. There were several great tea masters, most notably one called Sen Rikyu, and the manner in which these great masters conducted the tea ceremony—their deportment, dress, conversation and

Japanese-English Glossary

MISO: *fermented-soybean paste*
MISOSHIRU: *soybean-paste soup*
SASHIMI: *slices of raw fish*

level of esthetic appreciation—set the standards for patterns of behavior throughout Japanese society. They were in effect Japan's arbiters of taste.

The rules laid down by the great masters for the tea ceremony are, in large measure, still observed by the Japanese. These rules embraced everything from the ideal dimensions for the tea hut to the ideal number of guests, three to five. There were rules for the order in which dishes should be presented, so that each dish would appear at the precise moment in the meal when its texture, flavor and temperature would be best appreciated. Most of all there were rules for the heart of the ceremony, the preparation of the tea. The water had to be boiled in an iron kettle over a charcoal fire; the tea had to be whipped in the cup, or tea bowl, with a bamboo whisk until the froth on the top was exactly the right depth; the bowl was offered and sipped from with gestures as carefully choreographed as those of a dance.

The tea ceremony remains to this day a cultural ideal that has to do with how people live and what they consider important. It is concerned with tea, of course, and with food, but it is also concerned with the setting in which the two are served—the room, the plates, the utensils—and with the manners and conversation of the participants. In short, it is the Japanese idea of a truly pleasant social occasion. Because its standards of beauty and deportment profoundly influence all of Japanese life, the tea ceremony is sometimes treated as a cult and sometimes is conducted with a good deal of display. But in fact this ceremony, which was evolved by men who combined virility with sensitivity, is a search for harmony with nature and with one's self; it may also serve as a kind of entertainment.

Not everyone, to be sure, is entertained by it. Foreigners are apt to admire it extravagantly or consider it a complete bore. Frank Lloyd Wright, the great American architect, spent four years in Japan supervising the construction of Tokyo's Imperial Hotel (now, sadly, torn down) and came to admire "this science or art of most gracefully . . . getting a cup of tea made." Nonetheless he confessed that its fine points somewhat eluded him and that he eventually became bored by its severity and discipline.

To the Japanese, however, the tea ceremony is no less entertaining for being disciplined and severe. Take, for example, the demands of *kaiseki,* which of all the cuisines of the world puts special emphasis upon harmonious combinations of color—not only in the food itself, but between the food and the dishes. That is to say, the food must delight the eye delicately, as a Japanese painting does, or a flower. Similarly, it must give off a fragrance that does not leap up and startle the nose, but is elusive and hard to place. If the eye and the nose are not charmed, then—to a Japanese of any breeding whatsoever—the food simply does not taste good. A Japanese is not merely taking in food, he is taking in a complete sensory experience. To do so he must "pay attention" in a special way, and paying attention is what the tea ceremony is all about.

One can begin to learn about this special attentiveness by putting oneself in the role of the host—although properly speaking, no one can be a tea-ceremony host without years of intensive study. To start with, the host may have got up at dawn to pluck mushrooms or wild herbs from the nearby woods or to pick out a fish at the morning market. In any case, he will have chosen all the food himself, selecting only what is in season and available lo-

cally. He will also have swept and prepared his teahouse and his garden, sprinkling each stepping stone in the garden path, being sure that a few leaves or a few pine needles remain in order to present an appearance of natural, seasonal charm. For the tea hut itself, which is made of the simplest but most exquisite materials, he will have chosen a hanging scroll and arranged a few seasonal flowers to please the tastes of his particular guests.

In the same way he will prepare the food with great care, according to the season, decorating the rice in the springtime with tiny cherry blossoms and flavoring chopped squid with the leaf buds of little fresh Japanese peppers. The food will also be appropriate to the time of day—often the formal tea ceremony starts at noon, but dawn and evening also make beautiful settings—and the food will look well in the dishes he has chosen to use. He is, in other words, creating a mood, and every part of the meal, even the timing with which he serves it, must further that mood.

The essence of the tea ceremony is harmony—harmony between host and guest, between the meal and the season, between the food and its containers, between the flavor and texture of one food and another. The host may, for in-

In a corner of her home, a Kyoto matron instructs her two daughters in the tea ceremony. The purpose of such lessons is to help the girls reach the level of proficiency required of refined and capable Japanese hostesses. The mother, seated in the position prescribed for a hostess, watches as one daughter sips tea. Then the cup will be set down, refilled and offered to her sister.

stance, decide to create a tea ceremony around a particularly flavorful mushroom, the *matsutake,* which is found under pine trees in October, when the frost has turned the leaves to splendid colors on the forest hillsides. Since the *matsutake* is available for only a short time, he will serve it in as many ways as he can. He may start by offering his guests—on an orange and yellow tray that matches the autumnal colors of the season—a lacquer box of rice cooked with chestnuts, a lacquer dish holding pieces of *horenso* (Japanese spinach) boiled with sliced *matsutake* caps, and a soup garnished with more *matsutake* caps combined with small pieces of raw sea eel. To further set off the taste of the mushrooms he may follow these dishes with one of cooked chicken in which the *matsutake* caps are combined with *togarashi* (a small, pungent red pepper) and with *zuiki,* the crisp white stem of the taro plant.

This still leaves the *matsutake* stems unused, a waste that would be considered bad form. Being less delicate, they are not cooked with the caps, but instead are served separately. First they are sliced longitudinally. Then they are chopped and placed inside a circle of cooked sea eel, and arranged on fresh fern leaves in a shallow basket, a countrified container more in keeping with the relative coarseness of the stems than fine lacquer would be. Into the basket also goes a bit of grated red carrot called *momiji oroshi* (literally "maple leaves," because that's what they look like), along with a few richly flavored leaves of the beefsteak plant *shiso,* cooked *tempura* style.

In this meal the *matsutake* mushroom has been used in many ways—in a soup, with a green, with chicken and pungent peppers, with fish and aromatic leaves—yet no guest could possibly feel sated. For one thing, the mushrooms are in season too briefly for anyone to become tired of their taste; for another, the host has used them sparingly, adding only a few to each dish. The whole effect is very simple and very subtle, and this is what *kaiseki* is meant to be. It would not be considered proper, for instance, to serve something out of season, unless the host did so for the sheer joy of pleasing one particular guest, a friend known to have a passion for that food—and even then, that passion should be known to the rest of the guests.

Neither would it be considered proper to go out of the way to get a *kaiseki* ingredient, to send to another city for a certain fish, for example, or an unusual variety of chestnut. This confuses expense with imagination, and *kaiseki* is not based on extravagance. Rather it is something of a game, an exercise in style, in which the host seeks to create the most beautiful effects from the simplest possible means. Thus for flavoring one turns to wild leaves rather than cultivated ones—to the crisp green leaves of the *shiso* plant, for instance, which when chopped up add color to a dish and when used whole add texture. And if the meal is based on one stellar ingredient—on the sweetfish called *ayu,* for instance—then every part of the fish will be used, but in different guises: the flesh may be roasted, the skin and head served with boiled vegetables, the innards put into the soup. From this it follows, in theory, that a poor man can put on as fine a *kaiseki* as a rich man, since what is essentially required of the cook is inventiveness and imagination.

Theory does not always accord with practice. While emphasis is primarily on simplicity of form, it does not follow that the content of the meal is inexpensive. As a matter of fact, the ingredients used are often the most

Continued on page 145

TEA CEREMONY UTENSILS
Listed below are the Japanese objects in this photograph.

1 *Kensui*—bowl for waste water
2 *Hishaku*—water dipper
3 *Futaoki*—rest for kettle lid or dipper
4 *Kobukusa*—small silk napkin
5 *Fukusa*—another silk napkin
6 *Sensu*—fan
7 *Fukusa bassami*—handbag
8 *Chawan*—tea bowl
9 *Chakin*—linen tea cloth
10 *Natsume*—tea caddy
11 *Chashaku*—bamboo teaspoon
12 *Chasen*—bamboo whisk
13 *Mizusashi*—cold-water jar
14 *Shikiita*—protective tile on which brazier stands
15 *Furo*—brazier
16 *Okama*—teakettle

A Time-Hallowed Ceremony That Nourishes the Japanese Soul

The simplest definition of the traditional tea ceremony is that it is an occasion when tea is made, served and sipped with graceful patterns of motion, as pictured on the following pages. Presiding over it are tea masters or their students, more than half of whom today are women. The ceremony may take place in the principal room of any home, but ideally it is held in a rustic tea hut, decorated only by a simple wall scroll and a flower arrangement. A subtle fragrance of incense fills the room. The guests inspect the objects of the tea service, often of great antiquity, and comment on their history and beauty. In sum, then, the tea ceremony is far more than the social occasion it appears to be. To the Japanese, it serves as an island of serenity where one can refresh his senses and nourish his soul.

After the guests have arrived, the host (the hostess in this case) brings in all of the utensils needed for the tea ceremony, except for the brazier and kettle, which are already in place. The various objects are then arranged in a harmonious and artistic pattern, and the hostess proceeds ritually to clean the immaculate teaspoon, tea caddy and the single tea bowl. One at a time she wipes the teaspoon and tea caddy with the silk napkin called the *fukusa*. Now she picks up the bamboo dipper—a brand-new dipper is used each time a tea ceremony is performed—and transfers a small quantity of hot water from the teakettle to the tea bowl. To wipe and dry the bowl, she folds a small oblong piece of pure linen cloth called a *chakin*, also brand-new, over the sides of the bowl, and turns it round and round in her hands. Done in a deliberate manner, the rotation of the bowl helps to steady her hands and clear her mind. Thus the hostess' public washing of these objects not only assures absolute cleanliness but also shows the thoroughness of her concern for her guests and helps to concentrate her attention on the demands of the ceremony to come.

When the tea bowl has been wiped dry, the hostess places the tea cloth on the rim of the kettle lid *(background)* and sets the bowl directly before her. Next, from its perch on the lacquered tea caddy, she lifts the teaspoon, a slender piece of bamboo curved at one tip and no more than eight inches long, and with gentle, careful motions she opens the caddy, trying not to disturb the slightly mounded shape of the tea, brilliant in its golden setting. Like all Japanese foods, the finely ground tea is a visual delight. Various blends of tea are used, depending upon the degree of formality of the occasion. The hostess measures two or three small scoops of tea into the bowl, delicately pouring the powder to form a minuscule mound that repeats the shape of the tea in the caddy. When the last scoop has been tipped into the bowl, she taps the spoon against the bowl's inside rim to shake off any specks that might still cling to the spoon. The tea masters say that the soft sound of bamboo against the bowl—neither too sharp nor too muffled—helps focus the minds of the hostess and guests on the ordered procession of the ritual.

Now ready to add the water—the freshest, purest available—the hostess lowers the bamboo dipper open side down into the kettle. With a graceful, continuous motion, she rotates the dipper as it sinks into the water and so avoids disconcerting gurgles as the dipper fills. Then she lifts it out, places it over the center of the tea bowl and tips the dipper just enough to pour about one third of the boiling water over the tea. To assure the water's boiling to the proper degree, she takes great care beforehand to prepare a bed of ashes, either in a square sunken firebox or in a movable brazier, that will create just the right amount of draft necessary for a glowing charcoal fire. This assures an even heat under the singing teakettle. Guests listen appreciatively to this melodic sound, often likened to the wind sighing through pine trees or the plashing of a gentle stream. For the hostess, the kettle's song reveals whether the water has reached the proper temperature. If the bubbles should roll and surge excessively, the hostess will dip cold water from the chinaware jar *(right foreground)* into the hot kettle to "restore the youth of the water."

The final step in preparing the tea involves an object perfectly formed for its function. This is the *chasen,* a handmade whisk whose shape, developed many centuries ago, has defied improvement. The whisk whips the tea and water together into what one tea master has described as a "liquid jade froth." More than 50 steps are required to turn a single piece of bamboo into a whisk, formed at one end into a handle and curved at the other to form small tines, and the best whisks come from a town near Kyoto called Chasenmura, which literally means "tea-whisk village." Despite their beauty and utility, whisks frequently are used only once and then discarded. Since each guest drinks the entire contents of the bowl, the hostess whips a relatively small amount of tea and water for each serving. Her guests watch attentively, for to attain the technique required to whip the tea with a vigorous but graceful motion implies long hours of practice and years of actual experience. A simple ceremony like this one lasts about 40 minutes, but ceremonies that include the elegant meal called *kaiseki* may last for four hours.

When she has whisked the tea, the hostess places the tea bowl on the silk *kobukusa;* the guest picks up both in the manner illustrated below and raises it in thanks. Then the guest turns the cup to a suitable spot—dictated by the bowl's shape and decoration—and sips slowly, appreciatively noting the tea's froth and color as well as its taste and aroma.

expensive foods available. And while to the untutored eye the utensils, the trays and the bowls may seem simple and unassuming, this is a simplicity and lack of ostentation that may cost thousands of dollars to achieve. A single tea bowl that has the combined attributes of having been made by one of the great artists of the past, and of having pleased one of the legendary tea masters sufficiently for him to deign to sign it, can cost $100,000 or more. From the Western point of view, there is no art on earth that is less pretentious and more expensive than the utensils used in the tea ceremony.

However, the ceremony can be performed with bowls and kettles that are well within the reach of Japanese with modest incomes. Good contemporary bowls are available for $25, and better ones can be bought at prices ranging up to $2,000. Some of these objects may even have been made by craftsmen whose work is so fine that the government has conferred upon certain of these brilliant artists the title of "Living National Treasure."

Despite the inroads that increasing industrialization has made on tradition, the tea ceremony remains a national institution of Japan. Literally millions of men and women are enrolled in one or another of the schools of tea. The largest of the schools, Urasenke, also has a televised program of instruction, and has now even extended its activities to a branch in New York City. Intense rivalry characterizes the relationship of the major schools, and each of them claims to be the authentic transmitter of the purest traditions of simplicity and beauty.

Sometimes the simplicity of *kaiseki* is dictated not only by style, but by an exquisite concern for the occasion. Here, for example, is a menu for a September *otsukimi,* or moon viewing, when the moon is especially luminous and the fronds of the pampas grass are at their best. Because the guests' attention will be focused elsewhere—on looking at the moon—the meal has been chosen to enhance that experience and at the same time remain unobtrusive. It consists of a small heap of *shiso*-flavored rice in a lacquer bucket; two glowing halves of hard-cooked egg, which suggest the moon, on a pale, footed dish, set off by a few soy beans cooked in their pods; a small dish of stewed *ayu* and a similar dish of chopped mackerel lightly cooked in vinegar. Making magic of this quiet feast is a bowl of *misoshiru,* brown as the earth, in which is floating a white circle of fish cake *(shinjo)*—another echo of the moon—decorated with a few Chinese pea pods and brown beans that have been arranged to look like a spray of flowering bush clover.

The desire to make everything in *kaiseki* absolutely perfect for the occasion extends, of course, to the perfect pleasure of the guests. Nothing should startle their eyes; nothing should make them gasp. One of the host's first considerations should be what his guests are used to, what they can appreciate and enjoy. He is supposed to cater to their tastes rather than his own—an excellent principle in entertaining—and he should make sure beforehand that they all like what he plans to serve. He should not, for instance, offer some extremely refined dish to people who would find it more impressive than good to eat. And he should manage the meal so subtly that no one really notices how marvelously it has been planned and executed. His guests should feel, not notice; anything noticed may have been overdone.

To a foreigner unfamiliar with *kaiseki,* its delicacy is sometimes too overwhelming for him to appreciate. He may not see, for instance, that the colors of the dishes placed before him pick up the colors of the garden he has just walked through. Nor may he realize that the vegetables he is eating in early spring are the young shoots of bamboo and butterbur and fiddle fern, all of them picked wild. But in summer, when it is almost too hot to eat, even an untutored guest can appreciate the light *kaiseki,* almost a picnic, placed before him by a thoughtful host. On a simple black tray, accompanied by a clear-glass *sake* cup that looks like a piece of sculptured ice, there may be a little ceramic dish with a few pale slices of *sashimi,* slightly cooked and cooled to make it more tender; the *sashimi* will be set off by tiny cucumbers, still carrying their tender yellow blossoms. The main dish will make him think —as it was meant to—of a feast in a cool hillside grove. It will consist of delicious morsels of various foods, cooked ever so slightly, then cooled and arranged on the freshest green bamboo section obtainable: rice balls with fresh red ginger stems; golden eggs with green bell peppers; pale pink shrimp; tiny eggplants roasted in *miso.* As a pungent garnish to this soothing snack, there may be a few green leaves of *shiso.*

Such a meal invites nibbling, but in fact *kaiseki* food is not meant to be nibbled at. The economy practiced in its cooking extends to the eating as well; everything put before the guest is meant to be consumed. To make this simpler, the portions are kept small and very few things are served with bones or other inedible parts. Only rarely, and then for certain special occasions, is lobster served in its shell. As a result, the plates at the end of a *kaiseki* meal will be quite clean-looking.

Behind this cleanliness is a principle—to be immaculate in one's surroundings contributes to purity of heart—and this principle, like all the others associated with *kaiseki* derives from the rituals of the tea ceremony.

When the tea ceremony was evolving, the patrons of the great tea masters were men of wealth and power, and the tea ceremony came to be surrounded by an aura of luxury. Every ingredient, every utensil, everything seen or touched or tasted was the finest obtainable. At the same time the ceremony was never ostentatious, for the great tea masters were followers of Zen and subscribed to the Zen ideals of simplicity, serenity, withdrawal and contemplation. We know, for instance, that the greatest of the tea masters, Sen Rikyu, always stressed the principle of "less is more," and served his noble guests meals of the utmost simplicity. There is a record, in a 16th Century diary, of one of Sen Rikyu's *kaiseki* menus for a tea ceremony given in the fall of the year 1556. It is not a frugal meal but it is far less elaborate than a similar meal would be today.

Sen Rikyu's *kaiseki* began with a group of four dishes in black lacquer bowls on a black lacquer tray: one contained raw carp and vegetables, another contained asparagus, a third contained a soup of crushed duck and vegetable, and the fourth was a bowl of rice. This was followed by a plate of sweets served on a legged table or tray. The meal was concluded with skewered quail and pepper in an earthenware bowl, accompanied by two pieces of raw sea bream on a plate and a few pickles. Today a typical meal would offer a much greater variety of taste sensations. The fish, possibly sea bass *sashimi,* would be served with needle-cut cucumber prepared with *wasabi* (horseradish) and vinegar. The bean-paste soup would contain rice-flour dumplings and a garnish of *shiso* leaves and pungent green pepper.

The soup and fish would be followed by a plate of cooked foods of various kinds—boiled egg, salted duck meat and citron-flavored broth. After this would come something broiled or baked, perhaps a broiled sweetfish such as *ayu* accompanied by its roe. A clear soup would follow, possibly of jellyfish with needle-cut ginger for seasoning, and this would appear with side dishes of plain-fried lobster and plain-boiled taro, a potatolike root vegetable. And all of this would be accompanied from time to time by rice and *sake.*

Whatever the menu, a good *kaiseki* meal should offer the same range of sensations to the eyes and nose as it does to the palate: this is the essence of *kaiseki.* And beyond that it should also offer the body nourishment appropriate to the season. There is a wonderful *kaiseki* menu devised to be served in late December around the turning of the year, a time rich in associations for the Japanese. New Year's is one of their most important festivals, and during the celebrations they also commemorate the death of a band of heroes, 47 faithful samurai who gave their lives to avenge a terrible wrong done their lord in the year 1701. Both these events, along with December's cold weather, are taken into account in a meal that is hearty enough to ward off the chill and delicate enough to tempt even the sternest warrior from his duties.

This December menu begins with one of the most thoughtful soups imaginable. It is made of *miso*—but a white *miso* rather than the common red variety. Floating in the snowy soup is a piece of *tofu,* bean-curd cake, that has been frozen outdoors and thawed so that it has acquired a special texture and flavor. The first frozen *tofu* came from a snowbound temple on Mount Koya, where its freezing—perhaps unavoidable—became the occasion for a new experience in taste.

Since there are few fresh vegetables in December, the giant radish, *daikon,* comes into its own and is served boiled, with a sauce of *miso* paste, as a side dish to the soup. After this there follows a dish that ingeniously commemorates the encirclement and death of the ancient heroes. A slice of red snapper has been salted in the morning, and by evening it has contracted into a circle. Into its center goes a small mound of boiled noodles, *soba,* because this is what the heroes are said to have eaten before attacking their lord's enemies —and also because *soba* is one of Japan's favorite winter foods. On top of the pale yellow *soba* is a little piece of dark-brown seaweed and a few slivers of scallions. Looking at this little composition one thinks, aha, the moon crossed by clouds—and remembers that the heroes set out on a moonlit night. Then, lest this allusion be carried too far, the final dish is a sturdy combination of octopus and sweet potatoes served on rough, country-style ware.

The effect of this meal, with its tones of brown and white—like snow on the roof of a wooden house—is quite extraordinary. Yet the ingredients that compose it are not in the least unusual in Japan—all of them are simple, seasonal, local and fresh. What transforms them into a memorable eating experience is spirit and thought. *Kaiseki,* they say, takes the right materials, the right flavorings and seasonings, and the right heart. Without the right heart there can be no true *kaiseki.* To think out a menu perfectly, to choose exactly the right dishes, to arrange the food with perfect artistry, to serve the meal with smoothness and finesse, to make every moment one of happy refinement—this is true *kaiseki.* No wonder so few people become great tea hosts. And no wonder people who care about food and style keep trying.

Tea-Ceremony Cooking

Overleaf: A meal like the one shown on the next two pages is an example of *kaiseki ryori* (tea-ceremony cooking), in which Japanese formal dining reaches its pinnacle. Following the rules laid down by the great tea masters of old, the host tries —under ideal conditions—to use only locally obtained, seasonal foods. The trays, bowls and serving dishes are chosen with the same care as the tea ceremony utensils *(see pages 141-144)* and each food must be perfectly complemented by its container. The *kaiseki* pictured is, by the choice of foods, an appropriate one for late spring or early summer. The courses, numbered in the order of serving, are as follows:

1 Rice in a black lacquer bowl comes with soup flavored with soybean paste, and above these is salted raw fluke garnished with asparagus.
2 A clear soup is dominated by a square of white *tofu* (soybean curd) with slivers of fish paste and crab meat and is garnished with *warabi,* a fern.
3 Broiled porgy is in a precious pottery bowl and steamed rice in the large black lacquer bowl.
4 In an antique china bowl, bamboo shoots and *fuki,* a Japanese vegetable, are garnished with *sansho* (pepper) leaf.
5 A clear kelp broth is served in a covered bowl.
6 Lima beans, from the fields, are coupled with shrimp from the sea, stuffed with egg yolks.
7 Pickles made from squash accompany white Chinese cabbage.
8 *Yuto,* a soup made from burned rice, is served from a red lacquer pitcher.
9 *Sake* pot and cups: the drink is served throughout the meal.

6
5
1

8
7
4
3
2

VII

Eating Out as a Way of Life

The Kawataro Restaurant, located in Fukuoka on Kyushu Island, serves only the freshest seafood. Caught in the nearby Inland Sea, the fish and shellfish are stored alive in the large fishpool directly behind the counter *(background)*. As the owner serves Ise lobster and sea bream to customers, a helper nets another sea bream to fill a new order.

The husband who takes six hours or so to make his way home from the office several times a week, and who often turns up somewhat unsteady on his feet, may automatically be suspected by Westerners of philandering. Not so in Japan, for it is an equally valid possibility, as we have seen in Chapter 5, that he has merely been eating and drinking and enjoying himself, and perhaps flirting harmlessly with a bar hostess. Far from bringing shame on himself and his wife, the Japanese who habitually dines out earns a reputation as an important fellow, someone who is tuned in to the affairs of the world and who knows how to live well. For in Japan good living means restaurant eating; in variety, in taste and in the esthetics of food presentation, restaurant meals are considerably above anything the average housewife can produce. And this generalization applies not only to the lofty establishments that serve as the guardians and exemplars of Japanese *grande cuisine* but also to thousands and thousands of tiny workaday eating places crammed together in the narrow beehive streets of urban Japan.

I have eaten thousands of restaurant meals in Japan—either delivered to my inn or at the restaurants themselves, and because my wife is Japanese I have eaten at innumerable places where the presence of a Westerner would ordinarily create a stir. Only twice has the food been disappointing, and never have I encountered a Japanese version of the "greasy spoon" joint. Moreover, I doubt that Japan's consistently high restaurant standards will ever decline—as have those of the French, for instance—because restaurants and drinking places play a crucial role in Japan's social and business life, serving many needs that are met in other countries by quite different institutions.

Japanese-English Glossary

DASHI: *all-purpose soup stock*
FUGU: *globefish*
KATSUOBUSHI: *dried bonito*
MIRIN: *sweet rice wine*
NORI: *laver seaweed*
PONZU: *soy-sauce and citrus-juice dressing*
SASHIMI: *slices of raw fish*
SUKIYAKI: *simmered beef dish*
TATAMI: *straw matting*
TEMPURA: *deep-fried food*
TERIYAKI: *broiling method using a "mirin"-and-soy-sauce marinade*
TOFU: *soybean curd*
TOKONOMA: *alcove with decorative items*
TORO: *belly flesh of tuna*
TSUKEMONO: *pickled things*
WASABI: *green horseradish*

For example, the grandest restaurants are in effect private domains for the affluent and powerful, the equivalent—but with much more grace and beauty—of the stuffy and exclusive clubs of London's Pall Mall or the private dining rooms maintained by large American corporations. In the isolated rooms of Japan's most elegant eating places, over *sake* cups and *sashimi* and a full array of meticulously presented formal dishes, cabinet ministers, bureaucrats and members of parliament and their financial backers come to most of the political and economic decisions that govern Japan. While geisha keep the *sake* flowing and artfully sustain the mood of harmony and good cheer through any arguments that might develop, political compromises are worked out, candidates for office selected, alliances forged, influence peddled and—occasionally—officials corrupted. Leading political figures hold court nearly every night at their favorite restaurants, and everyone in the political world knows which restaurant "belongs" to which party faction. In some cases the powerful politico may actually share the ownership of the restaurant, having set up a favored geisha as its proprietress.

Lower down the scale there are restaurants that are forums for the stylish and fashionable, like the salons of Paris and the penthouses of New York. Restaurants provide the setting for reunions, parties and banquets, for testimonial dinners honoring champions of judo or professors of history, and for receptions publicizing a new movie or a new mammoth oil tanker.

Entertaining in Japan is virtually synonymous with going to a restaurant. Most modern Japanese houses and apartments lack the uncluttered natural grace of the Japanese architectural ideal. Therefore they cannot provide the atmosphere that the Japanese consider necessary for the full esthetic enjoyment of a meal. But restaurants, even ordinary ones, specialize in atmosphere, for their proprietors realize they are supposed to fulfill the average person's yearning for the beautiful, uncrowded and harmonious—the better things of life that he cannot afford at home but for which he hungers deeply.

Conjuring up this atmosphere requires careful—and expensive—attention to every detail, not only to the food itself. Just as the articles that adorn the *tokonoma* are precisely arranged, so must a dish and tray be of the right color and material to bring out the hue and texture of the food upon it. Equal care and expense are lavished on what will be seen beyond the tray and dishes: the room, the garden, the view.

Even in the modest restaurants squeezed together like so many hand-crafted doll houses in the narrow alleys of the big cities, considerable effort is made to provide some kind of natural view, often when a space of only five or 10 square feet is available. In Kyoto, where attention to nature and atmosphere is at its zenith, customers at one small restaurant can rinse their fingers in a perfect miniature stream that babbles along the counter in front of them, landscaped with rocks and moss and dwarf trees. A neighboring shop seats its clientele in booths around a Lilliputian pond, fitted out with tiny bridges and teahouses and swarming with live and very active carp. Pond and dining area together take up an area less than 20 feet square, and traffic is roaring by just 50 feet away, but seated in that cameo garden, watching the carp jump and savoring the excellent food, you feel as if you have stumbled on a corner of Eden.

Japanese restaurants could not provide so elaborate an atmosphere if the customers had to pay for it out of their meager salaries. Fortunately, the restaurant business can depend on the huge patronage of the *sha yo zoku,* the "company business tribe," or, as we would say, the expense-account crowd. Expense-account eating and drinking is a much bigger enterprise in Japan than anywhere else; 90 per cent of the food and drink consumed in the better restaurants of Tokyo is paid for directly by one business firm or another, and not by the customers. The diner simply signs the bill, leaving his name card if he is not well-known to the manager, and at the end of the month his company's cashier will pay the bill.

It is safe to say that no deal is ever signed in Japan, no big sale ever concluded, unless the individuals concerned have eaten and drunk together at a restaurant or bar. The Japanese do not like to deal with strangers, and in order to avoid this necessity Japanese businessmen spend vast sums and long hours establishing and maintaining good personal relationships in every direction, with everyone in business or government whose affairs are likely to touch theirs in any fashion. The best way to do this is to take the other fellow to a bar or restaurant or cabaret—or preferably all three; he will reciprocate later, and a good time will be had by all. Once Japanese have dined and wined together they are friends, and business can then proceed on a basis of mutual personal obligation. To the Japanese an agreement confirmed personally is much more binding than the ironclad clauses of a contract; failure to meet a promise made to someone with whom you have exchanged *sake* cups and sung old songs is a breach of honor, but a written contract with a stranger is merely a piece of paper with no equivalent moral weight. Many Westerners, trying to deal with the Japanese in a no-nonsense, business-is-business manner, have discovered to their dismay that without personal relations and restaurant entertaining nothing gets done.

The recipients of expense-account entertainment are not only officials of the government or of other companies whose good will is important; Japanese executives may use tax-free company money to entertain department heads within their own companies, the department heads may do so for section chiefs, and so on quite a way down the line until the lowliest clerk can on occasion expect to be given his night to howl—all in the name of personnel relations and business efficiency.

The government tax office makes no effort to ensure that business matters are discussed at any of these great or small affairs: that would destroy the whole purpose of the exercise. The only limitation is on the overall amount spent. Every year each company is entitled to deduct from taxable income all "social expenses" up to one quarter of one per cent of its total capitalization, and half of such expenses over that. This unofficial subsidy to Japan's bars and restaurants adds up to more than $1.6 billion a year, a sum equal to one tenth of the national budget.

Important politicians and captains of industry are more or less obliged, because of their status, to take their guests to the great restaurants where dinner, drinks and entertainment can cost more than $50 per person. The lower echelons of the *sha yo zoku,* and those unfortunates who must bring their wallets with them, may rarely dine at the artistic summit, but what they miss in elegance and perfection they can more than make up for in the variety offered by everyday restaurant eating. For 20 cents hungry Japanese can fill up with a tasty bowl of *ramen,* Chinese-style noodles; for $10 or so they may

Many proprietors of Japanese restaurants entice customers inside by displaying remarkably realistic plastic facsimiles of their specialties outside the front door. Small labels give names and prices of the dishes and, in the larger cities, English translations. For example, at top right in this display case is *kanisu,* boiled crab, at 400 yen (about $1.10).

Continued on page 161

NOODLES TWO WAYS
At the Yabuizu noodle restaurant, diners enjoy *zarusoba*, noodles and soup served separately *(above, right)*, and *tempura soba*, noodle soup topped with a fried prawn *(above, left)*.

A SAMPLING OF *SUSHI*
The chef *(opposite)* at the Isogen Restaurant rolls up *sushi* (vinegared rice) in a sheath of seaweed to make cylindrical *makizushi*. In the center of the large bowl are slices of these rolls, now stuffed with tuna or cucumber. The other *sushi* morsels are mostly mounds of rice topped with a slice of raw fish. The small, round box on the left contains *chirashi*, loose rice covered with fish. The blocklike boxes, stacked upside down, are wooden *sake* cups.

A Sampling of Specialty Restaurants

The Japanese like to eat out—and they do, with a fervor and a frequency that are unmatched in the West. As a consequence, restaurants not only flourish by the thousands but also come in every size and description. They range from the elegant and expensive preserves of the wealthy and influential to tiny cubbyholes and mobile food bars. Of all the eating establishments, the public most often patronizes the restaurants that specialize in one way or another—perhaps in a distinctive cooking technique or in serving a single kind of food or in making the dishes associated with a particular region of Japan. On this and the following pages are shown some of Tokyo's most popular types of specialty restaurants. There are countless others as well, but despite their diversity, they share several qualities: the food is uniformly good both in preparation and presentation, the restaurants are immaculately clean, and the prices are fair and often inexpensive.

白鶴
剣菱

TEMPURA, PIECE BY PIECE

The chef at Ten-ichi serves each *tempura* item as it reaches deep-fried perfection, and is ready with a new piece when the customer finishes eating the previous one. Shown below are vegetables, ginkgo nuts and seafoods awaiting *tempura* frying.

SLICES OF RAW FISH
A cheerful chef at the Otomo *sashimi* restaurant poses proudly with a few of the many raw fish dishes advertised on the long, handwritten menu that lies on his counter. The fish used for *sashimi* not only must be as fresh as possible but also must be expertly sliced to make the most of its flavor.

GRILLS FROM THE WEST
The Western-style hat on a cook at the Ginsen, an expensive steak house *(below)*, is worn because this type of restaurant was originally designed to cater to foreigners. But these establishments quickly attracted many Japanese. The principal dish is steak and vegetables grilled on the large stainless-steel *teppan*.

BARBECUE, JAPANESE STYLE

Yakitori—food grilled on skewers over a charcoal fire—sends up a tantalizing aroma that has customers waiting eagerly for service at Torishige Restaurant. On the skewers *(from left)* are chicken, duck liver and ground-chicken patties.

SNACKS AND *SAKE* ON WHEELS
A late-night sight on Japanese streets is the food wagon. From its sizzling grill come fish, potatoes, eggs, giant radish and fried soybean curd. Hunched on stools, customers savor the *sake* and the snacks provided by the mobile eatery.

ONE-POT COOKING
The Junidanya Restaurant specializes in *shabu shabu,* one kind of *nabemono* (one-pot) dish made with thinly sliced beef and vegetables. The ingredients are first stirred in a bubbling broth. Then they are dipped in sauces, garnished with red pepper, salt and sesame seeds and eaten with assorted pickles.

1
2
3
4
5

treat their palates to an epicurean masterwork of raw *fugu* and *tempura;* in between those extremes stretches a bewildering choice of restaurants for every budget, every taste, every mood. Someone has calculated that in Tokyo alone there are 105,000 licensed restaurants (not counting bars and coffee shops), or more than one for every 100 people. However, that figure only proves that Tokyo is big, its restaurants small, and that the Japanese like to eat out. For the gourmet, a more interesting statistic would be the number of *kinds* of restaurants—which no one to my knowledge has ever totted up. My guess is that you could go to a different type of eating place every day and not even begin to repeat yourself for many months. Perhaps that is what we really mean when we call them "everyday" restaurants.

There are restaurants that serve a six- or seven-course meal in which the main ingredient of every dish is *tofu*—and it is not monotonous at all. Some restaurants handle only whale meat offered both as *sukiyaki* and raw *sashimi,* some specialize in crab (broiled, or vinegared, or boiled with vegetables and noodles), and some do all kinds of things with all parts of the turtle. One excellent Ginza eatery offers nothing but sardines—raw, fried, salt-broiled, soy-broiled, mashed, curried or steeped in broth. And up in the mountains, near the resort of Nikko, is an unpretentious country restaurant purveying only carp in dozens of styles ranging from *arai,* a kind of *sashimi,* to a thick-sauce melange resembling Chinese sweet-and-sour fish. Other seafood restaurants concentrate not on one species but on a single method of preparation such as broiling, cooking at the table or, of course, *sashimi.*

One of the most common restaurant foods is *yakitori,* skewered bits of chicken, chicken liver and scallions grilled over a charcoal fire *(Recipe Index.)* Four or five little chunks are impaled on each slim bamboo *kushi* and brushed with a *teriyaki* sauce before grilling. To eat, you pick up the skewer and bite off the tidbits one by one. Tiny quail eggs, ginkgo nuts, green peppers and other delicacies get the same treatment. Many *yakitori* shops are little more than open-air stalls, and you can easily find them by following your nose: their charcoal stoves face the street and the smoky, appetizing aroma of grilling chicken pervades the neighborhood. Fancier establishments do their grilling in a pit set in the middle of a *tatami*-carpeted room. They usually offer a complete and graduated meal, starting with tiny sparrows, grilled whole on the skewer (the bones are fine enough to chew), and going up through quail, chicken, duck livers and finally pieces of duck.

Then there is *teppanyaki,* a plain and hearty method of grilling meat and chicken on a metal plate. There are numerous ways of doing it, and one can find restaurants specializing in each: *okonomiyaki,* in which you get your own little gas or charcoal grill and a plate of meats and vegetables and then do it all yourself; *karibayaki,* or "hunters' grill," where your kimonoed waitress manages things on a perforated metal dome that lets just enough juices run off to keep the meat dry but tender; *ishiyaki,* in which a sizzling stone takes the place of the hot plate; and *batayaki* (*bata* being the Japanese' best approximation of "butter"), meats grilled in butter. Similar to these, and very popular in Japan, are restaurants offering "Genghis Khan barbecue," which is mutton grilled over charcoal, and a Korean beef barbecue, with a hot sauce, cooked the same way. In recent years the Japanese have adapted *teppanyaki* to Western-style steak, using the superb Matsuzaka and Kobe beef.

Restaurants like Tokyo's Sasagayuki *(opposite)* serve entire meals of *tofu* (soybean curd), one of the most versatile of Japanese foods. Although it has little flavor of its own, it absorbs other flavors easily, so *tofu* is used in innumerable dishes both for its soft, comforting texture and for the different tastes it adopts. Spread before three diners is an assortment of *tofu* dishes that includes: *giseidofu,* uncooked *tofu* topped by strips of deep-fried *tofu (1); namashoyu dofu, tofu* boiled in weak soy sauce flavored with lemon and ginger *(2); hiyayako dofu,* another uncooked but chilled *tofu,* this time with a spicy soy sauce *(3); iridofu,* or *tofu* scrambled with chicken and peas *(4); koyadofu,* dried *tofu* boiled in soy-sauce soup with mushrooms *(5).*

At these "Japanese steak houses," originally developed for the tourist trade but now popular with Japanese as well, the customers sit around a huge grill on which a chef deftly manipulates sizzling chunks of tender beef and parcels them out, done to order, with bean sprouts and *ponzu* sauce.

Many Tokyo restaurants serve food Osaka style, and Tokyo-style establishments can be found in Osaka, so that expatriates from both cities can eat happily far from home. (The two cuisines are fundamentally the same but differences do exist—Osaka food is richer and sweeter, for instance—and despite rapid modern transportation that has lessened the distance between the two cities, little blending of the two styles has taken place.) In Tokyo, moreover, one can find a seemingly endless yet ever-increasing number of restaurants specializing in foods from one region of the country or another. These regional restaurants cater primarily to the hundreds of thousands of homesick small-town lads who have come to the big city to make their fortunes. These places just ooze nostalgia: the excellent food is authentic, imported waitresses in traditional regional costume speak the local dialect and sing local folk songs, and dishes and décor reflect the region's culture and crafts. The dreamy expression in the eyes of the customers is a sure indication that the restaurant has evoked memories of home villages. By eating at a few of these places a foreigner can simulate a tour of Japan cheaply, quickly and without ever leaving Tokyo.

Sliding slightly down the epicurean scale to simpler fare, but still within the range of good eating, we come to restaurants specializing in *chazuke* (in which tea or *dashi* is poured over the rice after it is cooked) and others devoted to *chameshi,* rice cooked with other ingredients. *Chameshi* (the word means "tea rice") originated several centuries ago with Buddhist priests who cooked their rice with brewed tea instead of plain water, but nowadays soy sauce and *mirin* are used instead of tea, and in the fancier versions, usually called *kamameshi,* or "pot rice," many kinds of seafood, meats, vegetables and mushrooms, chopped fine, may be added. The better *kamameshi* restaurants offer a staggering selection of ingredients and combinations, and cook each portion to order in an individual pot that is then set before the diner in a scooped-out block of wood. Some Tokyo restaurants, like the crowded, lusty Tori-gin in the Ginza, serve both *yakitori* and *kamameshi;* with *sake* or beer it's a wonderful combination.

Other rice restaurants include those concentrating on *nigiri meshi,* which is a ball of rice pressed together around *katsuobushi* flakes or some kind of fish paste or *tsukemono,* and sometimes wrapped in a sheet of *nori,* and other shops specializing in any of a number of kinds of *domburi,* that bowl of rice with sauces and meats or fowl that housewives sometimes make for lunch out of leftovers. *Domburi* is often topped with a piece of shrimp *tempura* (in which case it is called *tendon*) or with a pork cutlet *(katsudon).*

The lowly pork cutlet, *tonkatsu* (*ton* is pork, *katsu* is the Japanese pronunciation of "cutlet"), is a standard workingmen's meal available in many inexpensive eateries, but there are restaurants that specialize in this dish. Breaded and fried lightly in oil, *tonkatsu* is commonly served with a thick, pungent sauce on a bed of shredded cabbage spiced with *shiso,* the beefsteak plant; the cabbage drains the grease from the cutlet and the *shiso* cuts the oiliness.

Over the doorway of every restaurant hangs a short curtain, a *noren,* which the customers have to duck under or brush through in order to enter. It is set at a tantalizing height, just below eye level, so that a passerby cannot see anything but the floor of the restaurant without ducking his head or holding aside the curtain and peering in. Once he does that, he will be greeted by a chorus of "irasshai" (welcome) from the staff and will find it embarrassing to turn away.

To the proprietor of a restaurant his *noren* is symbolic of the reputation of his establishment. Moreover, the *noren,* usually made of strips of heavy blue cloth, carries the insignia of the shop in bold white characters. Anywhere in Japan you can tell at a glance what kind of food the place serves from a glance at the curtain. Even a foreigner can soon learn to spot the particular lettering signifying an eel restaurant or a noodle shop. And if he sees a *noren* made of strands of rope instead of cloth, he will know that behind it lies a humble, inexpensive eatery catering to workingmen—and to smalltime neighborhood gangsters.

Most of Japan's eating places, and many of those I have been talking about, are counter restaurants. In Western countries counter restaurants usually provide fast service and so-so food at best, but the food served over the counters of Japan is almost invariably excellent, and for certain foods—the rice and seafood tidbits called *sushi* and *tempura* for example—you simply have to eat at a counter if you want to get the best.

At counter restaurants the foodstuffs and the preparations must be of high quality because the customer can watch almost every step of the cooking. Seated at the gleaming, scrubbed-wood counter (which in some places seats only half a dozen people), the customer can examine the foodstuffs closely, can talk directly to the chef to tell him what is wanted and then watch—and learn—as the food is prepared. He will see the care, almost reverence, with which each dish is cooked, arranged and garnished, and how the head chef, usually the owner, examines every portion before it is served.

A *tempura* chef usually works inside a horseshoe-shaped counter with up to 15 customers sitting around it. Besides shrimp, the menu will consist of about a dozen ingredients: squid, shellfish and various kinds of fish, plus an assortment of vegetables including green pepper, lotus root, carrots, scallions, eggplant, ginger and mushrooms. (An expert *tempura* chef will toss his batter-coated shrimp and leafy vegetables into the pan with a peculiar twist of the wrist; this prevents them from curling up and absorbing too much oil, which would make them soggy.) At the critical moment for each ingredient he plucks the pieces out with a pair of long serving chopsticks, puts the food into a flat basket covered with absorbent paper and places it in front of the guest, who dips the morsels in salt or a sauce of soy and *mirin* before eating.

When two or three guests come in together, the chef can easily remember who has had what, as he serves them simultaneously. But his memory is taxed when he has five or six groups of people who are being fed different stages of his multi-item menu; 15 customers at a time seems to be the limit for one chef. Large *tempura* restaurants like Tokyo's Ten-ichi therefore divide their premises up into many small rooms, with a chef and his circular counter in each. This preserves the intimate relationship between chef and diner that is so essential to counter eating. As Isao Yabuki, the owner of the Ten-ichi, points out, this relationship is just as important to the chef as to the customer. "The good cook is the flattered cook," he says in his book on Tokyo foods, "and what more flattering to a man than those murmurs of mm—mm—mm as the eager guests regale themselves?"

Another advantage of counter restaurants, particularly for the nervous Westerner who suspects that cleanliness is nonexistent outside his home kitchen, is that it lets one see just how clean Japan's restaurants actually are. Even in very small counter places the floors are sloshed down several times an hour, the workers wearing wooden clogs that keep their feet several inches above the wet floor. Wooden cutting blocks are washed after every use and grills scraped down immediately. Chopsticks are used once and thrown away and counters scrubbed repeatedly until the wood gleams white. No employee who touches the food will handle money, and since every Japanese bathes at least once every day, staff hygiene is never a problem. The kitchens of restaurants with private dining rooms are not open to public view, but having inspected many of them and found them just as spotless as the counter restaurants, I can say without reservation that Japan's standards of restaurant cleanliness are the highest in the world.

Stepping from the grimy street into one of these spick-and-span restaurants, the customer himself is likely to feel unclean, or at least bedraggled. The Japanese have an answer for this, too: *oshibori.* These are small, damp towels—nowadays sterilized and rolled up in cellophane—which every Japanese restaurant and bar sets before each customer as soon as he sits down. *Oshibori* come steaming hot through most of the year and provide a refreshing and highly civilized way to wipe the casual dust from your hands and make you feel ready to handle your food. A man—or a woman without makeup—can get even more refreshment out of the *oshibori* by rubbing it over the face and neck, especially in the summer when *oshibori* are handed out ice cold.

No other counter restaurants have as much to offer the adventurous gourmet as Japan's *sushi* shops. Some people consider the cold snacks collectively called *sushi (Recipe Index)* to be the national dish of Japan; there is nothing remotely like it anywhere else in the world. You can find it in one form or another in every corner of Japan and I have yet to meet a Japanese who says he doesn't like it. Even Westerners, once they have overcome their prejudice against raw fish, rave about *sushi* and argue with each other over the merits of their favorite *sushi* place. The *sushi* combination of rice and seafood is one of those gastronomic marriages that were obviously made in heaven.

The typical *sushi* restaurant is small, cheery and sparkling with scrubbed wood. The counter runs the length of the place, presided over by one or more white-garbed chefs, hands red from constant washing, towels knotted around their foreheads. "Irasshai," they shout as you duck under the *noren* and slide open the door, and as soon as you have seated yourself at the counter a huge cup of tea, an *oshibori* and a little mound of sliced ginger are set before you (the ginger is to clear your palate before starting and between selections). You wipe your hands with the *oshibori,* sip your tea and examine the offerings of the day spread out in a refrigerated glass case running along the back of the counter. There will be the dark-red lean tuna, the marbled fatty *toro,* little slabs of snow-white squid, chunks of a fish shiny and speckled like herring, blood-red *akagai* clams, mounds of caviar glistening like jewels, octopus tentacles, abalone still in the shell, pale fingers of shrimp and, in the midst of all this seafood, little yellow rectangles of omelet, in which certain *sushi* are wrapped and eaten. Take your time and enjoy the display; no one will rush you, no matter how busy the shop is.

When you are ready you point to what you want, or order by name. The chef's hands flash like a magician's, quicker than the eye; he has trained and practiced for years before he is permitted to serve customers. Out comes the delicacy you have indicated. If it needs cutting, the long knife smoothly slices off two even pieces. From a large tub beside him the chef grabs a handful of vinegared rice; deftly he kneads it, squeezing in a bit of *wasabi.* Two fingers of one hand press the rice in the palm of the other: one tiny loaf-shaped rice ball is ready. Then another. The flashing hands slow down. Gently the two slices of fish or whatever are pressed on the two mounds of rice. Then, with a proud flourish, the chef picks them up in one hand and whisks them onto a slanted, shelflike part of the counter, where they await your pleasure, two pretty little twins of goodness. The whole process has taken maybe 30 seconds. You pick up one mound, dip the rice part into a saucer of soy sauce, turn it over to keep it from dripping, and then place the whole thing on your tongue. Each piece of *sushi* is designed as a single mouthful, but anybody who wants to prolong the delight by nibbling is readily forgiven—though the rice ball will crumble in his fingers before he is through.

One portion of *sushi* at a counter is always two of these bite-sized balls. (Nothing that is sliced must ever be served singly or in threes, for one slice is *hito kire,* which can mean "kill," and three slices, *mi kire,* can mean "kill myself.") Since the portions are so small you can sample the entire menu at one sitting, or you can eat as much of your favorite as you like. A serving of each variety is priced according to the value of the fish, and you pay only for what you eat. The most expensive is usually shrimp; the cheapest, by volume, is *makizushi (Recipe Index),* in which a long sliver of tuna (or sometimes cucumber, at the end of a *sushi* meal) is wrapped in rice with an outer sheet of *nori;* this roll is then sliced crosswise, and six or eight squat cylinders are placed before you.

Sushi cuisine has a colorful vocabulary of its own, and the customer who uses the special words to order instead of the standard Japanese lexicon often gets favored treatment as a true *sushi* gourmet. Surprisingly, many Japanese do not know that at a *sushi* restaurant *wasabi* is called *namida* (tears), because it is hot enough to make you cry, or that octopus is *geso*—meaning "legs," of course. *Sushi* chefs refer to their egg item as *gyoku* (jewel), to tea as *agari* (meaning "up," for obscure reasons), and to cucumber as *kappa,* the name of a legendary river goblin who fancies that vegetable.

Of course, you don't have to go to a *sushi* restaurant to eat *sushi.* The *sushi* shops, as well as noodle and *domburi* restaurants, do a thriving send-out business. The *sushi* is beautifully arranged in opulent round lacquer boxes (which some esthetes say enhance the taste) and carried by bicycle and motorcycle to inns, offices and private homes. Moreover the box-lunch *bento* that are sold in infinite local and regional variations at train stations and at theaters and other amusement centers contain many *sushi*-type ingredients although they are not, strictly speaking, *sushi.* Like everything else prepared by the skilled and conscientious restaurant chefs of Japan, they are marked by fine materials, artful presentation and a broad and varied spectrum of tastes.

In Japan, where eating out is a national pastime, people are also fond of ordering prepared dishes to be sent in. Neighborhood restaurants do a thriving business delivering food to offices, factories and homes, often via bicycle. In the picture above, a noodle shop delivery boy dexterously balances lacquered boxes and very breakable pottery bowls that contain three different kinds of noodles and dipping sauces.

Much of the beef raised as described at left goes into the making of *sukiyaki.* This dish usually serves as the Westerner's introduction to *nabe,* or "one pot" cooking done at the table. To make beef *sukiyaki (Recipe Index)* the host first cooks the slices of beef, adding soy sauce as flavoring, then rakes them to one side of the pan. The other ingredients are then added and cooked briefly. *Sukiyaki* requires *(opposite, right of the beef, bottom to top):* sugar, eggs, soy sauce, soup. On the plate: green onions, bean curd, carrots, onions and mushrooms. Also on the table are a bowl of rice and chopsticks.

A Short but Happy Life

The beer-swilling steer above is enjoying the last months of a pampered existence on a de luxe ranch. Born of prizewinning parents, he was moved as a calf to another farm where climate, water and grazing offer optimum conditions for raising cattle. There he spent his days growing into a perfect three-year-old steer, receiving the sort of loving care that is usually lavished only on thoroughbred horses. He was curried daily and given a hand massage with *shochu* (Japanese gin) to knead his accumulating fat gently through his muscles and so impart the "marbled" look of great meat. His diet included rice, rice bran and beans. The beer was added shortly before his third birthday, after he reached his last abode, a ranch operated by the Wadakin Beef Restaurant of Matsuzaka for final fattening into perfect beef. His life is typical of those creatures destined to end up as *shimofuri* (fallen frost) beef, ranked by connoisseurs as the best in the world. This is a remarkable achievement, for the Japanese have developed their unique methods of beef-cattle raising only within the past century, after the ancient Buddhist injunction against the eating of meat began to fall into disuse.

Yakimono: BROILED FOODS

Mushimono: STEAMED FOODS

YAKIMONO: The recipes in the "yakimono" category are literally "broiled things." The broiling techniques are all familiar and simple, and the cooking times short. Variations that occur between recipes are mainly in seasonings and combinations of ingredients. Most of the recipes are suitable for outdoor cooking—over a charcoal fire or on the widely popular Japanese hibachi.

Horakuyaki 宝楽焼

STEAM-BROILED SHRIMP WITH CHICKEN, GINKGO NUTS AND MUSHROOMS

This method of broiling—on a bed of coarse salt—is in fact more a steaming or even a baking process than broiling as Westerners know it, and gives a delicate flavor to the food.

Although Japanese "horoku" are difficult to find in the United States, an excellent substitute would be the 12- to 14-inch Italian, Mexican or American unglazed earthenware casseroles equipped with tightly fitting covers.

To serve 4

- 4 medium-sized raw shrimp (16 to 20 per pound)
- 4 medium-sized white mushrooms
- 12 canned *ginnan* (ginkgo nuts), drained
- 1 whole chicken breast, boned *(see pages 176-177)* and cut into 1-inch cubes
- 8 chestnuts
- 1 to 2 cups coarse salt
- 2 to 3 sprigs fresh pine needles (about 1/4 cup)

DIPPING SAUCE

- 1/2 cup *chirizu (page 94)*

PREPARE AHEAD: 1. Shell the shrimp, but leave the last segment of shell and tail attached.

With a small, sharp knife devein the shrimp by making a shallow incision down their backs and removing the black or white intestinal veins with the point of the knife. Set the shrimp aside.

2. Wipe the mushrooms with a damp cloth and cut a small cross on the top of each.

3. Thread ginkgo nuts on each of 4 small (4- to 6-inch) bamboo skewers, and similarly thread 2 or 3 pieces of boned chicken on each of 4 other skewers. Set them aside.

4. Preheat the oven to 400°. With a sharp, heavy knife, make a deep cross on the curved top of each chestnut. Place the chestnuts on a baking sheet or in a shallow roasting pan and bake in the center of the hot oven for 10 minutes. Set them aside.

TO COOK: Pour a 1/2-inch layer of coarse salt into a 12- to 14-inch wide *horoku* or unglazed earthenware casserole. Sprinkle a few drops of water over the salt and place the casserole over moderate heat for 5 to 10 minutes, or until the salt is heated through.

Now spread a thin layer of the pine needles on the salt and arrange the shrimp, mushrooms, skewered chicken and nuts, and chestnuts on top. Scatter about 4 to 6 pine needles over the food, cover the casserole tightly (sealing the edges, if necessary, with a strip of aluminum foil), and steam undisturbed over moderately high heat for 12 to 13 minutes.

TO SERVE: Remove the pine needles and serve the food directly from the *horoku* or casserole, accompanied by small individual dishes of *chirizu* dipping sauce. *Horakuyaki* will serve four as part of a Japanese meal *(page 198)* or as a first course.

Chestnuts and pine needles add a hint of autumn to an aromatic *horakuyaki,* in which mushrooms, ginkgo nuts, chicken and shrimp are steam-broiled on a bed of coarse salt. The cooking utensil is a Japanese *horoku,* an unglazed earthenware casserole.

Miso Zuke 味噌漬

BROILED MACKEREL IN MISO MARINADE

To serve 4

1 pound fillet of Spanish mackerel or pompano with skin left on, cut into 2- to 3-inch pieces

MARINADE

1 cup *shiro miso* (white soybean paste)
5 tablespoons sugar
3 tablespoons *mirin* (cooking *sake),* or substitute 2 tablespoons pale dry sherry

GARNISH

Hajikami (bottled pickled ginger sprouts)

PREPARE AHEAD: Place the *shiro miso* in a small bowl and with a wooden spoon, stir in the sugar and *mirin.* Arrange the fish pieces side by side in a baking dish just large enough to hold them in one layer and, with a rubber spatula, spread the marinade evenly over them. Cover with plastic wrap and refrigerate for 2 days.

TO COOK AND SERVE: Preheat the broiler or light a hibachi or charcoal grill. With a rubber spatula and paper towels, gently remove the marinade from the fish and discard it. Place the fish about 4 inches from the heat and broil for 7 to 8 minutes, flesh side toward the heat, or until the fish is a light golden brown. Turn the fish carefully with tongs, a spatula or cooking chopsticks and broil for another minute. Serve at once on individual plates, accompanied by the pickled ginger sprouts.

This dish will serve four as part of a Japanese meal *(page 198)* or as a first course or luncheon dish.

To serve 6 to 8

A 2- to 2½-pound red snapper, cleaned but with fins, head and tail left on
Salt
MSG
1 tablespoon *mirin* (sweet *sake*), or substitute 2 teaspoons pale dry sherry

GOMAYAKI (sesame-seed broiled fish)
1½ tablespoons white sesame seeds
Vegetable oil
1 egg white, lightly beaten

UNIYAKI (fish with sea-urchin glaze)
1 tablespoon bottled *uni* (prepared sea urchin)
1 teaspoon egg yolk
1 teaspoon *sake* (rice wine)
MSG

Takara Bune 宝舟

TREASURE-SHIP FISH

"Takara bune" translates as and literally is a treasure ship—the steamed shell of a whole fish, shaped into a basket and filled with colorful fish tidbits. The recipe in its entirety is suitable for a buffet or formal dinner, but the three different broiled fish can be served as first courses or hors d'oeuvre without the treasure ship itself.

TO MAKE THE FISH BASKET, or treasure ship: Follow the pictures and step-by-step instructions below and opposite.

Preheat the oven to 350°. Sprinkle both sides of the fish lightly with salt and MSG. Encrust the fins and tail of the fish heavily with salt, pressing it on with your fingers. Using the ends of the skewers as handles, set the fish lengthwise across the top of a large roasting pan at least 6 inches deep. Make sure that the tail curls downward, and place an empty coffee or large juice can against it to prevent it from curling upward while it steams.

Pour enough boiling water into the pan to come ¼ inch up the sides, and drape two or three damp paper towels over the fish. Set the pan on the floor of the oven and steam for 45 minutes, or until the flesh is firm to the touch. Sprinkle the towels from time to time with hot water to keep them moist.

Remove the fish from the oven and raise the heat to 475°. Gently peel off the towels, moistening them lightly with cold water if they stick. Invert the fish on a large ovenproof serving platter—so that the tail curls upward and

To prepare a "treasure ship" fish, insert the tip of a knife at the back of the head *(above, left)* and cut down to, but not through, the center bones. Cut along the side to the tail, then across the top *(above, center)* and down the other side. Remove the fillet *(above, right)*, turn the fish over, and repeat on the other side. Wash the fish, pat it dry, and set aside the fillets. Insert 2 long metal skewers along either side of the fish: first down through the neck, then up and down through the center of the body, finally up at the base of the tail. With strong cord, tie a firm knot around the tail and then loop the ends around the head. Bring the ends of the cord back toward the tail, catching the fins to spread them, and tie another knot to secure the fish "basket."

the fish forms a basket. Brush the head, tail and skin with *mirin* and return the fish to the oven for about 5 minutes, or until it is lightly glazed. Then cool the fish to room temperature. Do not remove the skewers and string.

TO MAKE GOMAYAKI: Preheat the broiler to its highest point. Heat a heavy 8- to 10-inch skillet over high heat until a drop of water flicked across its surface evaporates instantly. Add the sesame seeds and cook for 3 to 4 minutes, or until they are lightly and evenly toasted. Then with a sharp, heavy knife, chop them fine. Spread them out evenly on a sheet of wax paper.

Cut one of the snapper fillets into 1-inch pieces, place them skin side down in a lightly oiled baking dish and broil 3 inches from the heat for 2 to 3 minutes. Turn the pieces over and broil 2 minutes. Remove from the heat, dip the flesh side of the fish into the lightly beaten egg white, then into the chopped sesame seeds. Return to the baking dish and broil 1 to 2 minutes longer, or until the seeds are a golden brown. Set aside.

TO MAKE UNIYAKI: Combine the *uni* with 1 teaspoon of egg yolk and 1 teaspoon of *sake* in a small mixing bowl. Sprinkle lightly with MSG.

Cut the second snapper fillet into 1-inch pieces and place them skin side down in a lightly oiled baking dish. Broil 3 inches from the heat for 2 to 3 minutes. Turn the fish over with chopsticks or tongs and broil another 2 minutes. Brush the flesh side of the fish with the *uni* glaze and broil 1 minute, flesh side up. Brush again with the glaze, broil 1 minute, brush once more with the glaze and broil another minute. Remove and set aside.

KIMEYAKI (fish with egg-yolk glaze)
6 medium-sized raw shrimp, shelled and deveined but with tails left on *(see page 168)*
Salt
1 egg yolk

A treasure-ship fish, bearing *goma, uni* and *kimeyaki*—pieces of broiled fish *(above and following page)*—nestles atop a pine bough.

TO MAKE KIMEYAKI: Sprinkle the shrimp with salt and insert 2 skewers (4 to 6 inches long), about 1 inch apart, crosswise through the middle of each shrimp. Broil 2 to 3 minutes on each side, or until the shrimp turn pink. Then brush the curved top of the shrimp with egg yolk and broil another 2 minutes. Brush again with egg yolk; broil 2 minutes; brush once more with egg yolk and broil for a final 2 minutes. By this time the top of the shrimp should have a rich golden glaze. Remove from the oven, remove the skewers, and set the shrimp aside.

TO SERVE: Carefully slide the skewers out of the fish basket and cut away the strings. Fill the hollowed-out center of the fish with a neatly cut paper doily, rice paper, or a bunch of parsley. Arrange the chunks of broiled fish decoratively in the basket, and serve hot or at room temperature.

Yuan Zuke 柚庵漬

BROILED MACKEREL IN SOY-AND-RICE-WINE MARINADE

To serve 4

1 lemon, sliced thin
1 pound fillet of Spanish mackerel with skin left on, cut into 2- to 3-inch pieces

MARINADE
1/3 cup *sake* (rice wine)
1/3 cup Japanese all-purpose soy sauce
4 teaspoons sugar
2/3 cup *niban dashi* *(page 54)*

PREPARE AHEAD: 1. For the marinade, combine the *sake* and soy sauce in a 1½- to 2-quart saucepan and bring to a boil over moderate heat. Stir in the sugar and *dashi,* return to a boil, then cool to room temperature.

2. Add half the lemon slices and the fish to the marinade and turn them about to moisten them well. Marinate for 2 to 3 hours at room temperature, or in the refrigerator for 5 to 8 hours.

TO COOK: Preheat the broiler or light a hibachi or charcoal grill. Remove the fish and lemon slices from the marinade. Discard the lemon and strain the marinade through a sieve into a small saucepan. Broil the fish flesh side first for 6 to 8 minutes, or until golden brown. Carefully turn the fish over with tongs or chopsticks, brush with the marinade, and broil for about 2 minutes, or until the skin is a deep golden brown.

Meanwhile bring the marinade to a simmer on top of the stove.

TO SERVE: Divide the fish among 4 small serving dishes and moisten each with a teaspoon of the hot marinade. Garnish the fish with a fresh lemon slice.

Serve *yuan zuke* hot, as part of a Japanese meal *(page 198)* or as a first course.

Dengaku Tofu 田楽豆腐

GRILLED SOYBEAN CURD WITH MISO DRESSING

To serve 4

2 cakes fresh *tofu* (soybean curd), cut into 8 pieces each 3/4 inch wide by 3 inches long
1/4 pound fresh spinach leaves, stripped from their stems
4 ounces (1/2 cup) *shiro miso* (white soybean paste)
Kona sansho (Japanese pepper)

The appearance of skewered "tofu," decorated with white and/or green "miso," may remind Americans of an ice-cream popsicle. There, of course, the resemblance ends, although "dengaku tofu" is treated as a sweet course by the Japanese. The green-colored "miso" is made, in Japan, with ground "sansho" leaves, which are not available in the United States. Spinach makes an admirable substitute, with packaged "sansho" powder added for flavor.

PREPARE AHEAD: 1. Preheat the broiler to its highest point. Place the pieces of *tofu* side by side in a flameproof baking dish just large enough to hold them in one snug layer. Add enough cold water to come halfway up the sides of the *tofu,* then slide the dish under the broiler, as close to the heat as possible. Sear the *tofu* for a few seconds, then turn the pieces with a spat-

Bamboo-skewered *tofu,* spread with plain and spinach-flavored soybean paste and speckled in broiling, is served as a sweet course.

ula and sear the other side. The *tofu* will be speckled but not evenly browned. Remove the pan from the broiler and set aside.

2. In a $1\frac{1}{2}$- to 2-quart saucepan, bring 2 cups of water to a boil. Add the spinach leaves and boil uncovered for about 2 minutes. Then drain in a sieve and run cold water over the spinach to cool it quickly and set its color. Squeeze the spinach firmly to rid it of all its moisture and chop it fine.

In a *suribachi* (serrated mixing bowl) or with a mortar and pestle, pound or mash the spinach to a paste. Then with the back of a large spoon, rub it through a fine sieve into a mixing bowl.

3. Stir half of the *shiro miso* and a few sprinkles of *kona sansho* into the spinach, continuing to stir until the *miso* paste has turned a delicate green.

4. Place the remaining *shiro miso* in a small bowl and mix until smooth.

TO COOK AND SERVE: Over moderate heat, bring the pan of seared *tofu* (with the water still in the pan) almost to the boil. Remove from the heat and spoon the green *miso* dressing into a pastry bag equipped with a No. 47 ribbon tip. Squeeze the *miso* along the top of 4 pieces of *tofu,* covering the top of each piece. (Lacking a pastry bag, spread a thin film of *miso* on each piece of *tofu* with a spatula, and run the prongs of a fork down the *miso* to create serrated lines.) Cover the remaining *tofu* with the plain *miso.*

Insert two 4- to 6-inch bamboo skewers or small lobster forks halfway through the length of each piece of *tofu.* Return the *tofu* to the water in the baking dish and sear under the broiler for a few seconds. Serve at room temperature, as the sweet course in a Japanese meal *(page 198).*

Two flavorful dishes ideal for a summer barbecue: thinly sliced beef *teriyaki (above)* and skewered chicken and scallions.

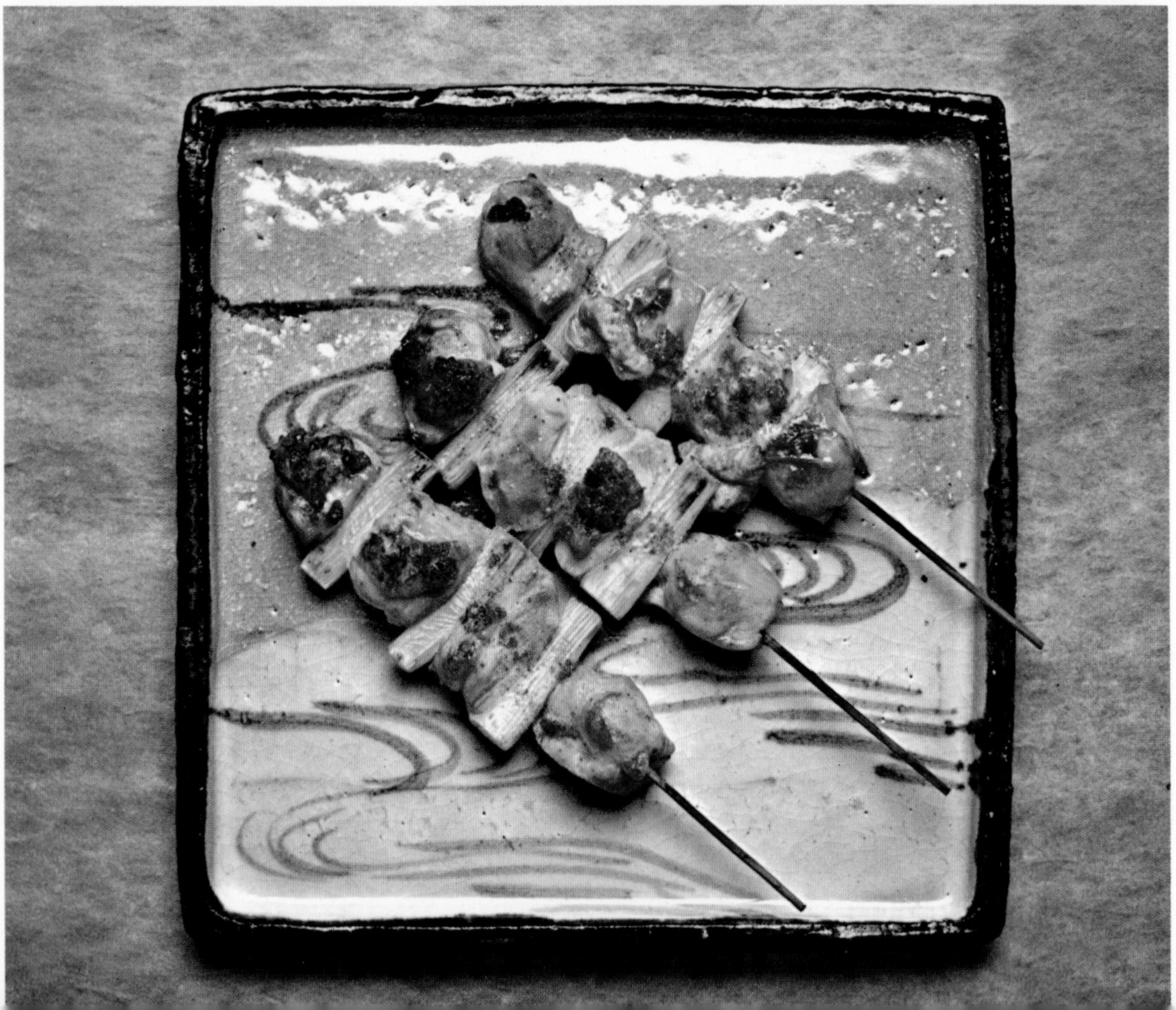

Gyuniku Teriyaki 牛肉てり焼

BROILED SLICED BEEF WITH A SOY-SEASONED GLAZE

Beef "teriyaki," like most of the "yaki" recipes, can be cooked not only in a broiler but also on a hibachi or charcoal grill. The sauce may be made in large quantities, covered, refrigerated and kept for as long as a month.

To serve 6

1½ pounds lean boneless beef, preferably tenderloin or boneless sirloin, cut in 12 slices ¼ inch thick

TERIYAKI SAUCE

1 cup *mirin* (sweet *sake*), or substitute 1 cup less 2 tablespoons pale dry sherry

1 cup Japanese all-purpose soy sauce

1 cup chicken stock, fresh or canned

TERIYAKI GLAZE

¼ cup *teriyaki* sauce

1 tablespoon sugar

2 teaspoons cornstarch mixed with 1 tablespoon cold water

GARNISH

4 teaspoons powdered mustard, mixed with just enough hot water to make a thick paste and set aside to rest for 15 minutes

12 sprigs fresh parsley

PREPARE AHEAD: 1. To make the sauce, warm the *mirin* or sherry in a 1½- to 2-quart enameled or stainless-steel saucepan over moderate heat. Off the heat ignite the *mirin* with a match, and shake the pan back and forth until the flame dies out. Then stir in the soy sauce and chicken stock, and bring to a boil. Pour the sauce into a bowl and cool to room temperature.

2. To make the glaze, combine ¼ cup of the *teriyaki* sauce and 1 tablespoon of sugar in an enameled or stainless-steel saucepan. Bring almost to a boil over moderate heat, then reduce the heat to low. Stir the combined cornstarch and water into the sauce. Cook, stirring constantly, until it thickens to a clear syrupy glaze. Immediately pour into a dish and set aside.

TO COOK: Preheat the broiler to its highest point, or light a hibachi or charcoal grill. Dip the beef, one slice at a time, into the *teriyaki* sauce. Broil 2 inches from the heat for 1 minute on each side, or until lightly brown. For well-done meat broil an additional minute.

TO SERVE: Slice the meat into 1-inch-wide strips and place them on individual serving plates. Spoon a little of the glaze over each serving, and garnish each plate with a dab of the mustard and a sprig of parsley. If you prefer, mix the mustard into the glaze before pouring it over the meat.

This will serve 6 as part of a Japanese meal *(page 198)* or 4 as a main course.

NOTE: Any leftover *teriyaki* sauce may be stored in tightly closed jars and refrigerated for as long as one month. Before using, bring to a boil and skim the surface of any scum.

Yakitori 焼鶏

BROILED CHICKEN, SCALLIONS AND CHICKEN LIVERS

To serve 4

3 tablespoons *sake* (rice wine)

1 tablespoon Japanese all-purpose soy sauce

2 teaspoons sugar

A 1-inch piece scraped fresh ginger root, cut into paper-thin slices

8 chicken livers, trimmed of all fat

2 whole chicken breasts or 4 legs, boned *(see pages 176-177)* and cut into 1-inch pieces

8 scallions, including 3 inches of the green stems, cut into 1- to 1½-inch-long pieces

1½ cups *teriyaki* sauce *(above)*

Kona sansho (Japanese pepper)

PREPARE AHEAD: 1. Combine the *sake,* soy sauce, sugar and sliced ginger in a 1- to 1½-quart mixing bowl and add the chicken livers. Turn them about in the marinade to moisten them well, and marinate at room temperature for at least 6 hours, or overnight in the refrigerator. Then remove the livers from the marinade and cut each one in half. Reserve the marinade.

2. On each of 4 small skewers, string 4 halved chicken livers. On each of 8 additional skewers, alternate 4 chunks of chicken with 3 strips of scallion.

TO COOK: Preheat the broiler, or light a hibachi or charcoal grill. Broil the skewered livers about 3 inches from the heat for about 4 minutes. Then dip them in the *teriyaki* sauce and broil for 4 to 5 minutes on the other side. Set the livers aside on a plate.

Quickly dip the chicken-and-scallion skewers into the *teriyaki* sauce and broil on one side for 2 or 3 minutes. Dip again into the sauce, grill for 2 minutes, dip once more, and grill on the other side for an additional 2 minutes. The entire grilling should take 6 to 7 minutes in all.

TO SERVE: Place 1 skewer of chicken livers and 2 skewers of chicken and scallions on each serving plate. Sprinkle with a little *kona sansho,* and moisten each skewer with a teaspoon or so of the marinade.

Tori Teriyaki 鶏てり焼

GRILLED CHICKEN WITH A SWEET SOY-SEASONED GLAZE

To serve 6

6 whole chicken breasts or 12 chicken legs
3 cups *teriyaki* sauce *(page 175)*
1/4 cup *teriyaki* glaze *(page 175)*
4 teaspoons powdered mustard, mixed with just enough hot water to make a thick paste, and set aside to rest for 15 minutes
12 sprigs fresh parsley

PREPARE AHEAD: Bone the chicken breasts in the following fashion: Hold the breast skin side down and bend it back until the spoon-shaped keel bone pops up. Pull it out and cut the breast in half with a heavy, sharp knife. One at a time, lay each half breast, bone side up, on a chopping board, with the tapered end toward you. Then slip the point of a sharp boning knife under the base of the slender single small rib bone attached to the rib cage. Press the flat of the knife up against the bone and cut the flesh away, freeing the bone. Hold the bone in one hand and pull it gently up toward you, meanwhile scraping away the flesh adhering to the adjacent ribs. Continue the scraping and cutting movement until the entire rib cage and adjacent small bones have been detached from the flesh. Pat the boned half breast meat back into shape and discard the bones. Repeat the entire process with the other half. Leave the skin intact on both of the pieces.

To bone a chicken leg, start at the drumstick end and, using the bone as a guide, cut the meat away from the bone in large pieces. Trim the meat of all cartilage and gristle, but leave the skin intact.

TO COOK: Preheat the broiler (or light a hibachi or charcoal grill). Dip the chicken breasts into the *teriyaki* sauce, coating them well, and broil skin side up 3 inches from the heat for 2 to 3 minutes, or until golden brown. Dip the breasts into the sauce again and broil on the other side for 2 to 3 minutes. Dip a third time into the sauce and broil—skin side up—another 3 to 4 minutes. The finished chicken should be a rich golden brown.

TO SERVE: Cut the chicken into 2- to 2½-inch pieces and arrange on individual serving plates. Pour the *teriyaki* glaze evenly over each portion and garnish the sides of the plates with a dab of mustard and a sprig of parsley.

Atsuyaki Tamago 厚焼玉子

BAKED FISH OMELET

To serve 8 to 10

2 ounces fluke, flounder or gray sole
9 eggs
2 tablespoons sugar
1/2 teaspoon salt
1/2 teaspoon MSG
Vegetable oil

PREPARE AHEAD: Put the fish through the finest blade of a meat grinder or purée it in an electric blender. Scrape into a large mixing bowl and, with a whisk or a rotary or electric beater, beat in the eggs 1 at a time. Then beat in the sugar, salt and MSG.

TO COOK: Preheat the oven to 300°. With a pastry brush or paper towel, lightly oil the bottom and sides of a 2-inch-deep flameproof baking dish or 8-inch skillet. Heat the pan over moderate heat until a drop of water flicked across its surface instantly evaporates. Pour in the egg-and-fish mixture and cook for about 3 minutes, or until the bottom is lightly set. Then place the pan in the center of the oven. Bake for 10 minutes, then turn the heat down to 200° and bake 1 hour, or until a toothpick inserted into the center comes out dry and clean.

TO SERVE: Run a sharp knife around the sides of the omelet and place a flat serving dish upside down over the pan. Grasping pan and plate firmly together, quickly turn them over. Rap the plate on a table and the omelet should slide out easily.

With a sharp knife, trim the ends of the omelet and slice the omelet into 1-inch-wide strips. Cut the strips crosswise into ½-inch-wide pieces and serve at room temperature.

Shioyaki 鹽燒

SALT-BROILED FISH WITH DIPPING SAUCE

"Shioyaki" is perhaps the simplest of Japanese recipes. Salting the fish before broiling causes the fat under the skin to break down, thus adding moisture to the flesh. Fish cooked in this fashion has such intense natural flavor that many Japanese prefer to serve it without a dipping sauce.

To serve 4

4 fresh trout, 6 to 8 ounces each, cleaned and scaled but with head and tail left on, or 1 pound fish fillets of any type with skin left on
Salt
Vegetable oil

DIPPING SAUCE FOR TROUT
3 tablespoons *ichiban dashi* or *niban dashi (page 54)*
4 teaspoons rice vinegar, or substitute 4 teaspoons mild white vinegar
A pinch of salt
MSG
½ teaspoon finely chopped parsley

GARNISH FOR FISH FILLETS
¼ cup finely grated *daikon* (Japanese white radish), or substitute ¼ cup grated icicle radish or white turnip
⅛ teaspoon finely chopped fresh parsley
½ teaspoon Japanese all-purpose soy sauce

PREPARE AHEAD: 1. To prepare the small whole fish, dip the tail and fins into salt, then wrap them in small pieces of aluminum foil to prevent them from burning. Salt the exposed surface of the fish lightly and let them rest at room temperature for about 30 minutes.

Although the fish may be broiled as they are at once, you may skewer them in the Japanese manner. One at a time, insert the tip of a long skewer completely through the side of each fish at the point where the head meets the body, then force the skewer back through the center of the body, and out through the base of the tail. After broiling, the skewered fish will appear to be swimming.

2. To prepare fish fillets, simply salt them lightly on both sides and let them rest at room temperature for 2 hours.

3. To make the dipping sauce for the whole fish, combine the *dashi,* vinegar, a pinch of salt, a sprinkle of MSG and the chopped parsley in a small bowl and mix thoroughly.

4. To prepare the garnish for the fish fillets, mix the grated *daikon,* parsley and soy sauce together in a small bowl.

TO COOK: Preheat the broiler, hibachi or charcoal fire. Oil the grill lightly and broil the trout for 5 minutes on each side, turning them carefully with the aid of the skewers. The fish fillets should be broiled with the flesh side exposed to the heat for 5 to 6 minutes, or until a golden brown.

Remove the skewers from the trout and serve the whole fish accompanied by individual dishes of dipping sauce, or the fish fillets accompanied by their garnish.

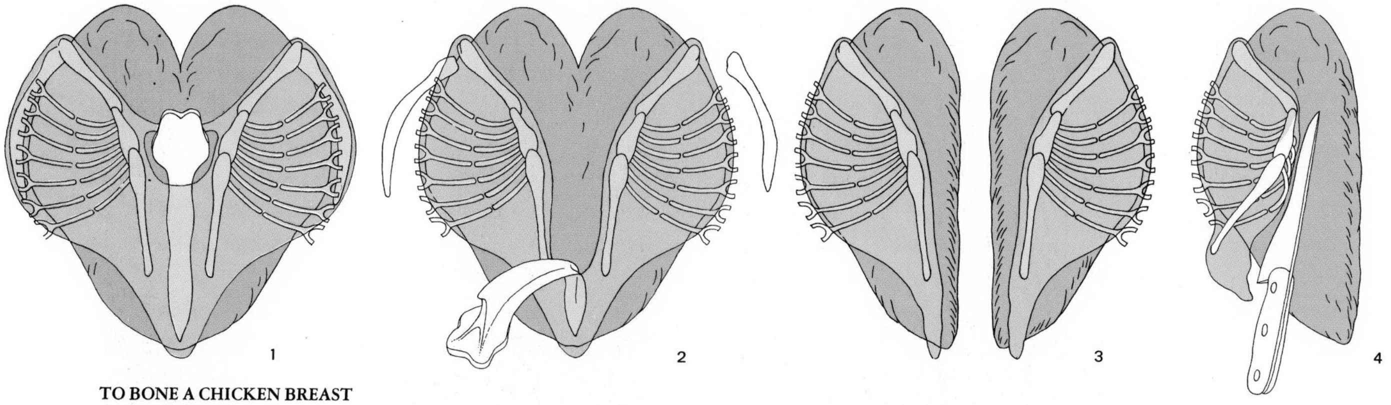

TO BONE A CHICKEN BREAST

Hold the breast skin side down and bend it back in half until it is flat *(1)* and the spoon-shaped keel bone in the center pops up. Pull it out *(2)* and cut the breast apart *(3)*. Slip the point of a sharp knife under the base of the slender rib bone *(4)* attached to the rib cage. Press the flat of the knife up against the bone and cut and gently pull the bone up toward you, meanwhile scraping away the flesh adhering to the adjacent ribs. Continue these scraping and cutting movements until the entire rib cage and adjacent bones have been detached from the flesh.

1 Pour a thin layer of egg into an oiled pan, top three quarters of it with *nori* and cook until lightly set.

2 With chopsticks or rubber-tipped tongs, gently roll over the egg layer into thirds, enclosing the *nori*.

To serve 1

Vegetable oil
3 eggs, well beaten (about 3/4 cup)
1/3 cup *niban dashi* or *ichiban dashi* *(page 54)*
1/8 teaspoon salt
MSG
1/2 teaspoon *usukuchi shoyu* (light soy sauce), or substitute 1/4 teaspoon Japanese all-purpose soy sauce

GARNISH
1 tablespoon finely grated *daikon* (Japanese white radish), or substitute 1 tablespoon grated icicle radish or white turnip
1/4 teaspoon Japanese all-purpose soy sauce
MSG
A sprig of parsley

ISOBE TAMAGO YAKI
1 to 2 sheets *nori* (dried laver)

Tamago Dashimaki 玉子だし巻

FLAKY ROLLED OMELET

PREPARE AHEAD: 1. In a mixing bowl, combine the 3 well-beaten eggs with 1/3 cup of *niban dashi,* 1/8 teaspoon of salt, a few sprinkles of MSG and 1/2 teaspoon of *usukuchi shoyu.*

2. Prepare the garnish in advance by mixing the 1 tablespoon of finely grated *daikon* with the 1/4 teaspoon of soy sauce and a sprinkle of MSG. With your fingers, shape the *daikon* into a ball and set aside.

TO COOK: With a pastry brush dipped in oil, lightly brush the bottom and sides of a rectangular Japanese *tamago* pan or heavy 10- to 12-inch skillet, preferably with a nonstick surface. Heat the pan over moderately high heat until a drop of water flicked across its surface evaporates instantly.

Pour in just enough of the egg mixture to coat the bottom of the pan lightly. Tip the pan back and forth over the heat for about 10 seconds, or until the eggs begin to set. Then, holding the pan about 2 inches above the heat, roll the omelet over into thirds or quarters, about 2 inches at a time, using chopsticks, tongs or a spatula. Slide the completed omelet to the far end of the pan and lightly oil the pan again. Pour in a little more of the egg mixture, letting some of it run under the first completed egg roll. In another 8 or 10 seconds, you will be able to roll again, this time starting with the first egg roll. Roll it toward you, over the new layer of egg and roll again, enclosing the new egg as you proceed. Repeat with the remaining eggs, oiling the pan lightly after each roll is completed and enclosing the whole roll in each new layer.

With a spatula, transfer the completed rolled omelet to a serving plate and cut it in half crosswise (or cut it in thirds, if it was made in a skillet). Garnish the omelet with a sprig of fresh parsley and a small ball of the soy-flavored *daikon.*

TO MAKE ISOBE TAMAGO YAKI, a variation of *tamago dashimaki:* Pass one side of a sheet of *nori* over a flame to intensify its color and flavor. Cut the *nori* into thirds. Proceed with the omelet as above, but just before rolling up each layer, cover the layer first with a strip of *nori* and then roll them up together. The cut finished omelet will have bands of the greenish-black *nori* between the egg layers.

Serve *tamago dashimaki* for breakfast or with soup as the main course of a light lunch or supper.

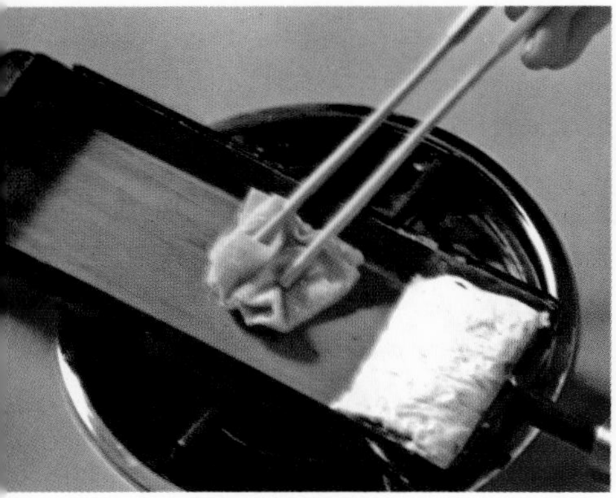

3 Slide the rolled omelet to near side of pan and, with paper towel or pastry brush, lightly re-oil pan.

4 Slide omelet back to far side, pour in more egg, and lift first omelet to let the new layer of egg run under.

5 Top again with *nori* and, starting with first omelet, roll in thirds again. Repeat with remaining egg and *nori*.

The light, fluffy omelet, halved to reveal its many layers of *nori* and egg, is garnished with grated white radish and served for breakfast or lunch.

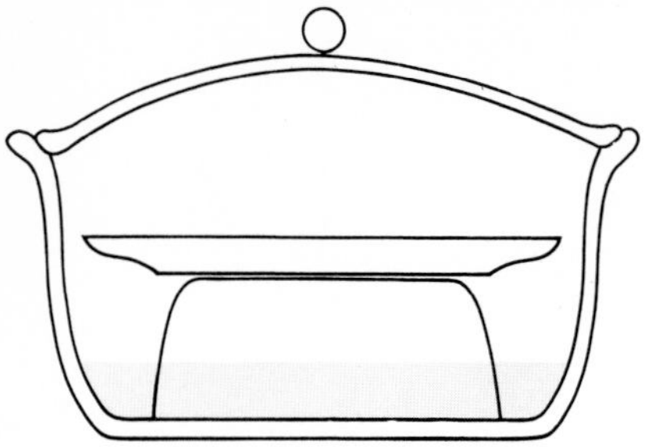

"MUSHIMONO" are steamed foods. They range from such simple combinations as chicken and shrimp steamed in egg custard (Recipe Index) to the elaborately constructed treasure-ship pumpkin described below.

Oriental steamers are available in many parts of the country, but lacking one, a substitute is easily improvised (left). Pour enough water into a large, heavy pot to come 1½ inches up the sides. Set a heatproof bowl upside down in the pot and place a plate with the food to be steamed on top. Bring the water to a boil, cover the pot tightly, and steam the food for the time specified in the recipe.

Takara Mushi 宝蒸

TREASURE-SHIP PUMPKIN, FILLED WITH SHRIMP, MUSHROOMS AND VEGETABLES

To serve 8 to 10

- 1 pumpkin (about 6 pounds)
- 1 teaspoon *ajishio* (equal parts salt and MSG)
- 4 medium-sized *shiitake* (dried Japanese mushrooms)
- 5 tablespoons sugar
- 1 tablespoon Japanese all-purpose soy sauce
- 1¾ cups *niban dashi (page 54)*
- ¼ cup *sake* (rice wine)
- 1 teaspoon *usukuchi shoyu*, or substitute ¾ teaspoon Japanese all-purpose soy sauce
- 18 small shrimp in their shells (26 to 30 to a pound)
- Salt
- 16 to 20 snow peas, or substitute 16 to 20 string beans
- 1 tablespoon *mirin* (sweet *sake*), or substitute 2 teaspoons pale dry sherry
- 30 canned *ginnan* (ginkgo nuts)

PREPARE AHEAD: 1. Scrub the pumpkin vigorously under cold running water with a stiff brush. With a large, sharp knife, cut off the top of the pumpkin to make a lid, leaving the stem intact as a handle. Remove the lid and, with a large metal spoon, scrape the seeds and stringy fibers from the lid and pumpkin shell. With a melon-ball cutter or small spoon, scoop out small balls of pumpkin meat, but leave a ¾- to 1-inch-thick wall of the flesh intact in the shell. Set the pumpkin balls aside.

Sprinkle the flesh side of the lid and the inside walls of the pumpkin evenly with *ajishio*.

To give the pumpkin a preliminary steaming place it and its lid in a colander with small supports, and set the colander in a deep pot large enough to enclose it completely. Pour enough water into the pot to come within 1½ inches of the bottom of the colander, and bring the water to a boil over high heat. Then cover the pot tightly, and steam the pumpkin for 10 minutes. Remove the colander and pumpkin from the pot and set them aside.

2. Place the *shiitake* in a small saucepan and soak in 1 cup of cold water for about 1 hour. Bring to a boil, then simmer uncovered for 15 minutes. Cool to room temperature, strain the liquid into a bowl and set it aside. Remove and discard the hard stems; cut the mushrooms into 16 or 20 half-inch pieces.

In a 1-quart saucepan, combine ½ cup of the mushroom liquid with 1 tablespoon of sugar and 1 tablespoon of soy sauce. Bring to a boil over high heat, add the mushrooms and, stirring frequently, cook briskly, uncovered, for 10 to 20 minutes, or until all of the liquid has evaporated. Set aside.

3. In a 2-quart saucepan, combine 1 cup of the *niban dashi*, 2 tablespoons of the sugar, ¾ teaspoon salt and the pumpkin balls. Bring to a boil, stir in 1 tablespoon of *sake* and sprinkle lightly with MSG. Boil uncovered for 5 minutes, then remove the pumpkin balls with a slotted spoon and set them aside.

Reduce the liquid in the pan by boiling it over high heat until it becomes a thick syrup. Watch for any sign of burning and regulate the heat accordingly. Then stir in 1 teaspoon of *usukuchi shoyu*, remove from the heat, and stir in the pumpkin balls.

4. In a 2-quart saucepan, bring 2 cups of salted water to a boil, drop in the shrimp and boil for 3 or 4 minutes. Drain in a colander and run cold water over the shrimp to stop their cooking. Peel the shrimp and make a shallow incision along their backs with a small, sharp knife. Remove the intestinal vein with the tip of the knife. Cut the shrimp in half crosswise.

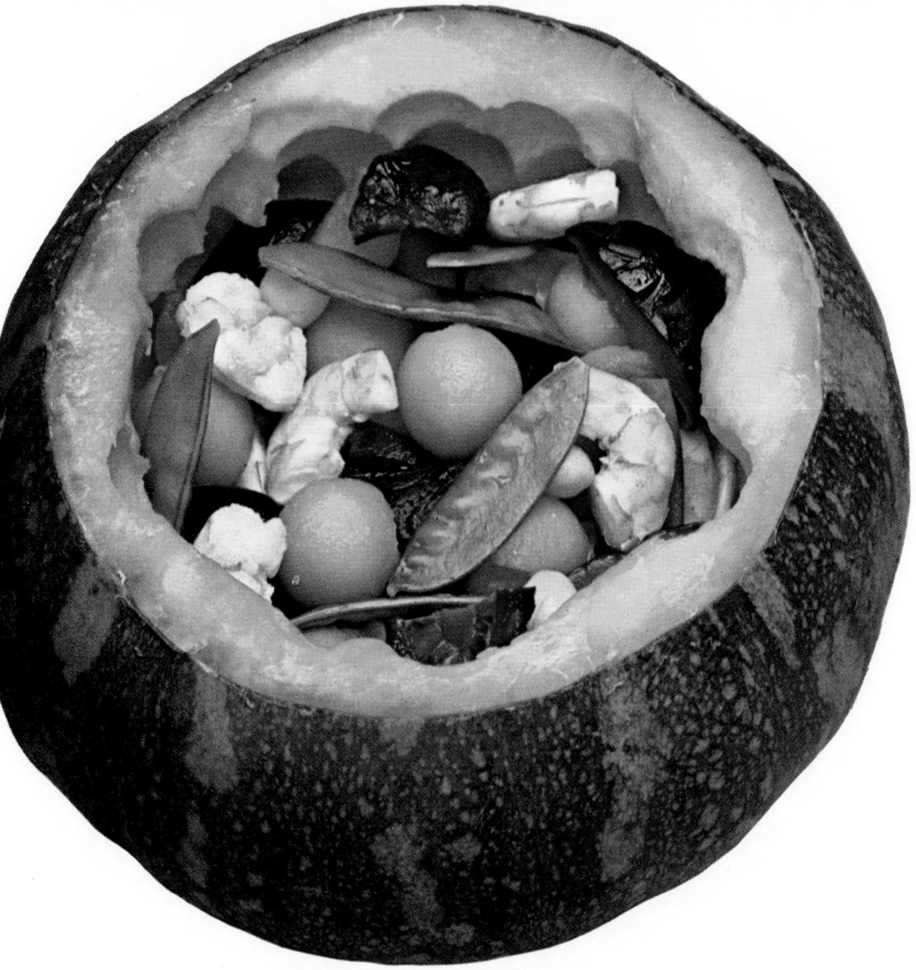

A colorful treasure-ship pumpkin, hollowed out and filled with delicately flavored shrimp, pumpkin balls, mushrooms, snow peas and ginkgo nuts, is often the highlight of a Japanese banquet. It would be equally dramatic at a Western buffet.

In a 2-quart saucepan, combine ½ cup *niban dashi,* 2 tablespoons *sake,* 2 tablespoons sugar and ¾ teaspoon salt, and sprinkle lightly with MSG. Bring to a boil and cook down to about half the volume. Remove from the heat. Add the shrimp, stir to moisten them thoroughly and set the pan aside.

5. In a 1-quart saucepan, bring 1 cup of salted water to a boil. Drop in the snow peas (or string beans), return to a boil, then drain in a sieve. Run cold water over the peas (or beans) to cool them quickly and set their color.

Combine ¼ cup *niban dashi,* 1 tablespoon *sake,* ⅛ teaspoon salt and a sprinkle of MSG in the saucepan and bring to a boil. Drop in the flavored snow peas (or beans), return to the boil, then remove from the heat. Cool by placing the pan in a large bowl of cold water.

6. In the 1-quart pan, combine 1 tablespoon of *mirin,* ⅛ teaspoon of salt, a sprinkle of MSG and the ginkgo nuts. Cook over high heat for 1 to 2 minutes, shaking the pan almost constantly until all the liquid evaporates. Remove from the heat.

TO ASSEMBLE AND STEAM: With a large knife, cut a thin slice from the base of the pumpkin to prevent it from rocking. Place the mushrooms, pumpkin balls, shrimp, snow peas and ginkgo nuts in the pumpkin, cover with the pumpkin lid, and carefully transfer it to the colander. Return the colander to its pot, add enough water to come within 1½ inches of the bottom of the colander, and bring the water to a boil. Cover the pan tightly and steam 5 minutes, then serve at once.

VIII

Magnificent Meals in Elegant Settings

I remember with pleasure an afternoon in early fall some years ago when I had lunch at the famous Kitcho Restaurant in Kyoto. The lovely garden outside our private dining room and the gently rolling, wooded hills in the distance combined to form a breathtakingly beautiful picture. Noticing my preoccupation with the view, my Japanese host leaned over and asked, "What in particular in that scene attracts your attention?" I nodded toward the hills where the leaves on a few maple trees on the highest ground were beginning to change color. "I'm fascinated," I said, "with the contrast those small patches of yellow and red provide to all the soft green in the foreground."

My host smiled approvingly, like an art teacher who has received a perceptive answer from a student. "Now," he said, "look at the plate in front of you." I glanced down and was astonished to see an asymmetrically shaped, pearl-gray dish decorated with skillfully painted maple leaves ranging in color from lush green through pale yellow to vivid red.

"This could hardly be a coincidence," I said.

My host shook his head. "Someone once described an artist as a man with an infinite capacity for detail," he said. "I think you will find that the description also fits the owners of fine restaurants in Japan."

I agree wholeheartedly with this observation. In no other nation in the world do the great restaurants make a comparable effort to provide the patron with a rewarding esthetic experience as well as an excellent meal. The platter that duplicated the autumn scene was an instance of this concern; and matched sets of china, like those prized and used the year round in the West, strike the Japanese as the height of monotony. "It is as though you

This elegant seven-course meal, served at Kyoto's celebrated Doi Inn, shows the beauty of the dishes in Japanese cuisine. For example, a low wooden box on a black lacquer tray holds shrimp *tempura* *(center)*. Next to it, a red and black tray holds an individual hibachi, with two kinds of trout broiling.

had a closet filled with clothes, all of them of the same material, cut and shade," a Japanese friend once said to me. "Can you imagine yourself wearing the same color and texture the year round, and having exactly the same style of dress for a walk in the country and a dinner dance?"

To provide the proper setting for the variety of foods served—in a good establishment 10 courses are usually served, but there can be as many as 18—fine Japanese restaurants have dishes that span the color spectrum, vary enormously in shape and size, and range in materials from coarse pottery to stoneware to fragile porcelain to basketry, bamboo and lacquered wood.

All of these dishes are carefully packed away in boxes after each use, labeled to indicate the season and food for which their contents are appropriate. To equip a restaurant with such tableware obviously requires a substantial investment. In fact, the dishes are sometimes worth more than the combined value of the building and the land on which it stands. "All of us haunt antique shops in search of replacements for the dishes that are inevitably broken and can't be replaced because the artist is dead," one Japanese restaurateur said. "This, of course, is in addition to the commissioning of new work by the finest living artists."

The meticulous choice of tableware is only one of the subtle ways in which an outstanding Japanese restaurant seeks to make dining a pleasurable experience for the eye and spirit as well as the palate. Time favors the top Japanese restaurants in the achievement of their goals. You simply do not make a spur-of-the-moment decision to have lunch or dinner at such a place; usually a reservation must be made several days in advance. Even then a stranger probably would not have his reservation accepted—though, of course, the refusal will be phrased so politely that the snub will not be immediately apparent. In effect, the first-rank dining places are operated much like private clubs and are supported by a devoted and regular clientele. The clublike atmosphere is heightened by the absence of a check at the end of the meal; monthly statements are sent to the diner. A newcomer seeking admission to these temples of eating must be vouched for by a longtime client whose manners are known to be beyond reproach. But whether the party is to be made up of habitués, novices or a mixture of the two, the restaurant insists on having ample time to create a proper setting and atmosphere and to prepare the many dishes that will be served. (The menu is either agreed upon in advance or, more often, left to the discretion of the manager.) A dinner at an excellent restaurant, like Hannya-en in Tokyo, will prove that the time required to enjoy the meal has been well spent.

Although Hannya-en is only a 10- or 15-minute taxicab ride from the city's business district, the quiet, dimly lit street on which its classic, 19th Century building is located seems wholly divorced from the frantic hubbub of downtown Tokyo. When guests enter Hannya-en, they are greeted at the gate by several of the serving girls, all dressed in handsome kimono of colors suited to the season. The patrons remove their shoes inside the door, are given felt slippers to wear, and then are led through a series of corridors to their private dining room. This, incidentally, is one of the principal ways in which the great Japanese restaurants differ from their Western counterparts; each group of guests has its own room, even if there are only two in the party.

Once in the dining room, the eye is struck by a lovely garden, so artfully landscaped that it seems a happy accident of nature. All the rooms at Hannya-en face on this garden with its ancient pine trees, beautiful shrubs and flowers, winding streams and great, fantastically shaped rocks. But the garden has been so designed that each room enjoys an unobstructed and seemingly private view of a particular section. If the weather is chill, the view is seen through floor-to-ceiling glass doors, but if the temperature is mild, the doors will be open and the guest is free to wander outside before the meal is served. At night, when the garden is softly lighted by the traditional Japanese stone lanterns, it takes on an oddly dreamlike quality, like a stage setting for an ancient Oriental legend.

The room itself is simply but richly furnished. A low lacquered table about 18 inches high is in the center. This is flanked by floor-level cushioned chairs, each with its own armrest to lean against. Inset in one wall is a *tokonoma,* the ever-present alcove in which is hung an elegant picture scroll, and beneath it, a delicately executed flower arrangement that complements the painting. The entire setting creates a mood of timeless tranquillity.

Once the guests are seated, serving girls enter with baskets of *oshibori*—steaming face towels, frequently scented with cologne. After everyone wipes his hands and face, the towels are returned to the basket and removed by the girls. When they return, each bears a tray holding small dishes for soy sauce, chopsticks and a small ceramic bar on which to rest the chopsticks between courses. There is a rare kind of grace in the way in which one of these well-trained girls serves the guests. Supporting a lacquered tray with the palms of her hands, she advances to within three feet of the table, kneels and places the tray gently with both hands on the mat-covered floor, lets her hands rest momentarily on her knees, and bows to the guests. Somehow the effect is one of unbroken movement. Incidentally, the girls will be with the guests through most of the meal, leaving only to return dishes to the kitchen after a course is finished and then to bring on the next course. If encouraged by the customers, they will join in the conversation and, since the party probably will be comprised exclusively of men, even flirt a bit. Except for a few fortunate Western women who, under suitable auspices, have had the pleasure of dining in this grand style, the patronage of the great, expensive restaurants in Japan is as exclusively male as that of YMCAs.

To see what is included in a fairly typical dinner at Hannya-en, I would like to have you join me as I recall the delights of a meal I had there with some Japanese friends. The first course was *sakizuke,* appetizers consisting of cashew nuts, an arrowroot cracker, a dried fish called *kisu,* fried sea tangle and crunchy ginkgo nuts carved in a hexahedron shape. An hors d'oeuvre followed. Each guest was served a hard-boiled quail egg rolled in bacon, a chicken ball, a cod-roe canapé, a raw oyster and salmon eggs nesting in a piece of melon carved into the shape of a ship.

Then in a black-and-gold lacquer bowl came a clear soup with a slice of carrot, cut in the shape of a maple leaf. A spectacularly served *sashimi,* succulent slices of raw fish, was next. In the setting of a miniature seashore—small potatoes entirely covered with seaweed serving as black rocks, polished white rice grains suggesting sand and pebbles adding an authentic touch—the chef had placed slices of raw tuna, sea bream, young yellowtail and shellfish. The fifth course, served in a shallow red lacquer bowl with a cover, was *tempura* that included prawns, eel, *kisu* (an Asiatic fish), asparagus and ginkgo nuts.

Continued on page 193

The working day at the Kitcho ("Good Omen") Restaurant in Kyoto begins *(above)* with a top-level conference on menus. Gathered around the low table, master chef Koji Yuki, in white, his wife Junko *(left)* and Sosei Takahara *(right)*, Kitcho's tea-ceremony expert, listen as spectacled Teiichi Yuki asks their opinions before making a decision.

Hospitality as a Fine Art

Patrons of Japan's finest restaurants expect—and receive—much more than mere gratification of their appetites. Starting with the selection of raw ingredients, proprietors meticulously supervise every detail in order to satisfy all five senses of the diner and above all to create an atmosphere of tranquility. Thus the appeal to the diner's eye extends beyond the room by providing him with a view of a garden and a section of the natural landscape. In their effort to avoid any jarring note that might disrupt this peaceful ambiance, the great restaurants train their staffs in the skills of preparing and serving foods that are both beautiful and good; over and beyond this the employees are schooled in comporting themselves with charm and grace. The décor, the table service, the esthetics of food preparation and the serving rituals derive largely from the rules laid down in the 16th Century for the tea ceremony. Shown here and on the following pages are a few behind-the-scenes glimpses of the work that precedes dining at Kitcho, a renowned Kyoto restaurant, considered one of the best in Japan.

Flower arrangement is a highly regarded skill in Japan, and Kitcho calls upon the services of an expert, Sosei Takahara *(above right),* to decorate the *tokonoma* in one of the dining rooms. Mrs. Takahara, the wife of an Osaka tea-ceremony master, also gives the staff a weekly lesson in tea-ceremony ritual *(right).* As the teakettle in front of her steams, she demonstrates the proper handling of the napkin used to wipe the tea utensils, while apprentice chefs in white jackets and kimonoed serving maids observe. The apprentice farthest to the right is Ohba, the first Japanese woman to be accepted for training as a master chef.

Two serving maids kneel in attendance as visiting American patrons begin the second course of a New Year's luncheon at Kitcho. Even though they are at the moment intent on their bowls of clear soup, the diners are always aware of the garden outside and the magnificent ceiling inside. The preceding course consisted of sliced abalone, the next one will be *sashimi* and the fourth a platter of assorted foods, each of which has a symbolic connection with the New Year. As arranged on the platter at left, they are *(counterclockwise from bottom):* egg patties; bean-curd patties; *chisha,* a Japanese vegetable; bamboo shoots; black beans on pine-needle skewers; salmon eggs in kumquat shells; boiled prawns; and raw fish wrapped in seaweed.

The host-chef Koji Yuki *(opposite)* drops in to wish his guests a prosperous year to come. The festive baskets on the table contain various tidbits from the New Year's platter at left.

A diner at Doi, a fashionable Kyoto inn, takes his eyes from the entertainment long enough to refill his *sake* cup, a gesture that ordinarily would be performed by one of the dancing geisha. The two girls who strike the stylized traditional poses are *maiko,* or apprentice geisha, who dance to the music provided by the samisen player in the corner. At Doi, noted for its food and its comfortable lodgings, geisha entertainment is not a regular feature. But like all fine restaurants and inns, Doi will bring in the girls at the request of patrons. When they have finished dancing, the geisha return to converse, play table games, pour drinks and light cigarettes for the guests.

This geisha displays the proper blend of docility and reserve as she presents a light to a diner in a Tokyo restaurant.

A beef dish with noodles, onions, broiled bean curd, Chinese cabbage, bamboo shoots and an egg served with a Japanese green pepper was the next offering brought in by the serving girls. Then came a lighter dish—a delicious salad of crab meat and fresh vegetables. *Chawan mushi,* a hot egg custard made of eggs, chicken, lily bulbs, boiled fish paste, ginkgo nuts and trefoil greens, followed the salad. The ninth course was fruit: melon, a peeled and sliced orange, and large, flawless, superbly succulent strawberries.

The 10th and final course consisted of two kinds of tea, a powdered, opaque variety that is served with a bean cake surrounding a chestnut center, and a clear tea. Although such a meal seems gargantuan in the recounting, it does not require the appetite of a lumberjack. The portions are small and the food is eaten at a leisurely pace. My own experience is that I usually feel pleasantly filled but not stuffed after such a banquet. The price of a dinner like this at Hannya-en or any of the other leading restaurants was about $45 per person, not including drinks. And given the Japanese enthusiasm for alcohol both before and during a meal, drinks would almost certainly be a substantial additional item.

Sake, the rice wine, which is generally served warm, is more or less the national drink, and a fine dinner is incomplete without repeated rounds of this beverage. Since it has an alcoholic content of about 15 per cent, making it slightly stronger than Western table wines, the atmosphere around the table can become extremely jovial by the time the last morsel of food has been eaten—especially since diners often alternate tall glasses of the excellent Japanese beer with the tiny cups of *sake.* Scotch whisky—either imported or a very acceptable domestic equivalent—is also much in demand in Japan.

The visitor who wishes to sample Japanese cuisine at its highest level can do so in the course of a dinner at one of the great restaurants and then return to his Western-style hotel to sleep and—perchance—to dream of exquisite dishes in endless profusion. But if he wishes to have a truly Japanese experience, I heartily recommend a stay at one of the superb Japanese inns whose reputation for all-enveloping hospitality equals the excellence of its table. There are only a limited number of hostelries that can meet both of these requirements: Doi in Kyoto, one of this select group, was where an American couple I know recently spent some time and returned with the following glowing report.

"When my wife and I arrived at Doi," the husband told me, "we were met at the door by Kakuko Yamada, one of the inn's five serving maids. Following instructions, we removed our shoes and replaced them with slippers set out on the floor. This pleasant custom, we learned, serves the hygienic purpose of leaving all street-dirtied footwear outside, and also protects the delicate *tatami* matting inside the inn from damage caused by sharp-edged heels. Then Kakuko led us into a kind of parlor and served us clear tea. After we downed this ceremonial refreshment, which is a traditional indication of intention to stay, she led us to our second-floor room whose large windows offered a fine view of Doi's serenely classical inner garden on one side, and the briskly modern Kyoto skyline on the other. Like all traditional Japanese rooms, this one served both as a living room and as a bedroom. Its furnishings were sparse—a lacquered table about two feet high in the center of the room, four cushioned chairs without legs, and a *tokonoma,* with its elegant yet simple adornments. (At night, as we discovered later, Kakuko would push the table and low chairs to one side and in their place set up beds consisting of thin but soft mattresses called *futon,* sheets and pillows, all brought from a closet in the corridor.)

"Kakuko then seated us at the table and served us a powdered green tea. As we drank it, she kneeled next to the table, a Japanese-English dictionary by her side, and asked us about our travels, our family and other matters. Soon, of course, we were asking her questions about herself. She was never intrusive, merely friendly and eager for us to enjoy ourselves. At about five in the afternoon Kakuko announced it was time for our baths."

The first stop in a Japanese bath is the dressing room, decorated with a Japanese print and a flower arrangement, and furnished with brushes, combs and cosmetics. Sliding doors open to the bath itself, a steamy room of about seven by twelve feet built entirely of carefully joined cypress planks. This aromatic wood adds its fragrance to the vapors rising from the hot water and gives the room a wondrous forest aroma. The sunken tub is about seven feet long, four feet wide and four feet deep—ample for two. But before getting in, the bather observes a very sensible Japanese custom: he washes himself with soap and hot water and then rinses until no soap suds remain to defile the clean water of the bath. Only then does he step into the pool.

To Western skins, the temperature of the water seems better suited for boiling lobsters than for bathing. Surprisingly, the body does make an adjustment after a few moments. At one end of the pool there is a small bench raised a few inches off the bottom. Seated on this slat, with only his neck and head above the surface of the water, the bather soaks luxuriously, feeling the tensions of the day melting under the heat of the water. When he emerges, he dons Japanese clothes provided by the inn and returns to his room.

When my friends arrived in their room, Kakuko again seated them at the table and took their orders for drinks. This was the only ordering done; the meal had been arranged beforehand. In a few moments she was back with glasses, bottles and an ice bucket. The bar and kitchen are on the first floor, which meant she made about a dozen trips on those stairs just to serve that one meal. Yet despite all the climbing and kneeling, she continued to look as fresh and dainty in her kimono as she had when she first appeared.

The dinner began with boiled shrimp on a slice of lemon, accompanied by a cube of *daikon* that had been hollowed out and filled with bean paste. Raw sea bream and crisp celery, served in exquisite blue-and-white Ming bowls followed. A clear fish soup with half a mushroom and strips of bright-green spinach stems floating on the surface was the next dish offered by Kakuko. After another trip to the kitchen, she returned with mushrooms covered with egg and a small buttonlike morsel of fish paste. A delicious *tempura* was next. Now Kakuko brought in two charcoal braziers on which she broiled sliced mushrooms and fish coated with the white of an egg. Also served with this course were pieces of roast quail. Next, Kakuko brought on a pungent soybean soup called *akadashi.* Pickled vegetables—eggplant, cucumber and radish leaf—served with fluffy white rice were next. Then came fresh fruit and, finally, tea.

"It was a magnificent dinner," the husband said later, "but the atmosphere contributed enormously to our enjoyment of it. The lights in the garden projecting shadows of maple leaves on the window, the simple elegance of the room, the graceful service, the moments of absolute silence when even the distant voices faded away—together they induced the great sense of intimacy, which is an essential part of a fine meal in Japan."

The artistic serving of excellently prepared food in a gracious atmosphere is, as we have seen, a serious art in Japan's outstanding restaurants. Like all great art, the finished product rarely betrays the effort that went into its making. We can get some idea of the care required to produce the best Japanese food by following the manager of one of these establishments as he selects the raw materials for his chef's masterpieces.

Shortly after 5 a.m. on most days, Koji Yuki, master of Kitcho in Kyoto—there are also Kitcho restaurants in Tokyo and Osaka—is in his station wagon rolling down the Kyoto-Osaka superhighway en route to market. Koji has two major reasons for making these trips: to confer with his father-in-law, Teiichi Yuki (who owns and retains overall supervision of the Kitcho restaurants) and to get fish for the Kyoto branch. All the fish for the three branches come from the small fishing village of Akashi, some 30 miles down the coast from Osaka. By 4 a.m., the previous day's catch is delivered to Kitcho's headquarters in Osaka; the fish destined for Tokyo has already gone off by air by the time Yuki has reached Osaka to pick up the portion earmarked for him. Although Japan teems with excellent fish markets, the Kitcho restaurants cling to this expensive system to be certain they are serving the best and the freshest fish available.

Similar care is shown in the buying of vegetables. For instance, on many mornings Yuki loads his station wagon with locally produced vegetables before leaving for Osaka. "Some of the vegetables are better in Kyoto than anywhere else," he explains, "particularly bamboo shoots and mushrooms." But no matter where the best vegetables are grown, the owners of Japan's top restaurants, or their representatives, will be there as buyers.

Fruits are especially cultivated and packed for these restaurants. As growing peaches, grapes and pears ripen, they are tied in little paper sacks to protect their skins from birds and bees. When the fruit is picked, each piece or bunch is cradled in white cotton batting and carefully placed in small wooden boxes only one layer deep to avoid bruises or tears during shipment.

The master chefs who perpetuate their restaurants' fame usually serve a 10-year apprenticeship before they are accorded this honored title. Serving maids, too, must serve an apprenticeship, although the period is much shorter than for chefs. Anyone who has ever observed the ballerina-like movements of these girls knows that the training is effective.

All of the chefs, serving maids and apprentices at Kitcho's in Kyoto live in quarters provided by the management, and when the work is finished at night, they gather with Koji and his wife, Junko, to watch television. Every staff member takes an interest in all aspects of Kitcho's operation, from menus to flower arrangements. This clannishness is a holdover from the long Japanese feudal tradition, but Kitcho is not entirely bound by the past. One of the apprentice chefs is a girl in her twenties, the first of her sex to wield a knife in any of the Kitcho kitchens.

Kitcho's staff does not include geisha but, like most of the great restaurants in Japan, Kitcho is happy to bring in geisha at the request of a patron. The geisha serves as a combination of entertainer and companion. She may dance, sing, play musical instruments, recite poetry or draw pictures for the guests, talk with them or listen sympathetically to their troubles, light their cigarettes, pour their drinks and, if invited, drink with them. But casual amorous advances to her are against the rules.

Although the average age of the geisha is about 27, neither youth nor beauty is a requisite for following the profession. One popular geisha is in her eighties. "Sometimes our clients request her specifically," I was told by a Tokyo restaurant owner. "She treats them like sons, and if they want to reminisce about the good old days, she can tell them about the romantic scandals involving the political figures of the prewar period."

At one time, girls were apprenticed to the profession when they were six; now the law requires that they complete junior high school, so the average starting age is 16. The apprentice, called a *maiko,* is supposed to be a virgin, and she wears a kimono with an extra fold over each shoulder to denote her maidenhood. (As a full-fledged geisha, she will probably acquire a rich patron who will assume her sizable debt to the *okiya,* or training residence for geisha, help pay for her wardrobe of kimono—which can cost up to $12,000 each—and generally provide her with financial security.)

The training period usually lasts for several years and emphasizes the development of poise, charm and wit. During this time, the apprentice also studies flower arranging and the tea ceremony, learns to perform the classical geisha dances and becomes proficient in playing various instruments. She must also master an elegant, circuitous vocabulary favored in *karyukai,* "the world of flowers and willows," of which she will be a part. When customers relax with a geisha in the evening, they enjoy the brilliant verbal play implicit in the poetic, evocative Japanese language. In the other-world atmosphere of a fine restaurant or geisha house, *shoyu,* for instance, is far too blunt a word for soy sauce. One should ask for *murasaki,* "the purple." Even salt has a lyrical name: *nami no hana,* which means "crest of the wave."

After completing her training, much of the geisha's work will be done in geisha houses. Since his company will pick up the entire tab, the businessman has no objection to the geisha's fee of about $3.20 per hour—the going rate in most big cities. She receives the entire amount; the house makes its money on the sale of food and drinks. But though geisha houses serve food, most of them bring it in from nearby restaurants whose standards are usually not up to those of the really fine dining places.

Therefore the ideal arrangement is to have dinner at an outstanding restaurant like Kitcho and enjoy the company of geisha there. I must quickly acknowledge that if you are a Western woman a good deal of what you will learn about geisha parties must come from Japanese and American men friends. While women have indeed attended such affairs, it is quite evident that their presence has an inhibiting effect on the festivities. Even so, the atmosphere is delightful enough that foreign ladies can see why Japanese men continue to cherish the custom—no matter how much it may be resented by young, increasingly emancipated Japanese wives.

Geisha parties will often start at a geisha house where the men may stay for a short while and have a few drinks and some light-hearted conversation with the girls before they go on to a restaurant or a nightclub. But if the party is being held at Kitcho, or some other great restaurant, it will probably begin and end there.

Once in the private room that has been reserved by the host, the guests relax with *sake* and beer, take off their jackets and loosen their neckties; some of them may shed all their Western clothing and get into comfortable kimono. The geisha, resplendent in their gorgeous finery, welcome the guests with smiles and bows and small talk.

Now the wonderful Kitcho food is brought in, course after exquisite course, and the party grows noisier as the *sake* cups are refilled with graceful gestures by geisha whose trained eyes immediately spot any empty cups. Faces grow flushed, and jokes, puns, snatches of poetry are flung back and forth across the long low table. By this time the geisha, too, glow as the warm *sake* they have been offered makes itself felt. The jokes become more elliptically suggestive. The food disappears and more is brought in. When the American guest protests that he can no longer keep up with his Japanese friends and their nearly continuous cries of "kampai!"—bottoms up—his half-serious complaint produces boisterous laughter and a challenge by one of the geisha to try his hand at a game. A tiny *sake* cup is placed before him and the girl fills it halfway to the brim. Tilting a *sake* flask, the American adds a little wine to the cup. Then the geisha does the same. After a few turns, the cup is full, then brimming, and then the convex surface of the wine trembles slightly as, drop by drop, the players strive to avoid adding the fatal dash that will make the bulging cup overflow. For the loser will have to drink a tall cup of *sake* with everyone at the table, guests and geisha alike. With a roar of delight the company watches the geisha's last move create a small cascade on the table. She bows to the foreign guest, compliments him on his steady hand, and with wonderful aplomb exchanges drinks with each member of the happy group.

As the meal reaches its end, an older woman comes in carrying a samisen, a lutelike instrument, bows and seats herself at one side of the room. The other geisha have gathered at the end of the room and stand in picture-book postures. The music begins and the girls dance, a highly formal set of graceful movements recapitulating a thousand years of tradition. When the dance is over, the guests applaud vigorously, and the geisha perform another stylized dance. Again they acknowledge the compliments, and after one more dance they return to the table and rejoin the guests.

More toasts are proposed, and other games are played. Some of them are ingenious puzzles like the one in which matchsticks are rearranged into prescribed patterns by adding or moving a limited number of sticks. Others involve great digital delicacy in manipulating carefully erected but teetering structures made of cigarettes without destroying the entire creation. Always there is good-humored laughter when one of the players loses, and loud praise when he wins. Finally it is time to go. The men get back into their dark suits, and the American is astounded by the swift transformation of his recently disheveled dinner companions into sedate Japanese businessmen, clothed in the respectability required by the world outside. Thinking about the party back in the quiet of his hotel room, the Westerner realizes that he has once again been made aware of the Japanese gift for living each aspect of life in complete harmony with the atmosphere of the occasion.

How to Use Japanese Recipes

One day a famous Kyoto chef visited a Zen monk.

"Tell me in a few words," the monk said, "the reasoning behind your cuisine."

"To reflect nature precisely."

The monk was silent. "Is it only nature you reflect," he corrected gently, "or is it your awareness of nature? When you slice a radish, shouldn't you be aware of where it grew, of the rain that fell on it, of the farmer whose toil produced it?"

This tale—true, not apocryphal—sums up why Japanese cuisine is so satisfying on so many levels. As you begin introducing Japanese dishes into your menus, you will find yourself shopping with an increased awareness of the foods that nature provides to celebrate the cycles of the year; even in this age when most foods are available frozen or canned all year round, you can find ways to bring the seasons to your table. Handling your ingredients in the kitchen, you will be more conscious of their shape, texture and color, since the Japanese believe—and who would contradict this?—that food should look as good as it tastes. More than most, Japanese cuisine is a challenge to all the senses.

It is, however, far from an overwhelming challenge. Anyone approaching Japanese cuisine for the first time will find that there is a wonderful clarity to almost every dish. Though some ingredients may seem unfamiliar, they are easily obtained in Oriental food stores—by mail order if necessary—and all except a few fresh vegetables can be stored almost indefinitely. If an ingredient proves to be totally unavailable in your area, you can often use a substitute. Even if the recipe calls for an item as universal as spinach, you can substitute watercress, for example, and a new taste will have been added by your ingenuity.

For obvious reasons, most Westerners would not even want to try to reproduce the atmosphere of a Japanese room, with its *tatami* mats, sliding wood panels, and scroll hanging in the *tokonoma*. But there is no reason why you should not try, if you wish, to serve your foods on different plates, bowls and saucers. Even small, decorative ashtrays can be used to serve dipping sauces or garnishes. As the photographs in this book show, the Japanese strive for a direct yet delicate balance of color and form.

Basic Rules of Meal Planning

The Japanese do not divide their meals as we do into one main course preceded by soup and accompanied by a salad and vegetables. The order of the Japanese formal meal often places soup near the end, and usually includes both fish and meat, or several kinds of fish and numerous vegetables treated in different ways. In this sense, the Japanese meal is similar to the Chinese, on which it was consciously patterned many centuries ago.

Westerners are likely to think of such menus as "a large number of small dishes." So at first it may be wise to plan your Japanese meal much as you would a Western one, by selecting a main dish and building around that. Most of the lunches and dinners listed on this page have, in fact, been planned around one main course. While it will be understandably tempting to settle on one of the more familiar *teriyaki, tempura* or *sukiyaki* dishes as a main course, you should not overlook the *nabemono* (one-pot) dishes, which are delicious and relatively simple to make.

A word here about salads and desserts. The Japanese do not eat salads in our sense of raw greens tossed with a dressing. The *aemono* and *sunomono* dishes *(Recipe Index)* are roughly the equivalent of salad, and several of them appear in these sample menus. They may be served as you would a salad, or even as a first course.

There is no dessert section in this book, since the Japanese normally end their meals with fresh fruit. A sliced orange, pineapple, canned mandarin oranges or strawberries will make a fitting close to any of the menus presented on this page.

Experimenting with Japanese Food

Since an all-Japanese meal requires a careful balance of foods, it might be a good idea to use the recipes in this book—at least initially—to supplement a Western-style meal. There are many Japanese soups, salads and main dishes that can substitute for equivalent Western courses. In this way, you can perfect your Japanese cooking techniques one at a time.

One great advantage to experimenting with Japanese recipes is that so many of the dishes may be served at room temperature; consequently they may be prepared at leisure, hours before serving.

A cautionary note: The number of guests that a dish will serve depends on whether it is part of a Western or Japanese menu. Western-style portions generally tend to be larger, and the Japanese dishes may serve fewer people in a Western meal than indicated.

Planning an All-Japanese Menu

Don't be afraid of trying multi-course meals. It's not really that much harder to prepare a half dozen small courses than it is to make a few hefty ones—if you plan your cooking operation in advance. The trick is not to be caught at the last minute with too many unfamiliar operations underway. This is true in all cooking, but it is particularly so in Japanese cuisine. A dish like *tempura* will demand all your attention while you're frying the shrimp and vegetables. The heat must be adjusted so that the temperature of the oil doesn't drop; the oil must be kept clean; the frying time must be quite precise. Consequently, if *tempura* is to be the main course, it might be preceded and followed by dishes that may be made hours in advance—leaving you free for a virtuoso performance as a *tempura* cook.

The various courses in a Japanese dinner are ordinarily brought to the table at the start of the meal. If you wish to eat as the Japanese do, you can give each of your guests an individual tray containing the various courses and accompany the meal with warm *sake,* which has about the same alcoholic content as most Western table wines. If you are preparing a more elaborate dinner with five or seven courses, you'll probably find it easier to serve two courses at a time. If the course is a big one, like *zensai* (Japanese hors d'oeuvre), it might be more convenient to serve it by itself.

Sample Japanese Menus

Spring luncheon:
Kinome-ae: bamboo shoots with green soy dressing
Mazezushi or *fukusazushi:* vinegared rice mixed with vegetables and seafood
Aka misoshiru: red *miso*-flavored soup

Fall luncheon:
Shira-ae: tofu-and-sesame-seed dressing with string beans
Shioyaki: salt-broiled fish with dipping sauce
Satsuma jiru: miso-flavored stew
Gohan: steamed rice

Winter luncheon:
Suzuko mizore-ae: red caviar with "sleet" dressing
Tori gohan: chicken and rice with mushrooms
Chawan mushi: chicken and shrimp in egg custard

Summer luncheon:
Kani kyuri ikomi: cucumber stuffed with crab meat and pickled ginger
Sashimi: sliced raw fish
Hiyashi somen: cold summer noodles

Spring dinner:
Nuta-ae: seafood and scallions in *miso* dressing
Hamaguri ushiojitate: clear clam soup with mushrooms
Sashimi: sliced raw fish
Kamo yoshino-ni and *fuki no nitsuke:* duck and coltsfoot simmered in *sake*-seasoned sauce
Tori teriyaki: grilled chicken with a sweet soy-seasoned glaze
Gohan: steamed rice

Summer dinner:
Domyoji age: deep-fried shrimp coated with rice
Kamo sukamushi: sake-steamed duck
Kimini: sake-seasoned shrimp with egg-yolk glaze
Nigiri zushi: vinegared rice-and-fish "sandwich"

Fall dinner:
Igaguri: thorny shrimp balls filled with sweet chestnuts
Sumashi wan: clear soup with *tofu* and shrimp
Tatsuta age: sliced beef with red-pepper-and-radish garnish
Yuan zuke: grilled fish in soy-and-*sake* marinade
Umani: chicken and vegetables simmered in seasoned broth
Gohan: steamed rice

Buffet:
Yakitori: grilled chicken, scallions and chicken livers
Nanban zuke: fried fish in vinegared sauce
Domyoji age: deep-fried shrimp coated with rice
Zensai: assorted hors d'oeuvre
Oden: winter casserole with fish cake, *tofu* and vegetables
Makizushi: vinegared rice and vegetables rolled in seaweed
Takara mushi: treasure-ship pumpkin, filled with shrimp, mushrooms and ginkgo nuts

A Guide to Ingredients in Japanese Cooking

Most of the basic ingredients in Japanese recipes can be found at any market. Exceptions, described below, can be bought in an Oriental food market, if there is one nearby, or ordered by mail from sources listed on page 207. Except for a few foods, such as *daikon* and *tofu*, Japanese ingredients can be stored at room temperature, many for as long as a year. If an ingredient is not available and a substitute is not named, the best course is to omit it from the recipe.

AJI-NO-MOTO: Japanese trade name for MSG (monosodium glutamate), a flavor-enhancing agent used in very small quantities. Available in containers in Oriental markets, or sold in supermarkets as Ac'cent or MSG.
AONORIKO: Powdered green laver, a member of the seaweed family. Used as a seasoning agent. Available in bottles in Japanese markets.
AZUKI: Red beans, usually cooked in rice or made into a dessert. Available in Japanese markets.

BENI SHOGA: Red pickled ginger root, available bottled in Japanese markets. Used slivered or sliced as flavoring agent or garnish. Once opened, will keep refrigerated for several weeks if bottles are reclosed.

DAIKON: Japanese white radish, available fresh in Japanese markets, in sizes ranging from sections of 6 inches to several feet. It may be refrigerated for up to two weeks. A substitute is icicle radish, which most closely approximates the taste and texture, or white turnip.
DASHI NO MOTO: Instant *dashi*, available in packages in Japanese markets. *Dashi* is a basic soup and cooking stock and is made from powdered *katsuobushi* and *kombu*. Only cold water and MSG need to be added.

FU: Light cake made of wheat gluten, available packaged in different sizes, shapes and colors. Used principally as a soup garnish.

GINNAN: Ginkgo nuts, available canned in Oriental markets and specialty shops. The opened ginkgo nuts may be refrigerated, tightly closed, for weeks.
GOBO: Burdock, a long, slender root popular as a vegetable in Japan. Available fresh in Japanese markets, *gobo* may be kept for two weeks in the refrigerator.
GOMA: Sesame seeds, both black and white, available in boxes. A popular spice in Japanese cooking, sesame seeds are generally warmed in a pan to release their aroma and flavor, and are often ground. Italian sesame seeds are a good substitute.
GOMA-ABURA: Sesame-seed oil, available canned or bottled in Oriental markets. Middle Eastern sesame-seed oil, which may be more easily available, has a different taste and weight but may be used if diluted with lighter vegetable oils.

HAKUSAI: A Chinese cabbage that has 12- to 16-inch-long smooth white stalks and large green leaves. Sold fresh by the bunch or by weight in Oriental markets. Will keep for one week refrigerated in a plastic bag. Substitute celery cabbage or white cabbage.
HARUSAME: Bean-gelatin noodles, literally, "spring rain." This vermicelli, also called cellophane or transparent noodles, is available in Oriental markets. Usually softened in water before using.
HICHIMI TOGARASHI: Seven-pepper spice, available in small bottles. Powdered blend of hot mustard seed, sesame seed, pepper leaf, poppy seed, rape seed, hemp seed and dried tangerine peel.
HIYAMUGI: Thin noodles, usually eaten cold. Available in bags or boxes at Japanese markets. Substitute Italian vermicelli.

JUNSAI: Wild delicacy sold in glass bottles in Japanese markets. Translated as "water shield," *junsai* has a slippery coating and is used as a vegetable garnish in soups.

KANPYO: Dried gourd shavings, available packaged in Japanese markets. Usually softened before being used as a garnish.
KATSUOBUSHI: Dried bonito. Preflaked *katsuobushi* is available in bags or boxes in Japanese markets primarily for use in *dashi*—the basic soup stock. Keeps indefinitely, even after opening.
KOMBU: Dried kelp, a species of seaweed. Comes in hard black sheets, which are usually cut into pieces, washed, and used in stocks. Keeps indefinitely.
KONA SANSHO: Ground pepper from *sansho* (prickly ash) leaf. Substitute ground black pepper.
KONNYAKU: A hard, translucent loaf made from starch of tubers of the devil's tongue plant. Available canned in Japanese markets. Once opened, may be refrigerated for weeks.

MATSUTAKE: Large Japanese mushrooms, available canned in Japanese markets.
MIKAN: Mandarin oranges, available canned—packed in syrup—in Japanese and many American markets. Used as a dessert.
MIRIN: Sweet *sake* (rice wine), used only for cooking. Available in liquor stores on special order. Japanese markets will often arrange to get it from neighboring liquor stores. A good substitute is pale dry sherry, used in lesser amounts than the *mirin* called for by recipes.
MISO: Soybean paste, made from the fermentation of cooked soybeans, wheat or rice, and salt. The basic types are *aka miso* (a reddish color) and *shiro miso* (white). Used as a flavoring in soups and as the base for a dressing for vegetables. Available in containers in Japanese markets. Will keep, even opened, for as long as a year at room temperature.
MSG: *See* Aji-no-moto.

NAMEKO: Tiny wild mushrooms with slippery wet coating, available in cans in Japanese markets.
NORI: Dried laver, a species of seaweed. Available in thin greenish-black sheets resembling carbon paper. When warmed, becomes crisper and more purplish in color. Used as garnish or to roll around rice or fish. Sold in packages in Japanese markets. Will keep for up to six months once opened.

RENKON: Lotus root, sold fresh in sections about 2 to 3 inches in diameter and 4 to 6 inches long, and canned in various sizes. Store in the refrigerator.

SAKE: Although called rice wine, *sake* is more closely related to beer. When used as a beverage, it is usually heated gently in the bottle before serving. It is also an important seasoning ingredient in cooking. Available at liquor stores, in stock or on special order.
SHIITAKE: Japanese mushroom, available dried in bags or packages in Oriental markets. Can be stored indefinitely in their packages. They are usually reconstituted by soaking in water for at least 30 minutes before using.
SHIRATAKI: Literally, "white waterfall." Shredded form of *konnyaku*, long vermicelli-like threads available canned or in small cartons in Japanese markets.
SHOGA: Gnarled, brown fresh ginger root, about 4 inches long, available fresh in Oriental and Puerto Rican specialty shops. Will keep for a few weeks wrapped in paper toweling in the refrigerator.
SHOYU: Japanese soy sauce, a pungent brown liquid made of fermented soybeans, barley, yeast and salt. Japanese soy sauce is more delicate and less salty than the Chinese or domestic brands.
SOBA: Thin buckwheat-flour noodles, available packaged in Japanese markets.
SOMEN: Fine white wheat-flour noodles, usually eaten cold. Available in Japanese markets. A substitute is very thin spaghetti.
SU: Rice vinegar, available bottled or canned, in various sizes, at Oriental markets. A good substitute is cider vinegar, but mild white vinegar will suffice.

TAKENOKO: Young bamboo shoots, available whole in cans in Oriental markets. Chinese sliced bamboo shoots are more widely available in supermarkets.
TOFU: Custardlike cake of soybean curd, about 3 inches square. Sold fresh in Japanese markets. Will keep for two to three days if refrigerated and kept in fresh cold water, changed every day. *Tofu* is also available canned and in instant powdered form.
TSUKEMONO: Pickled vegetables, in bottles in Japanese markets.

UDON: Thick wheat-flour noodles, available in Japanese markets. A good substitute is No. 2 spaghetti.
UMEBOSHI: Small pickled plums, available bottled in Japanese markets.
UNI: Prepared sea urchin, available bottled in Japanese markets.

WAKAME: Long, curling dried strands of seaweed. Available packaged in Oriental markets. Reconstitute by soaking in water, then strip the leaves from the tough center vein and use as a garnish.
WASABI: Green horseradish, available canned in powdered form, to which cold water is added.

Recipe Index: English

An R preceding a page reference refers to the Recipe Booklet.

Stocks and Soups

Basic soup stock ... 54; R2
Clear clam soup with mushrooms ... 58; R11
Clear soup with porgy ... 61; R8
Clear soup with rolled egg, vegetables and fish ... 60; R6
Clear soup with sea bass ... 58; R9
Clear soup with soybean paste ... 59; R12
Clear soup with *tofu* and shrimp ... 55; R4
Clear soup with winter melon and shrimp ... 58; R5
Cooking stock for vegetables ... 54; R3
Miso soup garnishes ... 59; R12
Miso-flavored pork-and-vegetable stew ... 61; R10

Picnic Food and Hors d'Oeuvre

Chestnuts cooked in green tea ... 70; R16
Cooked kelp ... R21
Miso-marinated asparagus ... 70; R22
Red bean cake ... R24
Sake-seasoned clams ... 73; R15
Sake-steamed duck ... 68; R14
Shrimp *sushi* with egg yolk ... 69; R18
Shrimp wrapped in seaweed ... R17
Steak and scallion rolls ... 73; R22
Steamed fish loaf ... 68; R20
Sweet-cooked abalone ... 73; R16
Sweet-cooked clams ... 73; R15
Sweet-cooked snails ... R17
Taro potatoes rolled in crumbled seaweed ... R21
Thorny shrimp balls filled with sweet chestnuts ... 70; R19
Turnips in vinegar dressing ... R23

Mixed Foods and Vinegared Salads

Bamboo shoots with green soy dressing ... 67; R32
Chicken and parsley with horseradish sauce ... R30
Crab meat in vinegared dressing ... 62; R36
Cucumber stuffed with crab meat and pickled ginger ... 66; R34
Daikon and carrot in vinegar dressing ... 64; R35
Eggplant with mustard and *miso* dressing ... R25
Mackerel in vinegar dressing ... 65; R36
Red caviar with "sleet" dressing ... 64; R28
Seaweed-flavored fish with lemon sauce ... R37
Slippery mushrooms with "sleet" dressing ... 65; R29
Soy-and-sesame-seed dressing with string beans ... 62; R27
Spinach with toasted sesame seeds ... R33
Rice vinegar and soy dipping sauce ... 64; R29
Tofu-and-sesame-seed dressing with vegetables ... 63; R26
Seafood and scallions in *miso* dressing ... R30
White *miso* dressing ... 67; R31

Sliced Raw Fish

Delicate soy-based dipping sauce for *sashimi* ... 94; R41
Sliced raw fish ... 90; R38
Sashimi wrapped in *nori* ... 94; R40
Spicy dipping sauce for *sashimi* ... 94; R40
White radish and red pepper garnish ... 94; R41

Vinegared Rice Dishes

Rice in vinegar dressing ... 95; R42
Vinegared rice-and-fish balls ... 95; R48
Vinegared rice-and-fish "sandwiches" ... 101; R44
Vinegared rice and vegetables rolled in seaweed ... 100; R43
Vinegared rice mixed with vegetables and seafood ... 96; R46

Rice

Chicken and rice with mushrooms ... 125; R52
Chicken omelet over rice ... 124; R50
Dipping sauce for *domburi* ... 125; R50
Mixed rice and vegetables ... 126; R51
Red-cooked festival rice ... 126; R53
Steamed rice ... 124; R49

Noodles

Buckwheat noodles with laver ... 131; R57
Cold noodles with shrimp and mushrooms ... 128; R58
Cold summer noodles ... R59
Dipping sauce for noodles ... 128; R58
Fox noodles ... 127; R56
Hot noodles and broth ... R55
Hot noodles and chicken in broth ... 130; R54

Fried Foods

Deep-fried shrimp and vegetables in batter ... 103; R60
Deep-fried shrimp coated with rice ... 105; R64
Deep-fried shrimp in noodles ... R65
Deep-fried *tofu* in soy-seasoned sauce ... 105; R68
Fried eggplant with *miso* dressing ... R67
Fried fish in vinegared sauce ... R66
Lemon and salt dip ... 104; R61
Light dipping sauce for *tempura: See mirin*-and-soy dipping sauce for *tempura* and noodles
Mirin-and-soy dipping sauce for *tempura* and noodles ... 104; R62
Mixed deep-fried pancakes ... 104; R63
Sliced beef with red-pepper-and-radish garnish ... R68

Foods Cooked in Seasoned Liquids

Boston mackerel in *miso* sauce ... R72
Chicken and vegetables simmered in seasoned broth ... 123; R74
Chicken simmered with white-radish threads ... R73
Coltsfoot cooked in *sake*-flavored sauce ... R73
Duck simmered in *sake*-seasoned sauce ... R72
Fresh sardines cooked in *sake*-flavored sauce ... 122; R70
Sake-seasoned fava beans ... R75
Sake-seasoned shrimp with egg-yolk glaze ... 122; R71
Sweet chestnuts ... 123; R75
Winter casserole with fish cake, *tofu* and vegetables ... R76

One-Pot Cookery

Beef and vegetables cooked in broth with dipping sauce ... 135; R80
Beef and vegetables simmered in soy sauce and *sake* ... 134; R77
Bubbling *tofu* ... 132; R83
Chicken and vegetables cooked in broth with *ponzu* dipping sauce .. 134; R78
Pan-broiled duck and vegetables with dipping sauce ... R84
Seafood and vegetables in broth ... 132; R82
Temple of Jade *nabe* ... R81

Broiled Foods

Baked fish omelet ... 176; R95
Broiled chicken, scallions and chicken livers ... 175; R89
Broiled fish fillets in rice-wine sauce ... R93
Broiled mackerel in *miso* marinade ... 169; R91
Broiled mackerel in soy-and-rice-wine marinade ... 172; R90
Broiled sliced beef with a sweet soy-seasoned glaze ... 175; R87
Fish with egg-yolk glaze: *See* Treasure-ship fish
Fish with sea-urchin glaze: *See* Treasure-ship fish
Flaky rolled omelet ... 178; R94
Grilled chicken with a sweet soy-seasoned glaze ... 176; R88
Grilled soybean curd with *miso* dressing ... 172; R98
Salt-broiled fish with dipping sauce ... 177; R85
Sesame-seed broiled fish: *See* Treasure-ship fish
Steam-broiled shrimp with chicken, ginkgo nuts and mushrooms .. 168; R92
Treasure-ship fish ... 170; R96

Steamed Foods

Chicken and shrimp in egg custard ... R101
Sake-steamed fish with *tofu* and spinach ... R102
Seasoned egg custard ... R103
Steamed chicken, mushrooms and ginkgo nut packages ... R102
Steamed shrimp, mushrooms, chicken and ginkgo nuts ... R104
Treasure-ship pumpkin, filled with shrimp, mushrooms and vegetables ... 180; R99

Recipe Index: Japanese

Dashi and Owanrui (Stocks and Soups)

Botan wan ... 58; R9
Hamaguri ushiojitate ... 58; R11
Ichiban dashi ... 54; R2
Misoshiru ... 59; R12
Misoshiru no-mi ... 59; R12
Niban dashi ... 54; R3
Satsuma jiru ... 61; R10
Sumashi wan ... 55; R4
Togan-to ebi ... 58; R5
Umewan ... 60; R6
Ushio jiru ... 61; R8

Bento and Zensai (Picnic Food and Hors d'Oeuvre)

Achara zuke ... R23
Awabi sakani ... 73; R16
Ebi isobe yaki ... R17
Ebi kimizushi ... 69; R18
Gyuniku negimaki ... 73; R22
Hamaguri sakani ... 73; R15
Hamaguri shigure-ni ... 73; R15
Igaguri ... 70; R19
Karashi zuke ... 70; R22
Kamaboko ... 68; R20
Kamo sakamushi ... 68; R14
Koimo nori-ae ... R21
Mizuyokan ... R24
Shibu kawa-ni ... 70; R16
Shiro bai ... R17
Tenjo kombu ... R21

Aemono and Sunomono (Mixed Foods and Vinegared Salads)

Goma joyu-ae ... 62; R27
Horenso hitashi ... R33
Kani kyuri ikomi ... 66; R34
Kani sunomono ... 62; R36
Kinome-ae ... 67; R32
Kobujime ... R37
Nameko mizore-ae ... 65; R29
Namasu ... 64; R35
Nasu karashi sumiso-ae ... R25
Neri shiro miso ... 67; R31
Nuta-ae ... R30
Sambai-zu ... 64; R29
Shime saba ... 65; R36
Shira-ae ... 63; R26
Suzuko mizore-ae ... 64; R28

Sashimi (Sliced Raw Fish)

Chirizu ... 94; R40
Isobe zukuri ... 94; R40
Sashimi ... 90; R38
Some oroshi ... 94; R41
Tosa joyu ... 94; R41

Sushi (Vinegared Rice Dishes)

Fukusa zushi: *See* Mazezushi
Makizushi ... 100; R43
Mazezushi ... 96; R46
Nigiri zushi ... 101; R44
Sushi ... 95; R42
Temarizushi ... 95; R48

Gohan (Rice)

Domburi ni shiru ... 125; R50
Gohan ... 124; R49
Oyako domburi ... 124; R50
Maze gohan ... 126; R51
Sekihan ... 126; R53
Tori gohan ... 125; R52

Menrui (Noodles)

Hiyashi somen ... R59
Hiyamugi ... 128; R58
Kitsune udon ... 127; R56
Menrui no dashi ... 128; R58
Su udon ... R55
Tori nanban ... 130; R54
Zarusoba ... 131; R57

Agemono (Fried Foods)

Agedashi ... 105; R68
Ajishio ... 104; R61
Dengaku nasu ... R67
Domyoji age ... 105; R64
Ebi kobore matsuba age ... R65
Kaki age ... 104; R63
Nanban zuke ... R66
Soba tsuyu ... 104; R62
Tatsuta age ... R68
Tempura ... 103; R60
Ten tsuyu: *See* Soba tsuyu

Nimono (Foods Cooked in Seasoned Liquids)

Fuki no nitsuke ... R73
Kamo yoshino-ni ... R72
Kimini ... 122; R71
Kiriboshi daikon ... R73
Kuri fukume-ni ... 123; R75
Miso-ni ... R72
Nitsuke ... 122; R70
Oden ... R76
Otafukumame shoga-ni ... R75
Umani ... 123; R74

Nabemono (One-Pot Cookery)

Hakusai nabe ... R81
Okaribayaki ... R84
Shabu shabu ... 135; R80
Sukiyaki ... 134; R77
Tori mizutaki ... 134; R78
Yosenabe ... 132; R82
Yudofu ... 132; R83

Yakimono (Broiled Foods)

Atsuyaki tamago ... 176; R95
Dengaku tofu ... 172; R98
Goma yaki: *See* Takara bune
Gyuniku teriyaki ... 175; R87
Horakuyaki ... 168; R92
Kimeyaki: *See* Takara bune
Kinome yaki ... R93
Mizo zuke ... 169; R91
Shioyaki ... 177; R85
Takara bune ... 170; R96
Tamago dashimaki ... 178; R94
Tori teriyaki ... 176; R88
Uniyaki: *See* Takara bune
Yakitori ... 175; R89
Yuan zuke ... 172; R90

Mushimono (Steamed Foods)

Chawan mushi ... R101
Kabura mushi ... R104
Sakamushi ... R102
Takara mushi ... 180; R99
Tamago dofu ... R103
Tori mushiyaki ... R102

General Index

Numerals in italics indicate a photograph or drawing of the subject mentioned.

Abalone, *35, 79,* 80, 188; diving for, 77; sliced and cooked in *sake* and soy sauce, *72*
Ac'cent (MSG), 110, 199
Aemono (mixed foods in dressing), 48, 62, 108, 115
Agemono (frying), 48-49, *102*-103
Agriculture, 10, *12-13, 14-15,* 29, *30-31,* 39
Aji-no-moto (MSG), *45,* 48, 110, 199
Akadashi (red soybean-paste-flavored soup with radish and scallion garnish), *35, 56*
Aka miso (red soybean paste), *45*
Akashi (village), 195
Algae. *See* Seaweed
Ama (diving girl), 77
Anisakiasis (gastro-intestinal parasitic infection), 82
Aomori, *map* 11
Aonoriko (powdered green seaweed), 43, *45,* 199
Appetizers, *72,* 185. *See also Bento;* Hors d'oeuvre; *Zensai*
Asparagus: garnish for raw fluke, *148;* marinated in *miso, 72*
Atlantic Ocean, 76, 80; Gulf Stream, 75
Awabi. See Abalone
Ayu (sweetfish), 28-29, 32, 76, 140, 147; fishing for, with trained cormorants, 29, *81;* salt-broiling, 29
Azuki (red beans), 43, *44,* 120, 199

Bamboo: leaves, *34;* stalks, 19, 128, *129;* teaspoon, 141-143; whisk, *141-143*
Bamboo shoots, 27, *35,* 43, *44,* 106, 107, 147, *148, 188;* cutting techniques for, 52, *53*
Bancha (cheap-grade tea), 28
Banquet, 181; wedding, *118-119*
Barley: roasted barley grain tea, 32
Barracuda, 38
Bass, 90, *91, 92, 99;* how to slice, *93;* in clear soup with wild vegetables and lime, 110, *111*
Batayaki (food grilled in butter), 161
Bean, 166; black, 43, *44,* 188; green powder, 27; lima, *148; mame,* 121; paste, 27; red, 43, *44,* 120
Beef, 22, 38, 46, 76, 108, *157, 159, 167,* 193; beer-fed cattle, *166;* Kobe, 161; Matsuzaka, 161; rolled beef with scallions, *72; teriyaki, 174. See also* Beef; Liver; Pork; *Shabu shabu; Sukiyaki*
Beer, 162, 193, 197; fed to cattle, *166*
Bento (lunch or picnic box), *24,* 25, *40,* 41, 68, 109, 165
Bering Sea, 76
Beverages, 32, 193. *See also* Beer; Gin; *Mirin; Sake;* Scotch; Tea
Blowfish. *See* Globefish
Boiling, 43; in seasoned liquids, 46-47, 122
Bonito, 32, 76, *79,* 80; dried, *45,* 87, 110, 152. *See also Katsuobushi*
Botan wan (clear soup with sea bass, wild vegetables and lime), 110, *111*
Brazier, *141-143*
Breakfast, 109, 179; soup, 41, *56-57,* 109, 110, 138
British Isles, 16
Broiling, 43, 168; salt-broiling, 29, 43, *169*
Broth, 46, 116, *159;* beef, 116; chicken, 43, 116; kelp, 147
Buckwheat noodles, 38, *130*
Buddhism, 16, 17, 19, 22, 86, 120, 162, 166; Zen, 137, 146
Buffet, 181, 198
Burdock root, *35,* 42, 43, *44. See also Gobo*

Cabbage, 49, 82, 162; Chinese, 38, *149*
Cake: in cherry leaves, 27; Children's Day, 120; Girls' Day, 120; funeral, 121; nightingale, 26-27; rice cakes, 27, 36, 38, 121
Candy, *34, 120*
Carp, 82, 161; symbolism of, 86, 121
Carrots, *40,* 41, 50, *51, 57, 133,* 163, 166, *167;* cutting techniques for, *52*
Cattle, *166*
Caviar, red, *40,* 41, *99, 130*
Chakin (linen tea cloth), *141-143*
Chameshi (rice cooked with other ingredients) restaurants, 162
Chasen (bamboo whisk), *141-143*
Chasenmura (village), 143
Chashaku (bamboo teaspoon), *141-143*
Chawan (tea bowl), *141-144*
Chawan mushi (food steamed in egg custard), 47-48
Chazuke (rice soaked in tea), 110; restaurants, 162
Chefs: apprenticeship, 195. *See also* names of chefs
Cherry: leaves, 27; trees, 8, *9,* 27, *114*
Chestnuts, *24,* 25, 36, 121, 140, *169;* in deep-fried shrimp balls, *40, 71*
Chicken, 22, *34,* 38, 43, 47, 109, 112, 140, *169, 174;* barbecued with chicken liver and scallions, 161; broth, 43; grilled, *158;* grilled with scallions, *174;* how to bone a chicken breast, *177;* scrambled with *tofu* and peas, *160,* 161
Children's Day festival, 34, 86, 120
China, 10; early influence on Japan, 16-17, 19; origin of tea ceremony, 137
Chirashi (loose rice covered with fish), 154, *155*
Chopsticks, *33, 34, 35, 40, 66, 85,* 109, *111, 112, 113, 114,* 116, 129, *130, 131, 148-149, 150, 154, 156, 159, 160,* 163, 166, *167,* 169, *187;* for cooking, *50, 71, 105,* 132, *178-179;* how to use, *47*
Chrysanthemums, 29, *30-31,* 121
Clams, *24,* 25, 76, 77, *79;* soup, *57,* 118
Cod, 76
Coffee shops, 27
Cooking clubs, 188
Cooking methods, 10, 23, 41, 43; boiling, 43, 46-47, 122; broiling, 29, 43, 168, *173;* food cooked at dining table, 46, 132, 166, *167;* frying, 43, 48-49, *102,* 103, *105;* grilling, 43, *158-159,* 161, 168; ingredients kept separate, 10; "interrupted cooking," 47; simmering, 41, 46; steaming, 43, 47-48, 115, *125, 169, 180. See also Aemono; Agemono; Mushimono; Nabemono; Nimono; Shioyaki; Sukiyaki; Umani*
Cooking schools, 108
Cooking utensils, *50,* 51; automatic electric rice cooker, *125;* brazier, *141-143;* chopsticks, *50, 66, 105,* 132, *178-179;* for tea ceremony, *141-144,* 145-146, 147, 148-149, *187;* hibachi, 37, 132, *182,* 183; *horoku,* 48, 169; improvised steamer, *180; kushi,* 161; *nabe,* 108, 132; *suribachi, 50, 63; teppan,* 157
Cormorant fishing. *See Ayu*
Cottage cheese, 110
Cottonseed oil, 49
Crabs, 76, 80, 82, 86, 110, 147; cucumber stuffed with, *66, 111;* restaurants, 161
Cucumber, *34, 35,* 48, 49, *98,* 110, *111,* 115, 165; cutting techniques for, 52, *53;* in *sushi,* 154, *155*
Cutting techniques: for chicken breast, *177;* for display, *40,* 41; for raw fish, *92-93;* for vegetables, *52-53*
Cuttlefish, 80

Daidai. See Orange
Daikon, 199. *See also* Radish
Dashi (soup stock), 32, 35, 38, 48, 76, 87, 89, 109, 112, 116, 152, 162, 198
Dinner, 56, 110, *111,* 112-113, 115, 116, 185, 193
Dipping sauces, 47, 110, 128, *129,* 132; for noodles, 36, 165; *ponzu,* 46, 82, 90, *91,* 152; *sambaizu, 65; sashimi, 91;* for *shabu shabu, 159;* for steak, 46; for *tempura,* 49; *yuzu* juice, soy sauce and *sake,* 116
Dishes: seasonal table service, 26; tea ceremony, *141-144,* 145-146, 147, *148-149,* 198
Dobin mushi (steamed chicken, fish, *matsutake* and ginkgo nuts), 36
Doi (Inn), Kyoto: baths, 194; description of, 183, 193-195; food, 194; geisha party, *190-191;* meal at, *182*
Domburi (bowl), 112, 162
Domyoji age (deep-fried shrimp encrusted with dried rice and served with green pepper, eggplant and lemon), 110, *111*
Duck, *24,* 25, *34, 114, 115,* 161; and chrysanthemum leaves, 110, *111;* grilled duck liver, *158;* with noodles, scallions, caviar and radish, *130*

Eating habits, 16, 19, 165; esthetic influence, 26, 33, 110, *111,* 120, 138; food in season, 26-32, *33-35,* 109; restaurant entertaining, 107, 152; Western influence, 22
Edo (old Tokyo), 32
Eels, *35,* 76, 87, 140; broiled, 29; eel day, 29, 32; medicinal

properties, 29; restaurants, 32, 163
Eggplant, 110, *111,* 115, 163
Eggs, *35,* 49, 56, 81, 110, 112, 115, *159,* 166, *167;* cold noodles topped with shrimp, mushrooms, eggs and parsley, *129;* custard in soup, 26; fried in sesame oil, 43, 46; in omelet *178-179;* paddies, *188;* quail, *24,* 25; shrimp stuffed with egg yolk, *148;* steaming in egg custard, 47-48. *See also* Omelet
Emperor of Japan, 16; birth of grandson, 120
Empress of Japan, 16
Europe, 16, 19

Ferns, *35,* 147, *149*
Festivals: Chestnut, 36; Children's Day, 34, 86, 120; Fish, 10; Girls' Day, or Doll Festival, 120; Harvest, 16; Mushroom gathering, 36; New Year, 121, 147, *188-189;* Tsukimi, 35
Fish, 8, *9,* 16, 19, *24,* 25, 28, 38, 49, 75, *79,* 80-83, *84-85,* 86-88, 110, 115, *150,* 151, 163, *188,* 195; auction, *78,* 79, 80; boning and slicing knives, *50;* cooking methods, 43; dried, 87, 88; exceptional flavor of, 75; festival, 10; how to fillet, *93;* market, 76, *78,* 79, 80-81; paste, 87, 121, 147, *148;* preparation of "treasure ship" fish, *170-171;* raw, 26, *92-93,* 154, *155;* vinegared rice-and-fish "sandwich," *99, 101;* salad, 48; sausage, 87; uses for, 87; variety and abundance, 75-76. *See also* Abalone; *Ayu;* Barracuda; Bass; Bonito; Cod; Cuttlefish; Flounder; Fluke; Globefish; Halibut; Herring; Mackerel; Porgy; Salmon; Sardines; *Sashimi;* Sausage; Sea urchin; Shad; Snapper; Snipe; *Sushi;* Trout; Tuna; Whale; Whitebait; Whitefish; Yellowtail
Fishing, 75; for abalone, 77; for *ayu* with cormorants, 29, *81;* industry, 76-77, 80, 87
Flounder, 82
Flour, 49
Fluke: fried and seasoned with vinegar sauce, *72;* salted raw, *148*
Fowl, 42. *See also* Chicken; Duck; Quail
France, 10, 23
Fruit, 10, 19, 36, 193; grown for restaurants, 195; in season, 26; introduced from West, 36. *See also* Cherries; *Fuki;* Kumquats; Lemons; Limes; Melon; Oranges; Persimmons; Plums; Strawberries; Tangerines
Fu (wheat gluten croutons), 41, 43, *45,* 199
Fugu. See Globefish
Fuki (vegetable), *148*
Fukiyose (nuts, shrimp, mushroom and vegetables), 36
Fukugen Restaurant, Tokyo, *85*
Fukuoka, *map* 11
Fukusa (silk napkin), *141-143; bassami* (handbag), *141*
Fukusa zushi (rice, seafood and vegetables wrapped in an omelet), *97*
Furikake (bottled sauce for rice), 110
Furo (brazier), *141-143*
Futaoki (rest for tea kettle lid or dipper), *141-143*

Garnish, seaweed, 89; white radish and red pepper, 90
Geisha, 108, *192;* party, 196-197; training and duties, *190-191,* 195-196. *See also Maiko*
Germany, 23
Gifu, *map* 11, 28, 29, 81
Gin, 166
Ginger, *34,* 43, *45,* 46, 161, 163, 164; grated, *65;* red pickled, *66, 97,* 110
Ginkgo nut, 36-37, *40,* 41, 43, *44,* 156, *169, 181*
Ginnan (ginkgo nuts), 43, *44,* 199
Ginsen (steak house), Tokyo, *157*
Ginza, 80, 162
Girls' Day cake, 120
Giseidofu (uncooked *tofu* topped by strips of deep-fried *tofu), 160,* 161
Globefish, 25, 38, 76, *84-85,* 86, 87, 152; expense of, 83; poisonous qualities, 83, 85
Gobo (burdock root), 42, 43, *44,* 199; cutting technique for, 52, *53*
Gohan (rice), 37
Goma (black and white sesame seeds), 43-44, 170-171, 199; *-abura* (sesame oil), 43, *44,* 199
Gourd, 100; dried, 42
Grater, *50*
Guji. See Sea bream

Hakusai (Chinese cabbage), 38 199
Halibut, 76
Hamaguri (clam soup), 118; *ushiojitate* with mushroom and lime garnish, *57*
Hangetsu (half-moon box), *114,* 115
Hannya-en Restaurant, Tokyo: description of, 184-185; typical dinner, 185, 193
Harusame (cellophane or transparent noodles), 43, *45,* 199
Heian Shrine, Kyoto, *114,* 115
Herbs, 19
Herring roe, 121
Hibachi, 37, 132, *182,* 183
Hichimi togarashi (seven-pepper spice), 43, *45,* 199
Hijiki (seaweed), 89
Hiroshima, *map* 11, 80; Bay, 19
Hishaku (water dipper), *141-143*
Hiyamugi (thin noodles served cold), 43, *45;* topped with shrimp, mushrooms, eggs and parsley, 128, *129*
Hiyayako dofu (chilled uncooked *tofu* with spicy soy sauce), *160,* 161
Hokkaido, 10, *map* 11, 80
Holland: early traders, 19
Honshu, 10, *map* 11, 38, 87
Horakuyaki (steamed on salt), 48, *169*
Horenso. See Spinach
Horoku (unglazed pottery bowl), 48, *169*
Hors d'oeuvre, *34, 66, 72,* 185
Horseradish, 81; green, 42, 82, 109

Ice cream, 22, 32
Igaguri, 40, 41, *71*
Inari, the rice god, 13, 37
Indian Ocean, 76, 80
Inland Sea, 10, *map* 11, 29, 75, 80, 151
Inn. *See* Doi
Innoshima Island, 29, *30-31*
Iodine, 89
Iridofu (tofu scrambled with chicken and peas), *160,* 161
Isao Yabuki, 163
Ishiyaki (food cooked on sizzling stone) 161
Isogen Restaurant, Tokyo, 154-*155*
Italy, 23

Japan, 10, *map* 11; Chinese influence on, 16-17, 19; dairy products, 10; description of, 10, 12-13, 75; expense-account spending, 153; fishing industry, 10, 76-77, 79, 80; food of, 8, 10, 16, 19, 22, 23; history, 12-19; philosophy of harmony with nature, 13, 33, 86, 138; symbolism and superstition, 86, 116, 120-121; visual appeal of food, 8, 10, 12, 110, *111. See also* Eating habits
Japan Current, 75
Japan Sea, 27
Jesuits, 19
Jimmu, first Emperor of Japan, 13
Junidanya Restaurant, Tokyo, *159*
Junsai (slippery vegetables), 43, *44,* 199; in soup with sea bass, 110, *111*

Kabayaki (broiled eel), 29, 32
Kaichi Tsuji, 12, 33
Kaiseki ryori. See Tea ceremony
Kaki. See Persimmon
Kakuko Yamada (serving maid at Doi), 193-194
Kamaboko (fish paste), 87, 121
Kamameshi (pot rice), 162
Kamasu (species of barracuda), 38
Kani kyuri ikomi (cucumber rounds with crab meat, watercress and red pickled ginger), 110, *111*
Kanname Sai. See Festivals
Kanpyo, 199. *See also* Gourd
Kansai, 36
Karashi (mustard), *45*
Karibayaki (food grilled on perforated metal dome), 161
Katsuobushi (dried bonito), 32, *45,* 76, 87, 89, 110, 112, 116, 152, 162, 199
Kawamasu. See Trout
Kawataro Restaurant, Kyushu, *150,* 151
Kazunoko. See Herring roe
Kelp *(kombu), 25, 45, 74,* 75, 87-89, 116, 121; broth, 147; symbolism of, 120, 121
Kensui (bowl for waste water), *141*
Kimeyaki, 40, 41, 170, *171*
Kimini (shrimp boiled in *dashi, sake,* sugar and salt), 47

Kitcho Restaurant, Kyoto: description of, 183; geisha party, 196-197; marketing for, 195; staff, *186-187,* 195-196
Koban (lidded box), *114,* 115
Kobe, *map* 11
Kobukusa (small silk napkin), *141, 144*
Kocha. See Tea
Koji Yuki, *186,* 188, *189,* 195; wife Junko, *186*
Kombu, 45, 199. *See also* Kelp
Kome (Japanese rice), 43, *44*
Kona sansho (Japanese pepper), 43, *45,* 199
Konnyaku (vegetable), *35,* 43, *44*
Korea, 12
Koyadofu (dried *tofu* boiled in soy sauce soup with mushrooms), *160,* 161
Kumquats, salmon eggs in, *188*
Kuromame (black beans), 43, *44*
Kusamochi (green cake for Girls' Day), 120
Kushi (bamboo skewer), 161
Kushizashi (brochette grilled food), 113
Kyogashi. See Candy
Kyoto, 8, *map* 11, 13, 19, 28, 36, 120, 139, 143, 152; Doi Inn, *182,* 183, *190-191,* 193-195; Heian Shrine, *114,* 115; Kitcho Restaurant, 183, *186-189,* 195-196
Kyushu, 10, *map* 11, 87

Laver (seaweed), 26, 88, 108, 109. *See also Nori*
Lemons, 110, *111,* 161; juice and soy sauce, 46
Limes, 26, *40,* 41, *57;* in clear soup with sea bass and wild vegetables, 110, *111;* juice and soy sauce, 46
Liver: chicken, 161; duck, 161
Lobster, *79,* 82, 112, *113,* 121, *133,* 150, 151; symbolism of, 120
Lotus root, 43 *44,* 163; cutting technique for, 52, *53;* leaf, 121
Lunch, 56, 109, 110, 179; New Year, *188-189*

Maguro (tuna), 82
Maiko (apprentice geisha), *190-191,* 196
Mackerel, 38, *65,* 80
Makizushi (vinegared rice wrapped in seaweed), *98, 99, 100,* 109, 154, *155,* 165
Mame beans, 121
Mandarin orange. *See* Tangerine
Marinade, 41, 42; for *teriyaki,* 43
Marriage ceremony, *117-119*
Matsunoh Shrine, Kyoto, *18,* 19
Matsutake, 199. *See also* Mushrooms
Matsutake Meshi (rice cooked with mushroom), 36
Matsuyama, *map* 11
Matsuzaka, 166
Meat, 42, 110. *See also* Beef, Pork, Liver
Medicinal uses for food, 36, 38; eels, 29, 32; globefish, 83, 86
Mediterranean Sea, 76
Melon, 115
Mikan, 199. *See also* Tangerine
Mirin (sweet rice wine), 42, 43, *44,* 121, 152, 162, 199; and soy sauce marinade, 43
Miso (fermented soybean paste), 41, *45,* 48, 138, 146, 147, 199; -marinated asparagus, *72*
Misoshiru (soybean paste soup), 41, *56-57,* 109, 110, 138
Mizusashi (cold-water jar), *141-143*
Mizutaki (simmered chicken dish), 38, 108, 116
Mochi. See Rice cake
Mochi-tsuki (rice-pounding ceremony), 121
Mollusks, 79
Monosodium glutamate, *45,* 48, 110
Morimoto, Toshio, *4,* 50, *51*
Mount Fuji, 19, *map* 11
Mount Koya, 147
MSG. *See* Monosodium glutamate
Mugicha (roasted barley-grain tea), 32
Mushi (food steamed on suspended plate), 47-48
Mushimono (steamed foods), 115, 180
Mushiyaki (steaming without water), 48
Mushrooms, *34, 35,* 43, *44-45,* 128, *129,* 161, 163, 166, *167, 169, 181; matsutake,* 32-33, 36, 43, *44,* 140, 199; *nameko,* 43, 44, 199; *shiitake,* 32, *37,* 42, 43, *45,* 199
Mustard, *35, 45,* 115

Nabe (pot or saucepan), 108, 132, 166, *167*
Nabemono (food cooked at table), 46, 116, 132, *133, 159,* 166, *167*
Nagara River, *81*
Nagasaki, *map* 11
Nagoya, 10, *map* 11, 28
Namashoyu dofu (*tofu* boiled in weak soy sauce flavored with lemon and ginger), *160,* 161
Namasu (salad), *65*
Nameko. See Mushrooms
Nara, 10, *map* 11
Nara zuke (melons pickled in *sake* lees), 115
Natsume (tea caddy), *141-143*
Natto (fermented soybean), 115
New York City, 145
Nigiri zushi (vinegared rice-and-fish "sandwich"), *99, 101*
Nihon-cha. See Tea
Niiname Sai. See Festivals
Nikko, 117, 161
Nimono (boiling in seasoned liquids), 46-47, 110, *111,* 122
Noodles, 43, *44-45, 71, 133;* buckwheat, 32, 38, *130;* cold with shrimp, mushrooms, eggs and parsley, 128, *129;* duck, scallions, caviar and radish, *130;* restaurants, *154;* shops, 25, 165. *See also Harusame; Hiyamugi; Somen; Udon*
Nori (dried laver), 32, *34, 45,* 88, *89, 97, 98, 99, 100,* 109, 110, 112, *131,* 152, 162, 165, 199; gathering, *88;* in omelet, *178-179*
Nuts, 36. *See also* Chestnuts; Ginkgo nuts

Obi (broad sash worn with kimono), 26
Octopus, *35,* 76, 77
Odori (shrimp) dance, 82-83
Ohba (first female apprentice chef), *187,* 195
Oil: for *tempura,* 49, 103; sesame, 43, *44. See also* Olive oil; Cottonseed oil; Sesame-seed oil; Peanut oil
Okama (teakettle), *141-143*
Okinawa, 76
Okiya (geisha training residence), 196
Okonomiyaki (do-it-yourself grilling), 161
Olive oil, 49
Omelet, 46, 110; as wrapping, *97,* 165; how to roll, *178-179;* rectangular pan, *50, 178-179*
Onigiri (rice wrapped in seaweed), 89
Onions, 166, 167
Oranges, 121
Osaka, 10, *map* 11, 36, 186, 195; food in, 162
Oshibori (damp towel), 110, *111,* 164, 185
Otomo *(sashimi)* Restaurant, Tokyo, *157*
Oyako domburi (chicken and egg over rice), 112
Oysters, 76, 80; baby, 77; boat, 19, *20*

Pacific Ocean, 10, *map* 11, 76, 80
Peanut oil, 49
Peas, scrambled with chicken and *tofu, 160,* 161
Pepper, Japanese, 43, *45*
Pepper leaf *(sansho), 45, 57,* 147, *148,* 157
Peppers, red, 43, *45,* 140
Persimmon, *28,* 36
Philippines, 19
Pickles, 43, *44,* 112, 115; squash, 147, *149,* 198
Pine needles, *169*
Plum: cucumber stuffed with plum paste and raw prawns, *34;* red pickled, 109
Ponzu (soy sauce and citrus juice), 46, 82, 90, 152; with scallion and radish garnish, 83, *91*
Porgy, *57,* 147, *149*
Pork, 22, 112; cutlet, 162
Portugal: early traders, 19
Poultry. *See* Chicken; Fowl
Prawns, *34, 79, 154, 188*
Pumpkin, *181*

Quail, 161; eggs, *24,* 25

Radish, 26, *130;* cutting techniques for, *52;* in dipping sauce, 83; Japanese *(daikon), 35,* 42, 43, *45,* 46, 48, 49, 50, *51, 52, 56,* 82, 90, 108, 109, 115, 147, *179,* 199; yellow, *98*
Renkon (lotus root), 43, *44,* 199
Restaurants, 12, 22, 23, 25, 26, 27, 29, 36, 38, 42, 46, 76, 80, 81, 83, 88, 107-108, 109, 110, 112, *150, 153,* 186, *192; chameshi,* 162; *chazuke,* 162; cleanliness, 164; eel, 32, 163; entertaining at, 152; expense-account clientele, 153;

fugu, 25, 83, *85,* 86; rice, 162; *sashimi, 157;* specialized, *154-160,* 161; steak houses, *157,* 161-162; *sushi,* 81, *155,* 164-165; *tempura, 156,* 163; *tofu, 160,* 161; *yakitori, 158,* 161. *See also* names of restaurants
Restaurants: Fukugen, Tokyo, *85;* Ginsen, Tokyo, *157;* Hannya-en, Tokyo, 184-185, 193; Isogen, Tokyo, 154-*155;* Junidanya, Tokyo, *159;* Kawataro, Fukuoka, Kyushu, *150,* 151; Kitcho, Kyoto, 183, *186-189,* 195-197; Otomo, Tokyo, *157;* Sasagayuki, Tokyo, *160,* 161; Ten-ichi, Tokyo, *156,* 163; Tori-gin, Tokyo, 162; Torishige, Tokyo, *158;* Wadakin (for beef), Matsuzaka, 166, *167;* Yabuizu, Tokyo, *154*
Religious ceremonies, 86-87
Rice, 8, *9,* 10, 19, 26, *34,* 35, 37-38, 43, *44,* 81, 87, *97, 101,* 109, 110, *111,* 112, *114,* 115, 140, 147, *148-149,* 154, *155,* 162, 165, 166, *167;* automatic electric rice cooker, *125;* bran, 166; cakes, 26, 27, 109, 121; dried, 110; historic importance of, 13, 37, 42; paddies, *14-15;* red, 120. *See also Sake; Sushi*

Sake (rice wine), 13, 25, 26, *34, 35,* 36, 38, 42, 43, *44,* 46, 47, 83, 86, 115, 116, 128, *129,* 146, 162, *190-191,* 193, 197, 199; at wedding ceremony, *118-119;* blessing of, *18,* 19; food wagon, *159;* game, 197; shops, 87. *See also Mirin*
Sakizuke. See Appetizers
Salad, 48; crab meat and vegetables, 193; mixed, 48
Salmon, *34,* 82; eggs in kumquat shells, *188*
Salt, 42, 110; for steaming, 48, *169*
Sambai-zu (dipping sauce), *65*
Samisen (musical instrument), *190,* 191, 197
Samma (mackerel), 38
Sampei jiru (salmon soup with vegetables), 38
Samurai, 17, 19, *34*
Sansankudo (part of wedding ceremony), *118*
Sansho (pepper) leaf, *45, 57, 148*
Sapporo, 10, *map* 11
Sardines, 76, 80, 161
Sasagayuki Restaurant, Tokyo, *160,* 161
Sashimi (slices of raw fish), 26, 27, 43, *65,* 80-83, 86, 90, *91,* 108, 112, 138, 146, 152; restaurant, *157,* 161, 185, 188; knife and scabbard, *50;* popularity of, 81; preparation of, 81-82, *92-93*
Sauces, 38, 86, *112;* for rice, 110; for salad, 48; *tare,* 29, 113. *See also* Soy sauce; Dipping sauces
Sausage: fish, 87
Sayori (snipefish), 112
Scallions, 32, *56,* 109, 113, 116, *130, 133,* 163, *174;* barbecued with chicken and chicken livers, 161; in dipping sauce, 83; rolled beef with scallions, *72*
Scallop shells for cultivating oysters, 19, *21*
Scotch whisky, 193
Sea bream, *34, 35,* 76, *79,* 80, 82, 110, 120, *150,* 151; symbolic importance of, 86, 121
Seafood, 42, 56, *57,* 81, *97, 102, 105, 150,* 151, 156, 164; variety and abundance, 75-76. *See also* Fish; Octopus; Shellfish; Seaweed; Squid
Sea of Japan, *map* 11
Seasonal themes, 10, 26, 33-35; autumn, *35, 40,* 41; spring, 10, *24,* 25, *34, 120,* 147, *148-149;* summer, *34;* winter, *35*
Seasonings, 42, 47. *See also* Monosodium glutamate; Pepper; Salt
Sea urchins, *34,* 43, *45,* 76, 80, 115
Seaweed, 8, *9, 34,* 76, 81, 88-89, *188;* for *sushi,* 89, *98-99, 100,* 154, *155;* garnish, 89; medicinal value, 89; powdered green seaweed, 43, *45;* shrimp wrapped in seaweed, *72. See also Hijiki;* Kelp; Laver; *Nori; Wakame*
Sekihan (red rice): symbolism of 120, 121
Sendai, *map* 11
Sen Rikyu, 137, 146
Sensu (fan), *141*
Sesame: oil, 42, 43, *44,* 49; seeds, 38, 48, *63,* 110, *159*
Shabu shabu (simmered beef dish), 38, 108, 116, *159*
Shad, 82
Shellfish, 8, 75-76, 77, 82, 115, *150,* 151, 163; salad, 48. *See also* Clams; Crab; Lobster; Mollusks; Oysters; Prawns; Scallops; Shrimp; Snails; Spat
Shiitake, 45, 199. *See also* Mushrooms
Shikiita (protective tile on which brazier stands), *141-143*
Shikoku, 10, *map* 11
Shimofuri (fallen frost) beef, 166, *167*
Shimonoseki, 87
Shincha (first new tea leaves), 27
Shinmai (new rice), 37
Shinto: gods, 38, 121; prayer, 16, 76; priests, *18,* 19; religion, 13, 19; shrines, *18,* 19, *117-118;* wedding, *117-119*
Shioyaki (salt broiling), 29, 41, 43
Shirataki (vegetable), 42, 43, *44*
Shiro dashi (white soybean-flavored-soup with gourd and hot mustard garnish), *56*
Shiro miso (white soybean paste), *45,* 199
Shisha (vegetable), *188*
Shiso (beefsteak plant), 147, 162
Shiumani (vegetables and chicken, sautéed and then boiled), 47
Shizuoka (town and prefecture), 27, 38
Shochu (Japanese gin), 166
Shoga (ginger root), 43, *45*
Shoyu, 44, 199. *See also* Soy sauce
Shrimp, 22, *35, 57,* 76, 81, *99,* 128, *129, 133,* 162, *169, 181;* deep-fried and encrusted with dried rice, 110, *111;* deep-fried shrimp balls, *24,* 25, *71;* dried, 88; eating alive, 82-83; how to prevent curling, *69;* stuffed with egg yolk, 147, *148;* wrapped in seaweed, *72. See also Tempura*
Shrines: Matsunoh, Kyoto, *18,* 19; Toshogu, Nikko, 117-118
Siberia, 12
Skimmer, *50*
Snails, soy-seasoned in shells, *72*
Snipe fish, 112
Snow peas, *181*
Soba (buckwheat noodles), 38, 147, 199
Sodare (bamboo mat), *50, 100*
Somen (thin wheat noodles), 43, *45,* 199
Some oroshi (white radish and red pepper garnish), 90, *91*
Sosei Takahara, tea master, *186, 187*
Soup, 75, 115, *130, 154,* 166; burned rice, 147, *149;* clam, *57,* 118; clear, 56-57, 110, *111,* 147, 185, 188; egg, 26; flavored with soybean paste, 41, *56-57,* 109, 110, 138, 147, *148;* salmon, 38. *See also* Broth; *Dashi; Miso shiru*
Soybean: curd, 32, *34, 35,* 41, *45,* 108, *159, 160,* 161, 166, *167, 188;* fermented soybean paste, 41, 109, 115, 147, *173,* green, *34;* importance of, 16; red paste, 35, *45;* white paste, *45. See also Miso; Tofu;* Soy sauce
Soy sauce, 26, 32, *35,* 36, 41, *45,* 48, 90, *91,* 116, *160,* 161, 166, *167,* 196; with fish, 81, 82; ingredients, 42; and *mirin,* 43, 46, 162; multiple uses, 42. *See also Ponzu*
Spain, 19
Sparrow, 161
Spat (baby oysters), 77
Spice, 43, *45*
Spinach, 87; *horenso,* 140; salad, 48
Squash pickles, 147, *149*
Squid, 76, *79,* 80, 82, *92, 99,* 163; "fire fly," 27; how to cut, *92;* and pickled cod roe, *72*
Steaming: in egg custard, 47-48; on suspended plate, 47-48, *180;* over *sake,* 47; steam- or salt-broiling, 29, 43, *169*
Stock, 46; fish, 116. *See also Dashi*
Strawberries, 32, 38, *39;* popularity of, 25-26
Su (rice vinegar), 43, *44,* 199
Sugar, 46, 166, *167*
Suimono (clear soup), 110; wedding, 121
Sukiyaki (simmered beef dish), 22, 26, 27, 36, 38, 41, 108, 116, 152, 161, 166, *167;* origin of dish, 46
Sumo (professional wrestlers), 22
Sunomono (vinegared salad), 48, 108, 115
Suribachi (serrated mixing bowl), *50, 63*
Sushi (vinegared rice), 8, *9,* 26, 77, 80, 81, 89, *98-99, 100,* 108, 110, 115, 163; popularity of, 81; restaurants, 81, 154, *155,* 164-165; vocabulary, 165
Suzuko mizore-ae (red caviar and radish), *130*

Tableware, 183-184
Tai. See Sea bream
Takano tjume (small whole red peppers), 43, *45*
Takenoko (bamboo shoot), 43, *44*
Takuan (pickled radish over rice), 115
Tamago dashimaki (rolled omelet with grated *daikon),* 46, 110, *179*
Tamago dofu (seasoned egg custard in a soup), 26
Tangerines, 10, 38
Tare (sweet soy sauce), 29, 113
Taro, 110, *111,* 140
Tatami (straw matting), *148-149,* 152, 193
Tea, 17, 27-28, 38, 110, *111,* 112, 162, 164, 193; black, 27; cheap-grade, 28; green, 27, 32, *144;* harvest, *12-13;* plantations, *12-13,* 27; preparation of, 27-28, *141-144. See also Bancha; Shincha;* Tea ceremony
Tea ceremony, 17, *136,* 137-147; esthetics, 136, 138-139, 141, 145-146, 147; food, 26, 143, 145-147, *148-149;* leaf for, 27; masters, 137-138, 141, 142, 143, 145, 146, 147; menus, 145, 146, 147, 186; origin, 137; preparation, *141-144;* rules, 138, 144, 147; schools and lessons, *139,* 145, *187;* utensils and dishes, *141-144,* 145-146, 147, *148-149, 187*
Temarizushi, 40, 41
Temples: Sojiji, near Tokyo, 86-87. *See also* Shinto
Tempura, 19, 38, 43, 115, 116, 152, 162, 163, 185; dips, 49; ingredients, 49, *102;* oil, 49, 102; origin, 19, 22; preparation, 48-49, *102, 105,* 163; restaurants, *156,* 163; shrimp, *182,* 183
Ten-ichi Restaurant, Tokyo, *156,* 163
Teppanyaki (grilled meat and chicken on metal plate), *157,* 161, 162
Teriyaki ("shining broil"), 43, 152, 161, *174*
Tofu (soybean curd), 32, 36, 41, 42, *45,* 48, 87, 108, 109, 110, 116, *133;* 147, *148,* 152, 161, *173,* 199; assorted dishes based on, *160,* 161; instant powdered variety, 42; restaurant, *160,* 161; slicing knife, *50;* variety of uses for, 42, 161; with dried bonito, scallions, ginger and soy sauce, 32
Togarashi, 199. *See also* Pepper
Tokonoma (alcove with decorative items), 10, 26, 86, 108, 152, 185, *187,* 193
Tokyo, 10, *map* 11, 22, 27, 32, 77, 86, 107, 110, 115, 162; Bay, 87; fish market, 76, 79, 80-81; Imperial Hotel, 138; Shinjuku section, 83; restaurants, *155-160,* 161, 162, 163, 184-185, *192,* 193
Tonkatsu (pork cutlet), 162
Tori-gin Restaurant, Tokyo, 162
Torishige Restaurant, Tokyo, *158*
Toro (belly flesh of tuna), 152
Toshogu Shrine, Nikko, 117
Toyama, *map* 11; Bay, 27
Trout, 28, *182;* broiled rock trout, *35;* river, *34;* salt-broiled, 27. *See also Ayu*
Tsukemono (soaked things or pickles), 43, *44,* 115, 152, 162, 198-199
Tsukiji Central Market, Tokyo, 76, 78, 79, 80-81
Tsukimi Festival, 35
Tsukudani (fish and kelp mixture), 87, 89
Tsunokakushi (horn concealer hat), *117*
Tuna, 76, 81, 82, *92, 99,* 154, *155,* 165; buying, *78,* 79, 80; how to slice, *93;* red, 82, 90, *91, 98;* vinegared rice-and-tuna "sandwich," *101*
Turnips, 71; cutting technique for, 52, *53*
Turtle, 161
Udon (wheat noodle), 38, 43, *45*
Uguisu mochi (nightingale cake), 26-27
Ujidawara district, 13
Ukai (cormorant fishing). *See Ayu*
Ukemochi-no-kami (food goddess), 13
Umani (boiling in sweet liquid), 47
Umeboshi (red pickled plum), 43, *44,* 109
Uni (sea urchin), 43, *45,* 170
United States: influence on Japanese food, 22, 23
Urasenke (tea ceremony school), 145
Ushinohi. See Eels
Vegetables, 29, *30-31,* 42, 47, 48, 57, 71, 75, 81, 89, 109, 110, 116, *156, 157,* 159, 163, 195; canned, 43, *44;* cutting knife, *50, 51;* cutting techniques for, *52-53;* pickled, 110, *111;* slippery, 43, *44;* soaked, 115; steamed, 47; wild, 110, *111. See also* Asparagus; Bamboo shoots; Beans; Burdock; Cabbage; Carrots; Cucumber; Eggplant; Ginger; Gourd; Lotus root; Mushrooms; Onions; Peas; Potatoes; Pumpkin; Radish; Rice; Scallions; *Shirataki; Shisha; Shiso;* Snow peas; Soybean; Spinach; Squash; Taro; Turnips; Watercress
Vinegar, 72; rice, 8, 42, 43, *44;* salad dressing, 48
Vitamins in food: A, 29; C, 89
Wadakin beef restaurant, Matsuzaka, 166, *167*
Wakame (seaweed), *45,* 89, 109, 110, 199
Warabi (fern), 147, *149*
Wasabi (green horseradish), 42, 82, 90, *91,* 108, 115, 152, 165, 199
Wasabi zuke (vegetables pickled in green horseradish and mustard), 115
Watanabe family, *114,* 115
Watercress, *98, 100,* 110, *111;* cucumber stuffed with crab meat, watercress and ginger, 66
Whale, 76, 79; restaurants, 161
Wheat, 29, *30-31,* 42
Whitebait, 79
Whitefish, 76
Wine, 42. *See also Sake; Mirin*
Wright, Frank Lloyd, 138
Yabuizu noodle restaurant, Tokyo, *154*
Yakitori (food grilled on skewers over charcoal fire), *158-159,* 161, *175*
Yellowtail, 82
Yokohama, 10, *map* 11
Yosenabe (fish, vegetables, *tofu* and *dashi),* 116, *133*
Yudofu (steaming soybean curd), 116
Yuto (burned rice soup), *149*
Yuzu (citrus fruit similar to lime), 26, 109, 116
Zarusoba (buckwheat noodles), 32, *129*
Zen. *See* Buddhism
Zensai (hors d'oeuvre), 68, *72,* 198
Zuiki. See Taro

Mail-Order Sources for Foods and Utensils

The stores listed below are primarily food markets, but many of them carry utensils as well. All are firms that will accept mail orders. Write first to see if the items you want are available, and for current prices.

If you have difficulty getting items by mail from sources listed below, the Japan Food Corporation, a large importing firm, may be able to suggest stores in your area that carry Japanese foods and utensils but do not handle mail orders. For such information, write the Japan Food Corporation office nearest you:

900 Marin St.
San Francisco, Calif. 94119

1131 Mateo St.
Los Angeles, Calif. 90021

704 A St.
National City, Calif. 92050

1515 N. C St.
Sacramento, Calif. 95814

200½ White St.
Houston, Texas 77007

1850 West 43rd St.
Chicago, Ill. 60609

11-31 31st Ave.
Long Island City, N.Y. 11106

9179 Red Branch Rd.
Columbia, Md. 21043

Retail Stores

ALABAMA
Toni's Oriental Grocery
R.R. No. 2, Box 259
Daleville, 36322

CALIFORNIA
American Fish Market
1836 Buchanan St.
San Francisco, 94115

Uoki
1656 Post St.
San Francisco, 94115

Dobashi
240 E. Jackson St.
San Jose, 95112

Nishioka Fish Market
665 N. 6th St.
San Jose, 95112

Three Star Market
245 Washington St.
Monterey, 93901

Takahashi Company
221 S. Claremont Ave.
San Mateo, 94401

Enbun Company
248 E. First St.
Los Angeles, 90012

Ida Company
339 E. First St.
Los Angeles, 90012

Modern Food Market
318 E. 2nd St.
Los Angeles, 90012

Rafu Bussan Company
344 E. First St.
Los Angeles, 90012

COLORADO
Granada Fish
1919 Lawrence St.
Denver, 80202

Pacific Mercantile Company
1946 Larimer St.
Denver, 80202

FLORIDA
Oriental Imports
54 N. Orange Ave.
Orlando, 32801

Schiller's Delicatessen
3411 S. Manhattan Ave.
Tampa, 33609

Tropi Pac Food Products
3664 N.W. 48th St.
Miami, 33142

GEORGIA
Sachi's Japanese Rest. Market
3838 Cusseta Rd.
Columbus, 31903

ILLINOIS
Franklin Food Store
1309 E. 53rd St.
Chicago, 60615

Ginza & Company
315 E. University
Champaign, 61820

S & I Grocery
1058 W. Argyle St.
Chicago, 60640

Toguri Mercantile Co.
5358 N. Clark St.
Chicago, 60640

World Foods & Drug
312 S. Adams St.
Peoria, 61602

White Hen Pantry
150 Golf Rd.
Waukegan, 60085

York Super Foods
3240 N. Clark St.
Chicago, 60657

INDIANA
Fuji Oriental Food & Gift
1401 E. Markland Ave.
Kokomo, 46901

Smitty's Foodliner
1812 Northwestern Ave.
West Lafayette, 47906

Wilt's Food Center
100 Easy Shopping Center
Elkhart, 46514

KANSAS
Imported Foods
1038 McCormick
Wichita, 67213

Jade East Store
1030 Grant Ave.
Junction City, 66441

LOUISIANA
Oriental Trading Company
2636 Edenborn Ave.
Metairie, 70002

MASSACHUSETTS
Yoshinoya
36 Prospect St.
Cambridge, 02139

MICHIGAN
Goodrich's Spartan Shop
940 Trowbridge Rd.
E. Lansing, 48823

Kado's Oriental Imports
251 Merrill
Birmingham, 48011

Kuwahara Trading Post
3126 Cass Ave.
Detroit, 48201

Mt. Fuji Oriental Foods
22040 W. 10 Mile Rd.
Southfield, 48075

MINNESOTA
International House
712 Washington Ave., S.E.
Minneapolis, 55414

MISSOURI
Aloha Enterprises
1741 Swope Pkwy.
Kansas City, 64110

Maruyama's
100 N. 18th St.
St. Louis, 63103

NEBRASKA
Oriental Trading Company
1115 Farnam St.
Omaha, 68102

NEVADA
Terry's Oriental Gift Shop
& Imports
120 W. Second St.
Reno, 89501

NEW JERSEY
Haruko's Oriental Bazaar
Rt. No. 3, Box 3143
Browns Mills, 08015

NEW YORK
Japanese Foodland
2620 Broadway
New York, 10023

Japan Mart, Inc.
239 W. 105th St.
New York, 10025

Katagiri Company
224 E. 59th St.
New York, 10022

Nippon Do
82-69 Parsons Blvd.
Jamaica, 11432

Tanaka & Company
326 Amsterdam Ave.
New York, 10023

NORTH CAROLINA
Oriental Food Shop
P.O. Box 202 (N. Main St.)
Spring Lake, 28390

Oriental Market
307 Marine Blvd.
Jacksonville, 28540

OHIO
Dayton Oriental Food
812 Xenia Ave.
Dayton, 45410

Omura Japanese Food & Gift Shop
3811 Payne Ave.
Cleveland, 44114

Ida Oriental Foods & Gift
614 Yearling Rd.
Columbus, 43213

Soya Food Products
2356 Wyoming St.
Cincinnati, 45214

OKLAHOMA
Takara Oriental Foods
2012 Cache Rd.
Lawton, 73501

OREGON
Anzen Importers
736 N.E. Union Ave.
Portland, 97232

Soy Bean Products
P.O. Box 568 (336 S.W. 5th St.)
Ontario, 97914

UTAH
Sage Farm Market
52 W. First St. S.
Salt Lake City, 84101

Yamaguchi & Company
260 25th St.
Ogden, 84401

WASHINGTON
North Coast Supply
W. 27th Main St.
Spokane, 99201

Uwajimaya Inc.
422 S. Main St.
Seattle, 98104

WASHINGTON, D.C.
House of Hanna
1468 T St. N.W., 20009

Mikado
4709 Wisconsin Ave., N.W., 20016

WISCONSIN
Oriental Grocery & Gifts
821 North 27th St.
Milwaukee, 53208

Credits and Acknowledgments

The sources for the illustrations in this book are shown below. Credits for the pictures from left to right are separated by commas, from top to bottom by dashes.

All photographs by Eliot Elisofon except: 4—Horace Bristol, Monica Suder—Charles Phillips, Monica Suder. 11—Map by Kiyoshi Kanai. 14,15—Brian Brake from Rapho Guillumette. 28—T. Tanuma. 30,31—Orion Press from Free Lance Photographers Guild. 39—T. Tanuma. 46,47—Drawings by Albert Sherman. 51,52,53—Richard Jeffery. 63,66,69,71—Clayton Price. 81—S K Slide Company Ltd. 84,85—T. Tanuma. 92,93—Clayton Price, drawings by Matt Greene. 97,100,101,105—Clayton Price. 117,118,119—Ernest Heiniger from Rapho Guillumette. 125—Anthony Donna. 139—John Launois from Black Star. 153—Norman Wightman courtesy Japan National Tourist Organization. 154,158—T. Tanuma. 159—Top Jerry Cooke. 160—T. Tanuma. 170—Clayton Price. 177—Drawings by Matt Greene. 178,179—Top Clayton Price. 180—Drawing by Elise Hilpert.

For their help in the production of this book the editors wish to thank the following: *in Japan,* Takiko Kato, Ernest Satow, Mrs. Sochitsu Sen, Mr. and Mrs. Akira Watanabe, and the Ajinomoto Company, Inc.; *in New York City,* The Japan Society, Inc.; Hisashi Yamada, Director of the Tea Ceremony Society of Urasenke, Inc.; Genichiro Inokuma; Sondra Meadow; Mary Evans, for her assistance on the tea ceremony chapter; Teiji Tamaru; Maureen Herbert, Japan Airlines; Takatoshi Terahira, Japan Food Corporation; H. Hamano, Japan National Tourist Organization; Japan Trade Center; Ellen Sakata and Myyo Enoki, Japanese Foodland; Tatsuro Miyoshi, Miya Company, Inc.; Irwin Vladimir, Van Brunt & Company.

Sources consulted in the production of this book include: *They Came to Japan,* edited by Michael Cooper; *Typical Japanese Cooking,* by Tomi Egami; *Things Japanese,* by Mock Joya; *The Book of Tea,* by Okakura Kakuzo; *Japan Past and Present,* by Edwin O. Reischauer; *Japan, a Short Cultural History,* by George B. Sansom; *Japanese Inn,* by Oliver Statler; *The Romance of Tea,* by William H. Ukers; *We Japanese,* published by Fujiya Hotel, Ltd.

Printed in U.S.A.